Second Edition

COACHING FOOTBALL'S ZONE OFFENSE

Stan Zweifel

COACHES CHOICE™

©2004 Coaches Choice. Second edition. All rights reserved. Printed in the United States.

No part of this book may be reproduced, stored in a retrieval system or transmitted in any form or by any means, electronic, mechanical, photocopying, recording or otherwise, without the prior permission of Coaches Choice.

ISBN: 1-58518-904-9
Library of Congress Control Number: 2004108517
Book layout and diagrams: Deborah Oldenburg
Cover design: Jeanne Hamilton
Front cover photo: Courtesy of University of Wisconsin-Whitewater

Coaches Choice
PO Box 1828
Monterey, CA 93942
www.coacheschoice.com

Dedication

To my wife Diane and our four beautiful children—Saree, Shannon, Michael, and Mark. To all of the Warhawk players over the years who have made the Z-Train Zone go. A special note of affection to my youngest son, Mark, who has shown the courage and strength to go on, even while fighting a terrible illness.

—Stan Zweifel

Acknowledgments

The author is especially grateful to Brad Boll, who typed and edited this manuscript. Brad is duel a special thanks for all of his assistance on this project. Brad's efforts as an assistant when he was with the Warhawks were invaluable, and he is a fine football coach in his own right. I would also like to thank my two co-authors on the first edition of this book, Brian Borland and Bob Berezowitz, for their involvement with making this project a reality.

Contents

Dedication 3
Acknowledgments 4
Preface 6

Chapter 1: The Advantages of the Zone Offense 7

Chapter 2: Zone Formations 11

Chapter 3: The Inside Zone Play—Tight-End Sides 16

Chapter 4: The Inside Zone Play—Split-End Side 40

Chapter 5: The Outside Zone Play—Tight-End Side 54

Chapter 6: The Outside Zone Play—Split-End Side 70

Chapter 7: Zone Running Game: Trapping Game 91

Chapter 8: Zone Running Game: Misdirection Plays 106

Chapter 9: The Play-Action Pass: The Naked and Bootleg Series 126

Chapter 10: The Play-Action Pass: The Dropback Series 145

Chapter 11: Incorporating the Option Game in the Zone Offense 153

Chapter 12: Innovations in the Zone Running Attack 157

About the Author 170

Preface

The first edition of this book was originally written to provide football coaches at every competitive level with a tool that would enable them to develop, install, and execute the zone offense. In the years since its publication, this offensive structure has continued to be extremely effective against all kinds of defensive fronts.

The book presents a detailed overview of the advantages of the zone offense and details the various formations from which the zone offense is conducted. Chapters 3-6 review the zone running game from the two basic points of attack—the inside zone play and the outside zone play. Each point of attack is examined from both the tight-end side and the split-end side. Chapters 7 and 8 cover trapping plays and misdirection plays, respectively, for the zone running game. The next two chapters provide a comprehensive summary of how to effectively employ the play-action pass in the zone offense. Chapter 11 offers suggestions on how to incorporate the option game into the zone offense.

The final chapter (Chapter 12) discusses recent innovations in the zone running attack. The information presented in this book is designed to enable coaches to better understand how the extraordinarily unique and potent offensive structure inherent in the zone offense can help them. If in the process of using the techniques and fundamentals presented in this book, coaches are better able to maximize the abilities and talents of their players, then the effort to write *Coaching Football's Zone Offense* will have been well worthwhile.

I trust that the results you will achieve will speak for themselves. Keep on zonin'!

–Stan Zweifel

1

The Advantages of the Zone Offense

Following the 1993 football season, the staff at the University of Wisconsin-Whitewater began contemplating significant changes in our offensive approach and philosophy. We had just struggled through a 6-4 season in which our offense averaged only 325.5 total yards per game. As an offensive coaching staff, we were frustrated by our team's inability to adequately account for and block all of the multiple defensive structures that opponents were using, especially some of the attack, blitz, charge, and pressure fronts that began to emerge in the 1990s.

Initially, we had three primary concerns:

- We wanted our offensive linemen to be able mentally and physically to make the necessary adjustments to their blocking schemes and account for all of the defensive looks that they saw from week to week.

- We wanted to improve our play-action passing attack so that we could implement a high-percentage, ball-control passing game to counter defenses that attacked aggressively. We were looking for a simple and effective way to disguise our passing attack and move our quarterback out of the pocket and away from pressure against blitzing defenses.

- We wanted to significantly decrease (and hopefully even eliminate) assignment busts and technique mistakes. Given the fact that we had well over 100 missed assignments by our offensive linemen in 1993, we felt that they were not being aggressive enough nor playing as physical as we need to be against teams that played multiple defensive fronts because our linemen were confused and unsure about their assignments.

Philosophically, we felt that in order to be successful in the future, we needed to find an offensive scheme that:

- Was easy to implement and run.
- Allowed us to be aggressive, play physical, and wear down our opponents.
- Could account for every defensive structure we would face.
- Gave us the potential for a high-percentage, low-risk play-action passing attack.
- Could be run successfully with the personnel we typically recruited.

Subsequently, when we began to analyze successful football programs and investigate the offensive schemes they were using, one of the major trends in college football was the implementation and use of zone blocking schemes in the run game. Although they had been used on the professional level for more than five years, zone concepts just began to surface on the college level in the early 1990s.

As we began to analyze, examine, and seriously consider running the zone, we fortunately had one of the most successful Division I-A zone running teams in the country less than one hour away at the University of Wisconsin-Madison. That season, Wisconsin had won the Big Ten Conference championship and the Rose Bowl due largely in part to the zone running of Brent Moss and Terrell Fletcher, and the play action passing attack directed by Darrell Bevell. The coaching staff at the University of Wisconsin-Madison was very accommodating toward our staff as we began to investigate and ask questions about the zone. Throughout the process, the Badger's staff was a tremendous resource for us.

We also spent a great deal of time investigating professional teams who were running the zone offense effectively. We gathered as much film and compiled as much information from as many zone teams as we could find, and then analyzed that information. The result of this process was the development and implementation of the zone offense that has been run with great success for the past several seasons at the University of Wisconsin-Whitewater.

During our first four years in the zone offense, our team rushed for 11,032 yards in 40 games, for an average of 275 yards per game. The team also accumulated 17,198 yards of total offense, for an average of 429.9 yards per game. Our quarterbacks completed 483 passes in 756 attempts for a 63% completion percentage, throwing for

56 touchdowns and only 22 interceptions. In the three seasons after implementing the zone, the team scored 1336 points for an average of 33.4 points per game, representing an increase of more than 10 points per game from the season prior to when we went to the zone offense.

Most importantly, our teams have consistently performed well against some of the best NCAA Division III football teams in the country. As a coaching staff, and as an offensive football team, we have become better at running the zone each year since making the change.

As a staff, we strongly feel that the switch to running the zone has played a tremendous role in our success. My goal in writing this book is to share some of our ideas about the zone. In this book, I discuss what we have learned, review some of the schemes that we have developed and modified, and present the version of the zone offense that we employ.

In the process, over the years, I have become even more convinced by the effectiveness of what the zone offense allows our team to do. It addresses all of our initial concerns, and fulfills each of the five requirements that we were looking for in an offensive scheme. In addition, the zone concept:

- Provides a sound and simplistic way of running the football against any defensive front.
- Gives three basic points of attack on every play and forces the defense to account for all of them because each play starts exactly the same way.
- Allows emphasis on the aggressive and intense execution of basic fundamentals and techniques.
- Helps players be more physical and simply react to the defense by eliminating hesitation and the need to overanalyze different situations.
- Allows teams to block the line of scrimmage, deny penetration, and secure movement by using double-team combination schemes.
- Provides balanced split end-side and tight end-side running attacks.
- Allows teams to attack any hole or weakness in the defense.
- Can be run against any front or style of defense.
- Makes offenses difficult to prepare for because they are able to run a minimal number of base plays in conjunction with a wide array of formations, motions, shifts, and trades.
- Minimizes weekly adjustments and allows teams to perform the functions they do well, regardless of the opponent or defense being faced.
- Can be used in all field positions and situations (coming out of the end zone, red zone, short yardage, third and long, etc.).

- Complements the play action passing game as well as the naked series and the boot series.
- Allows offenses to dictate the tempo of the game and provides them the chance to pound the defense with patience and consistency.
- Relies on the success of the entire offensive unit instead of one or two individuals, and forces players to depend on one another and understand how they are all tied into the scheme.

The key point that should be emphasized is that the zone concept has given us great pride and tremendous confidence in our ability to run the football. It has helped our offensive unit improve year-by-year, week-by-week, game-by-game, practice-by-practice, and play-by-play.

2

Zone Formations

When we first installed the zone offense, we primarily ran our inside and outside zone plays from two-back formations. We have since advanced to the point where we can also run our base plays from one-back formations, but the zone is still primarily a two-back attack. Our one-back formation running attack is discussed and analyzed in later chapters.

The inside and outside zone plays are run primarily from eight formations. A multitude of motions, movements, shifts, and trades can be added to disguise the eight formations and make them appear different. The basic formations that we employ in the zone offense are:

- Queen Right and Queen Left
- King Right and King Left
- Queen Twins Right and Queen Twins Left
- King Twins Right and King Twins Left

The Queen Right and Queen Left formations are shown in Diagrams 2-1 and 2-2, respectively. Queen Right directs the tight end (Y) and the flanker (Z) to align on the side of the call (right), and the split end (X) to align on the side away from the call (left). Queen Right also directs the fullback (F) to align on the side away from the call (left). The fullback's heels are five yards from the line of scrimmage, while his outside

```
    X    O  O  O  O  O  Y
                O              Z
             F
                H
```

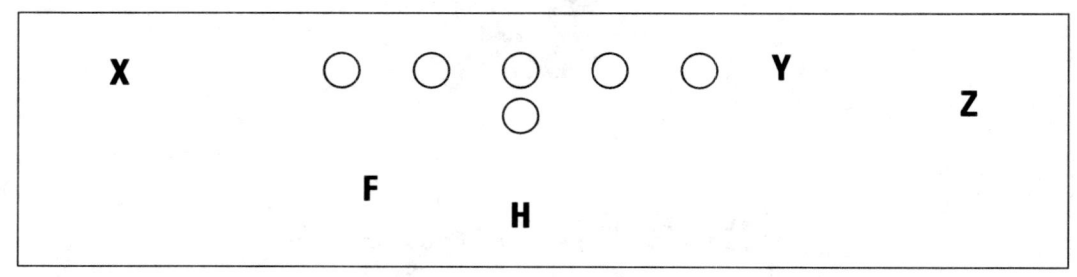

Diagram 2-1: Queen Right formation

foot splits the alignment of the weakside (left) tackle. The halfback (H) aligns directly behind the center in the footsteps of the quarterback, with his heels seven yards from the line of scrimmage. The normal line splits are:

- Center–guard .... 2 feet
- Guard–tackle .... 2 feet
- Tackle–tight end ...... 2-to-3 feet

The relationship that offensive linemen should have to the line of scrimmage is dictated by making one of three calls:

- "On" .... crowd the ball
- "Normal" .... normal depth
- "Off" .... off the ball

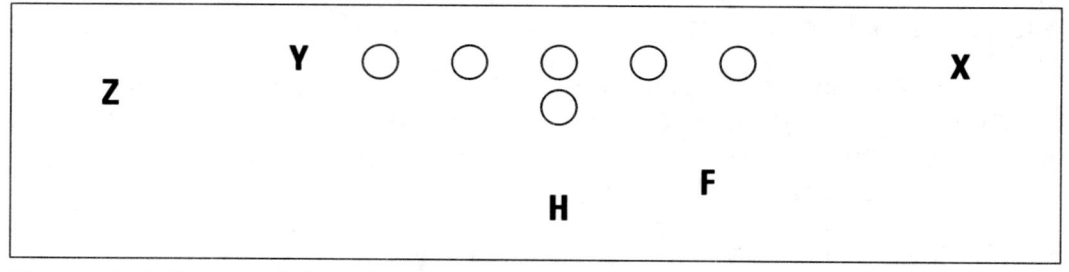

```
            Y  O  O  O  O  O
    Z              O                    X
                 H      F
```

Diagram 2-2: Queen Left formation

The King Right and King Left formations are also used extensively in the zone run game. All of the alignments and position rules remain exactly the same as they were in the Queen formations, except that the fullback now aligns on the side of the call. For our team, a Queen formation is a weak formation, and a King formation is a strong formation. The King Right formation is shown in Diagram 2-3, while the King Left formation is illustrated in Diagram 2-4.

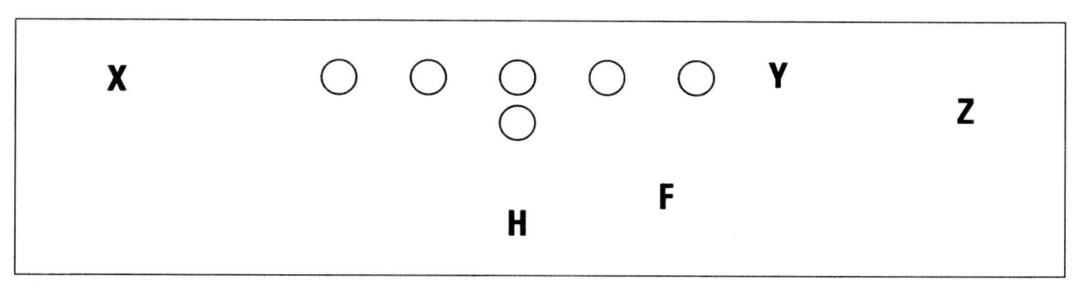

Diagram 2-3: King Right formation

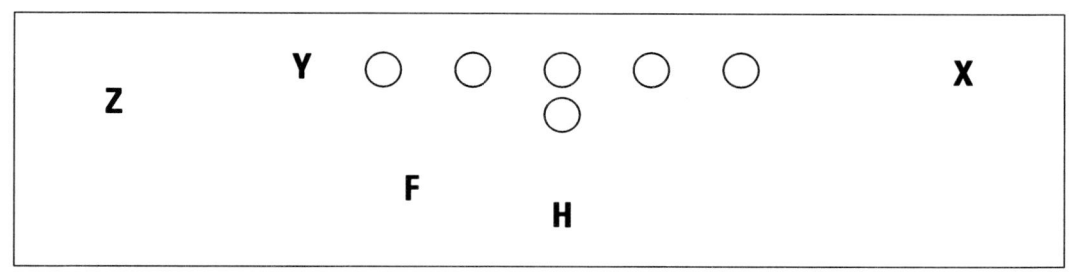

Diagram 2-4: King Left formation

The remaining two-back formations that are utilized in the zone run game are merely adjustments to the King and Queen formations that affect the alignment of the receivers. These formations are used to determine secondary coverages and to dictate second-level run support responsibilities. The first of these formations is Queen Twins Right, shown in Diagram 2-5. Adding the Twins designation to the Queen Right formation directs the flanker (Z) to align with the split end (X) on the side away from the call (left). The alignment of the split end (X) is exactly the same, but now the flanker (Z) is aligned to that player's inside. The tight end (Y) still aligns on the side of the call (right). The alignments of the halfback (H) and the fullback (F) are exactly the same as they are in the normal Queen and King formations. The Queen Twins Left formation is shown in Diagram 2-6.

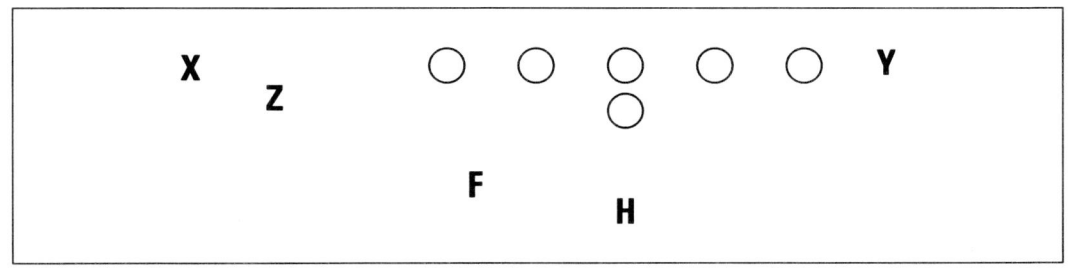

Diagram 2-5: Queen Twins Right formation

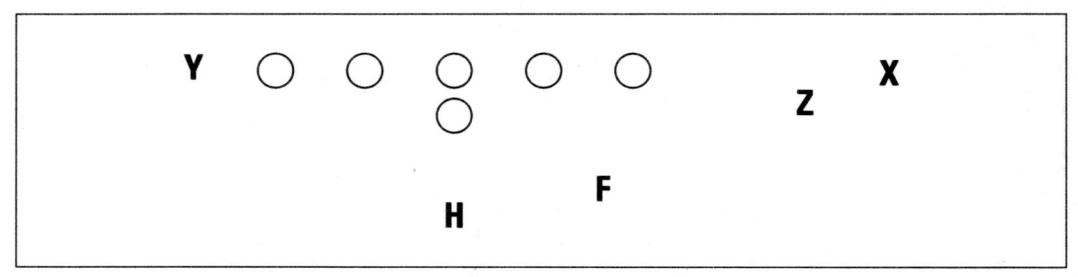

Diagram 2-6: Queen Twins Left formation

The final two formations that feature prominently in the zone attack are King Twins Right, shown in Diagram 2-7, and King Twins Left, illustrated in Diagram 2-8.

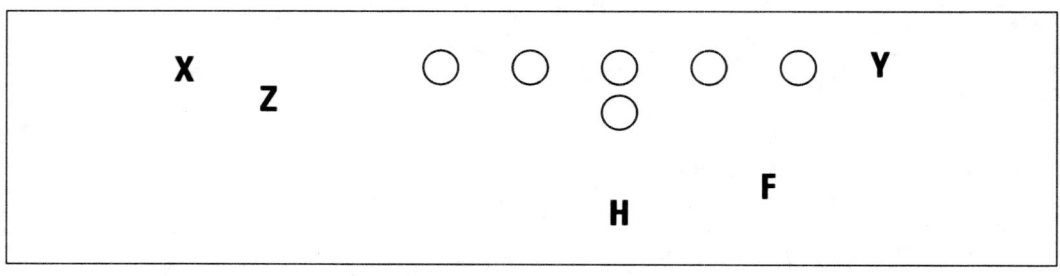

Diagram 2-7: King Twins Right formation

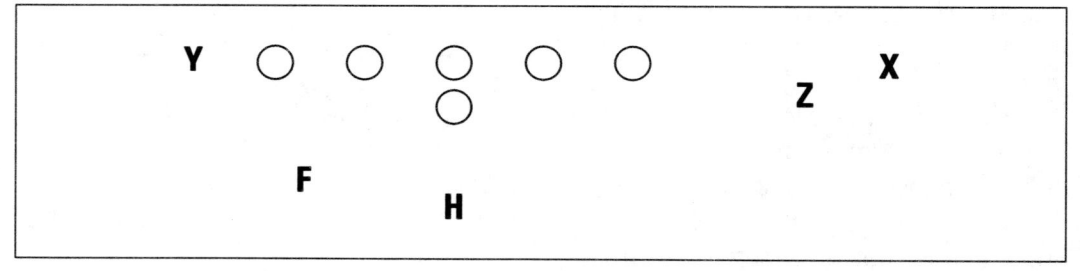

Diagram 2-8: King Twins Left formation

All inside and outside zone plays are called according to a numbering system that allows both the ball carrier and the initial point of attack for the play to be specified. The hole numbering system that is used to specify the point of attack is illustrated in Diagram 2-9. The running back numbering system that is used to specify the ballcarrier is illustrated in diagram 2-10.

This numbering system means that a play numbered 24, for example, would specify that the halfback (the 2-back) should carry the ball through the 4 hole, a direction which requires the halfback to attack the outside leg of the right tackle. This play is illustrated in Diagram 2-11.

Obviously, the way offenses huddle and call their cadences differs greatly from team to team, depending upon the preferences of each team's offensive coaching staff. As such, the zone system can easily be integrated with any previously established parameters involving cadence and the huddle.

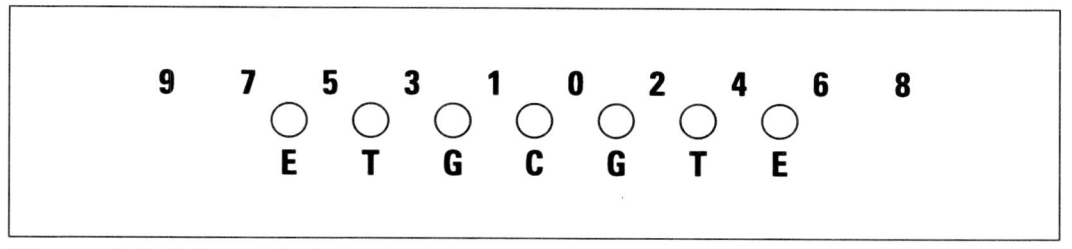

Diagram 2-9: Hole numbering system

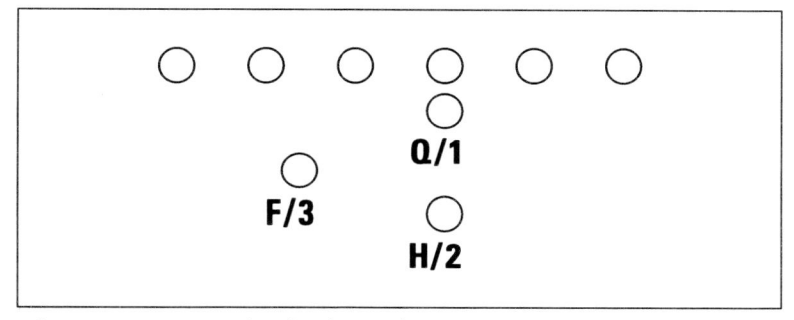

Diagram 2-10: Running back numbering

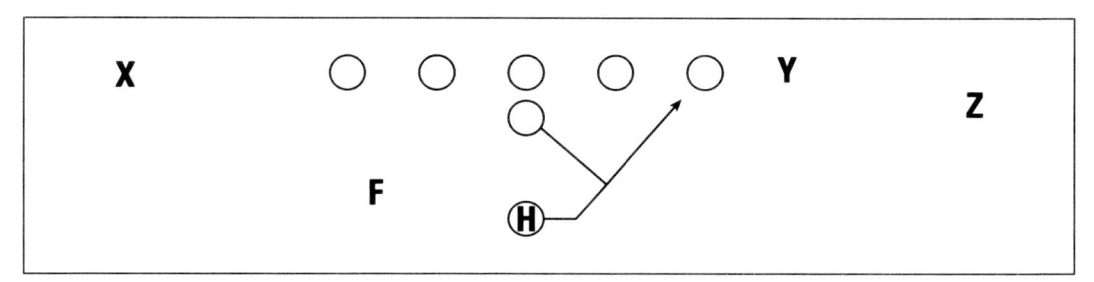

Diagram 2-11: Queen Right 24 Zone

3

The Inside Zone Play—
Tight-End Side

The zone running game really involves only four basic plays. These plays are run from many different formations to vary the anticipated point of attack. The four plays are:

- Inside Zone to the tight-end side
- Inside Zone to the split-end side
- Outside Zone (Stretch) to the tight-end side
- Outside Zone (Stretch) to the split-end side

One of our favorite running plays is the Inside Zone to the tight-end side. When it is run to the right, the play is called 24 Zone, and when it is run to the left, the play is called 25 Zone. This play is usually run from a Queen formation, although it can also be run from a King, Queen Twins, or King Twins formation, which will be discussed later in this chapter. The basic objectives of 24/25 Zone are:

- To utilize Inside Zone blocking schemes to attack the 4 and 5 holes, respectively.
- To attack either the split-end or tight-end sides of the defensive structure.

- To sink and drive the ball into the line of scrimmage, with the running back chasing the inside leg of the playside tackle as a landmark.
- To secure movement along the line of scrimmage with the offensive line, while accounting for any defensive blitzes, games, slants, and stems.
- To create running lanes for the running back by distorting and displacing the defense.
- To allow the defense to press the line of scrimmage and guess where the ball is going to be run, while forcing them to be wrong.
- To block zone to the call with the offensive line, and double team any look along the line of scrimmage.
- To read the first covered playside lineman with the running back, and "feel" the rest of the linemen.

Offensive Line Coaching Points

- The players should not be square; instead, they should work the angle of the ball.
- Two basic rules are followed:
    - If covered, then the linemen will drop step.
    - If uncovered, then the linemen will bucket step.
- Covered playside offensive linemen—drop step:
- The drop step lowers the linemen's center of gravity and allows them to cover up the defensive linemen.
    - They will lose ground to gain a blocking position.
    - They should drop step, sight the outside number, and punch it.
    - On the second step, they should knee the defender on the inside of that player's leg.
    - They should not cross over.
    - They should block flat-footed to sustain the block.
    - They should not allow color to show.
    - They should then finish, push, and pester.
    - Movement is desired.
- Uncovered offensive linemen—bucket step:
    - Getting depth buys linemen time.
    - The depth of their bucket step is based on the depth of the linebacker.
    - The linebacker should be keyed on a 3/5/9-technique call.

- The linemen should work the line of scrimmage first, helping adjacent linemen with a one-hand punch.
- The linebacker will press the line of scrimmage.
- They should keep a low center of gravity and work the angle.
- They should not square up when they get to the second level. They should dip and rip.
- Against a 2/4/6/7-technique call, they should bucket step and bring their hats and hands immediately to the target. The key goes directly to the down lineman.
- They should two-hand punch the outside number.
- They should get movement with adjacent linemen.

Drop Step

It is important to understand exactly what a drop step is, and perhaps more importantly, exactly what it is not. The offensive line and the tight end use precisely the same techniques when executing a drop step. On any play run to the right, the offensive line executes a right-footed drop step. On any play run to the left, the offensive line executes a left-footed drop step. The following coaching points should be emphasized concerning the drop step:

- The players should keep a wide base at all times, especially on contact.
- An instep push-off allows balance to come from the instep and create good power angles. Players should push off with the instep flat-footed, and step with the whole instep in a flat-footed manner.
- The drop step is designed for a blocker to lose ground in order to gain a blocking angle and position on a defender. Blockers should pick the foot up and put it down. The depth and width of the drop step are based on the alignment of the defender.
- The drop step allows blockers to create the best movement on the best angle. Blockers will not shrink the hole, because they will not be in the hole. They will not get flattened out or torqued.
- The drop step allows blockers to cover up a defender on the given angle.
- The drop step creates a slight shoulder turn or shoulder tilt that puts blockers on the proper angle to cover up the defender. Shoulders tilt and hips open according to how the defender is aligned. Shoulders turn and tilt relative to the defender's alignment. The drop step allows for the second step to get through.
- The second step has to get on the ground. The key lies in how fast blockers can get the whole foot down.
- The drop step allows blockers to lower their center of gravity and buys them time to sight the target.

- The drop step allows the linemen to stay gathered by keeping their shoulders between their ankles for balance and demeanor.
- The drop step allows blockers to lose ground to gain a wider base so that when they strike, they strike with a base.
- The drop step gives blockers better leverage by lowering their center of gravity and making them strike with stronger posture.
- The drop step gives blockers the ability to gather themselves and redirect to any inside movement. This demeanor allows them to maintain a base on blocking adjustments.
- Blockers should not step underneath themselves or cross over on the second step. If they step underneath themselves, they will shrink the hole.
- The drop step will time up with the running back's alignment, course, and chase lane. The running back has to complement the offensive line with the same turn and tilt. The running back will move the defense to influence his decision.
- The blocker's shoulders surge toward the defender—a blocker should not raise his shoulders up. His upper body is moving forward on the snap of the ball.
- Uncovered drop step rule: the deeper the linebacker, the deeper the drop step can be, because blockers have more time.

In the 24/25 Inside Zone to the tight-end side, the offensive line uses a series of technique calls and adjustments to communicate and block the different defensive structures. The way we communicate, describe, and teach the various alignment techniques that defensive linemen will play against our offensive linemen is shown in Diagram 3-1.

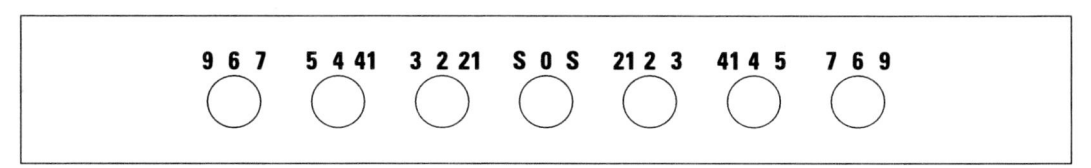

```
9 6 7    5 4 41    3 2 21    S 0 S    21 2 3    41 4 5    7 6 9
 O         O         O         O         O         O         O
```

Diagram 3-1: Technique calls

These technique calls give offensive linemen a way to communicate to each other what techniques the defensive linemen are using. If no down lineman is on a particular offensive lineman, that offensive lineman makes an uncovered call.

Calls and Adjustments

On every Inside Zone running play, each offensive lineman works with an adjacent player, based on the technique call that he receives from that player. The calls and adjustments for 24/25 Inside Zone are:

- Technique calls based on the alignment of the defense
- Hawk call (playside)
- Boss call (playside)
- Mate call (playside)
- Under call (backside)
- Man-it call (backside)

A Hawk call is made when a specific tight-end side alignment from the defensive structure is seen. The particular alignment is shown in Diagram 3-2. A Hawk call tells the offensive line that there is both a 3-technique and a 7-technique to the playside. The offensive line adjusts their blocking scheme—the playside guard base blocks the 3-technique, while the playside tackle one-hand punches the 7-technique, looking for the second-level linebacker. This blocking scheme is illustrated in Diagram 3-3.

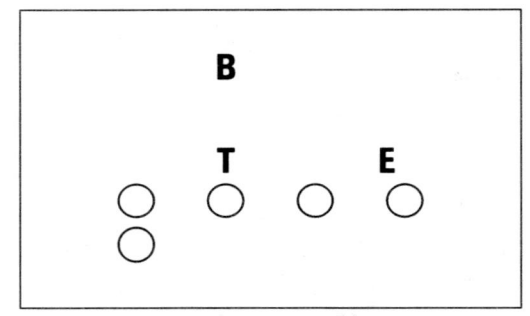

Diagram 3-2: Defensive structure that elicits a Hawk call

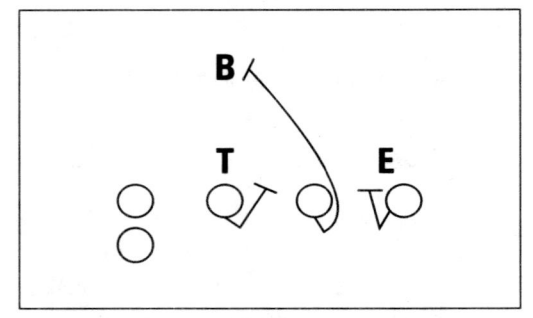

Diagram 3-3: The blocking scheme for a Hawk call

A Hawk call also instructs the tight end to wrong step on his release from the line of scrimmage. On any zone call to the right, the offensive line and the tight end normally make their initial drop steps with their right (playside) foot, but when a Hawk call is executed, the tight end makes his initial step with his left (backside) foot.

The Boss call is an adjustment used by the offensive line when the defensive structure is aligned in such a way that the offensive lineman can wrong step his release from the line of scrimmage in order to secure a double team block along the line of scrimmage and still get to a second-level player. Diagram 3-4 illustrates a defensive structure that would be blocked with a Boss call. Both the right guard and the tight end can wrong step their releases, secure a double team, and then cut off the linebacker.

Another playside adjustment that we make on tight-end side Inside Zone running plays is what we refer to as a Mate call. A Mate call tells the center that he will have to work with the playside guard to block a linebacker who is stacked behind a defensive lineman playing over the playside guard. Diagram 3-5 shows how a Mate call is used to handle this playside stacked look.

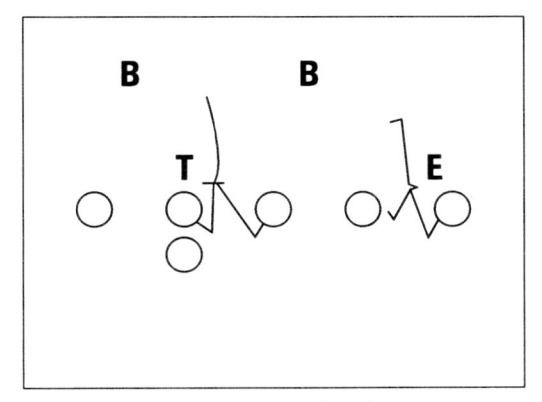

Diagram 3-4: A Boss call situation

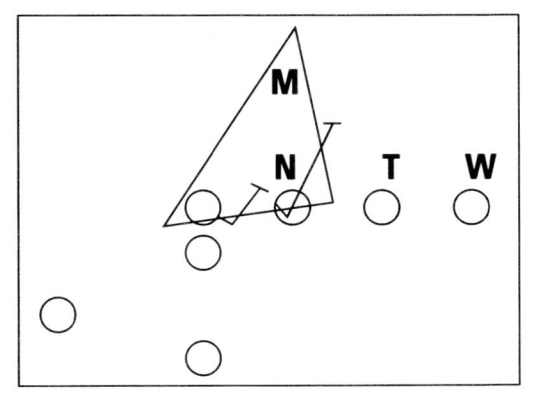

Diagram 3-5: Using a Mate call to handle a playside stacked look

The Under call is a backside adjustment that affects the fullback, backside guard, and backside tackle. Like the other adjustments, an Under call is employed against a specific defensive structure. Diagram 3-6 illustrates an Under call situation.

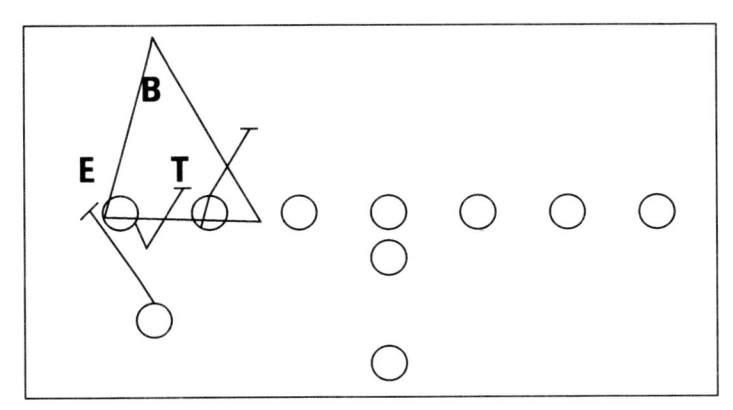

Diagram 3-6: An Under call situation

The final adjustment that we make on Inside Zone to the tight-end side involves a Man-it call. Like the Under call, it is a backside call that affects the fullback, the backside guard, and the backside tackle. It is used against defensive structures that incorporate a second-level player with a foldback defender. In a Man-it scheme, the fullback accounts for the second-level player. A Man-it situation is illustrated in Diagram 3-7.

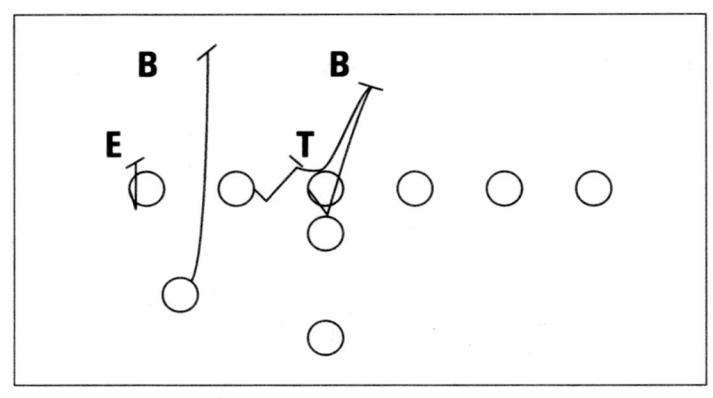

Diagram 3-7: Man-it call situation

Inside Zone Blocking Techniques and Rules

It is critical to understand the basic techniques that the offensive line should utilize when blocking Inside Zone. Two different techniques, which were introduced earlier in this chapter, are employed when blocking Inside Zone—covered at the point of attack and uncovered at the point of attack.

Zone Blocking—Covered at the Point of Attack:

- Assignment: reach block
- Technique: drop step and punch
- Target: two inches outside of the opposing player's midline; offensive linemen get pad under pad
- Players drop step and tilt their shoulders on an angle to cover up the defender. They should force the defender to make a decision. Blockers have to displace, distort, and stretch the defender.
- Blockers lead with their pads and fists. The upper body should go forward and surge on the angle. Blockers should punch, lift, and strain.
- The arms should be cocked and whipped for momentum. Blockers should thrust with their hands and then grab. They get their arms inside with upper-body violence and explosion.
- The second step should be put down immediately, slightly inside the defender. The blockers should knee the defender on the inside of that player's leg on the crossover, and get movement on the angle.
- On stalemates, the blocker's base should be widened quickly. The blockers activate their feet and finish when the defender moves to pursue the ball.
- If the defender slants, the blockers should stop and drop step with their inside foot to come back and get a piece of the defender.

- If the defender widens, or the blockers feel him beyond their center of gravity, then the blockers should twist that player out with the inside arm and the head. They should stay on the defender's body and finish.
- Ninety percent of the block is finish.

Zone Blocking—Uncovered at the Point of Attack:

- The drop step is based on the depth of the linebacker. If the linebacker is deep (i.e., three to five yards), then the blockers take a deeper drop step for depth and width. If the linebacker's depth is less than three yards, then the blockers drop step and waddle.
- Against a slow-flow linebacker, the blockers should key the linebacker. They should punch and grab the playside target or utilize the flipper technique. The linebacker should be blocked on or near the line of scrimmage.
- Against a fast-flow linebacker, the blockers should convert their hands to a two-hand punch and peak on the line of scrimmage. They should get movement and push with the outside blocker. Movement is crucial.
- The running back will set up the block. Therefore, the blockers have time. Accordingly, an understanding of timing is crucial. The running back will bring the linebacker to the blockers. The blockers should allow the linebacker to press the line of scrimmage.
- Shoulder angle and shoulder tilt should be maintained. The blockers should not get squared up; they should be alert to keep at the playside arm.
- The blockers should stay in their demeanor and maintain body control. They should understand that the best holes and creases are to the bubble in the defense.

Table 3-1 summarizes the blocking rules for 24/25 Inside Zone to the tight-end side.

Attacking a 5-2 Okie Front

Given the aforementioned blocking rules, the 24/25 Inside Zone should be considered against a variety of defensive fronts and structures. One of the defenses that should be considered is a standard 5-2 Okie front, as illustrated in Diagram 3-8.

Against an Okie front, the tight end and the playside tackle would base reach block the 5- and 9-techniques, respectively. The playside guard would follow his uncovered rule. The center would block the 0-technique, and the backside guard would execute a zone combination block with the center to account for the backside linebacker. It is important to understand the zone combination block executed by the center and the backside guard. This basic blocking scheme is the backbone of the entire attack.

Position	Assignment Rules/Coaching Points
Playside Tackle	• 4/5 call (covered rule). • Uncovered (uncovered rule). • Be alert for 6/7 call by tight end. • Be alert for Hawk call.
Playside Guard	• 1/2/3 call (covered rule). • Uncovered (uncovered rule). • Be alert for 4 call. • If 4 call, bring hat and hands.
Center	• Strong shade, 0 call, weak shade (covered rule). • Be alert for Hawk call, eyeball A gap, from the line of scrimmage to the second level.
Backside Guard	• 1/2 call (covered rule). • 3 call (uncovered rule). • Uncovered (uncovered rule). • Be alert for Under call or Man-it call against a 2- or 3-technique.
Backside Tackle	• 4 call (drop step and cut). • 5 call (drop and rip). • Uncovered (uncovered rule). • Be alert for Man-it call and communicate with running back.
Tight End	• Playside (base block). • Backside (cut off). • Players get movement up the field, then twist. • Players should not allow fold or quick chase, and they should be alert for crossing the opposing player's face.
Split End	• Playside (man on). • Backside (near safety).
Wide Receiver	• Playside (man on). • Backside (near safety).
Quarterback	• Open to play call. Drive the ball deep to halfback; point of aim is playside tackle's inside leg. Open to 10 o'clock and continue on naked fake after hand-off. Six-man rules apply in two-back formations.
Halfback	• Heels at seven yards. Open step at landmark 1 X 3 yards outside of tight end, second step at playside tackle, and continue on that path playside and "feel" the rest. If linebackers press, push helmet to playside tackle's outside leg. Chase the playside tackle's inside leg.
Fullback	• Heels at five yards. Regardless of position, block first defender outside of the backside tackle. Read first covered lineman.

Table 3-1: Blocking rules 24/25 Zone to the tight-end side.

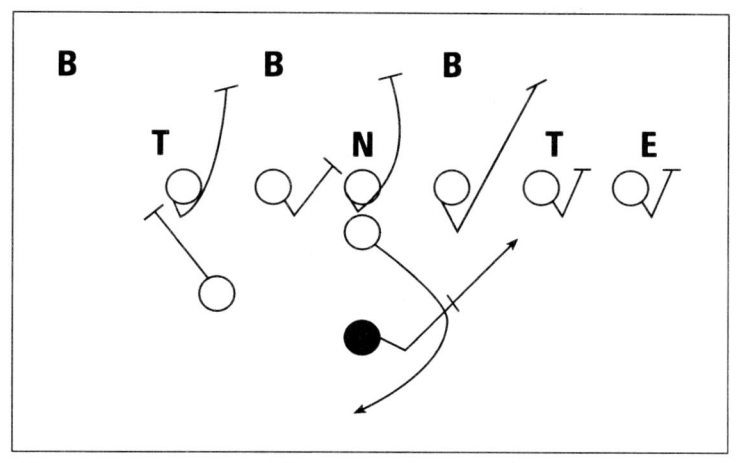

Diagram 3-8: Queen Right 24 Zone vs. an Okie front

Zone Blocking—Center-and-Backside Guard Combo:

- The center:
    - Against an O-technique, the normal zone rules apply.
    - Against an O-technique, the center will slant backside, stop, redirect, and put a body on the defender. He should maintain shoulder angle and key the backside linebacker with his eyes. The hands convert to a flipper.
    - Against a backside shade, the center will drop step and work bucket progression along the line of scrimmage to the second level. He should work his eyes and have a feel for second-level timing. On bucket progression, the backside guard will punch the nose guard into the center's lap. The center should be alert to grab it, especially on a slant move.
- The backside guard:
    - Against an O-technique or uncovered, the backside guard should drop step, punch, and peak. Slanting away will force the player to convert and waddle to the second level.
    - Against an O-technique shaded to the backside, the backside guard should drop step and two-hand punch the playside target. He will punch and peak. He should punch the nose guard back to the center and get movement, and then peek for the backside run-through. If the linebacker flows fast, the player should finish the nose guard hard and keep fighting his head inside.

The backside tackle and the fullback work the edge. The backside tackle drop steps and works up the field while the fullback blocks the edge.

Attacking an Eagle Strong Front

The next defensive structure that should be considered is the Eagle Strong. Against Eagle Strong, a Hawk call adjustment has to be made (Diagram 3-9). This adjustment allows the tight end to wrong step his release, and the playside tackle to block the second level. When we run Inside Zone against teams that play this type of defense, we expect that the running back will probably cut back, because the playside guard will have a very difficult time executing a reach block on the 3-technique.

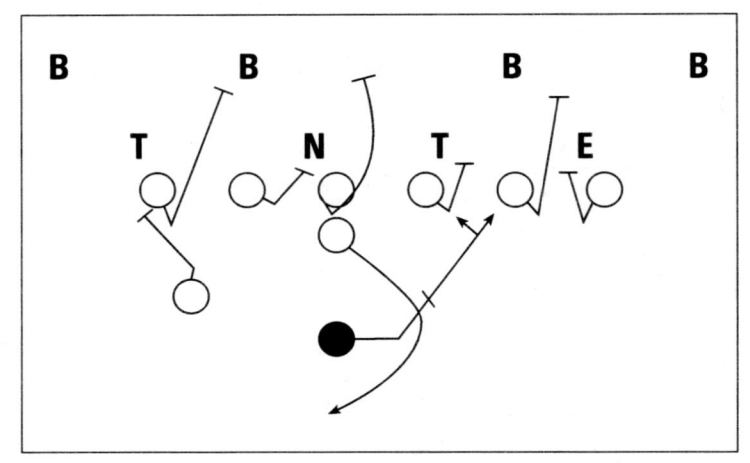

Diagram 3-9: Queen Right 24 Zone vs. an Eagle Strong front

Attacking a 4-3 Front

Another defensive alignment which must be considered is a 4-3 front. When a 24/25 Inside Zone is run against a 4-3 front, we expect the ball to be cut back inside of the 3-technique. We want the halfback to press the line of scrimmage and make the Mike linebacker attack him. The only possible adjustment against the 4-3 would be a Man-it call by the backside tackle and the fullback, allowing the fullback to attack the Will linebacker and keep the backside tackle on the defensive end. Diagram 3-10 illustrates 24 Zone against a 4-3 front.

Attacking a Reduced

An Eagle package on the split end-side is referred to as a Reduced front. Diagram 3-11 shows 24 Zone run against a Reduced front. The playside tackle and the tight end execute base zone blocks against a Reduced package. The playside guard follows his uncovered rule, and the center blocks the strong shade. The backside executes an Under call, with the backside guard getting off to the linebacker and the backside tackle blocking the 3-technique. The fullback blocks the edge, which would be the 5-technique.

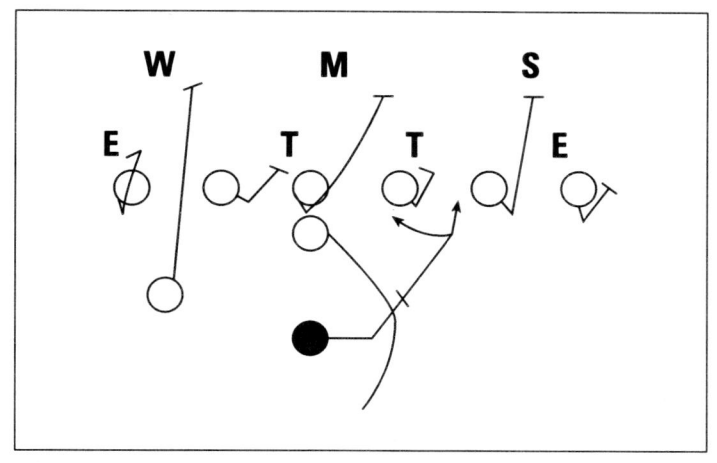

Diagram 3-10: Queen Right 24 Zone vs. a 4-3 front

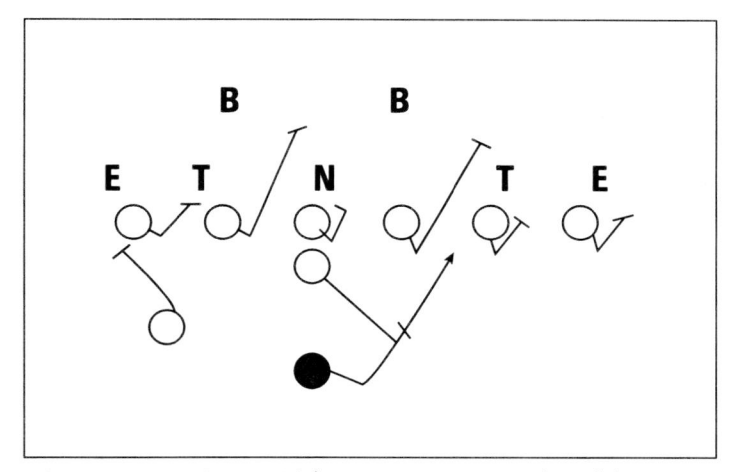

Diagram 3-11: Queen Right 24 Zone vs. a Reduced front

Attacking a Stack Front

Diagram 3-12 shows 24 Zone against a Stack front. It is a front in which everyone is covered by a defender except the center. A Stack front forces an adjustment to the center's normal Inside Zone blocking scheme. The center makes a Mate call, which tells the playside guard that he and the center will execute a zone combination scheme on the 2-technique and the linebacker. Diagram 3-13 illustrates this scheme.

The backside of the offensive line and the fullback will execute an Under call. If the backside guard has a 2-technique or a 2i-technique, then he can also block the play, as shown in Diagram 3-14.

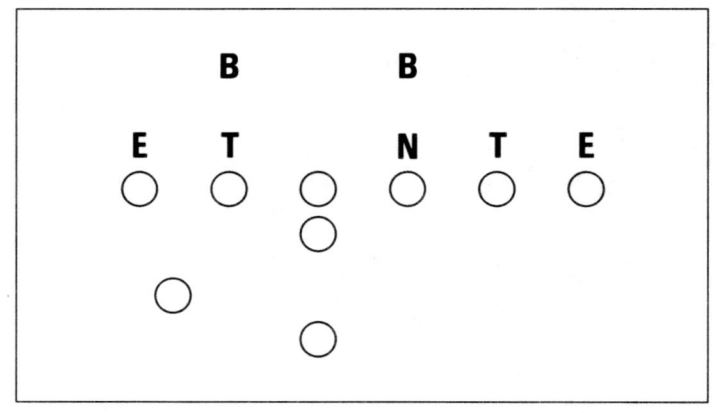

Diagram 3-12: Queen Right 24 Zone vs. a Stack front

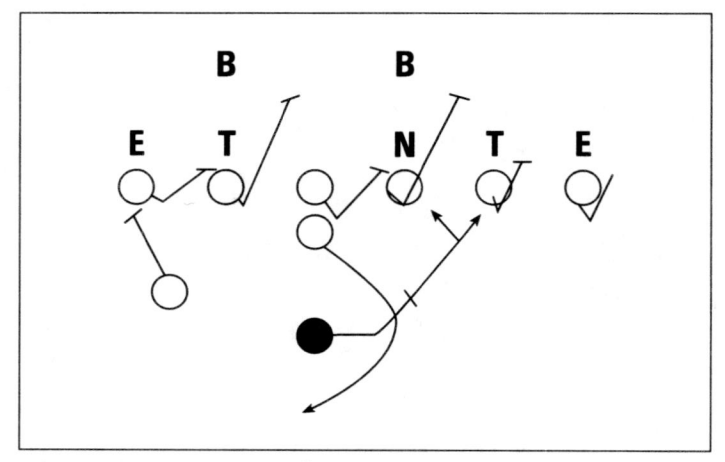

Diagram 3-13: A Mate call situation against a Stack front

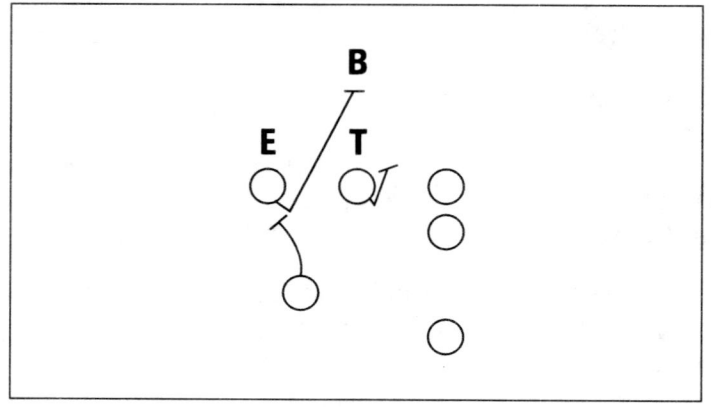

Diagram 3-14: Backside scheme vs. a Stack front

28

Attacking a Slide Weakside Front

Another defensive structure that must be considered is the Slide Weak, a true eight-man front. Because it is an eight-man front, the center will have to make a call that adjusts the blocking scheme. Diagram 3-15 illustrates the basic structure of a Slide Weak front.

Because only seven offensive players are available to block eight defenders, the scheme has to be adjusted. We will always let the strong outside linebacker go unaccounted for in the blocking scheme. Diagram 3-16 shows how we block 24 Zone against a team that plays a Slide Weak front.

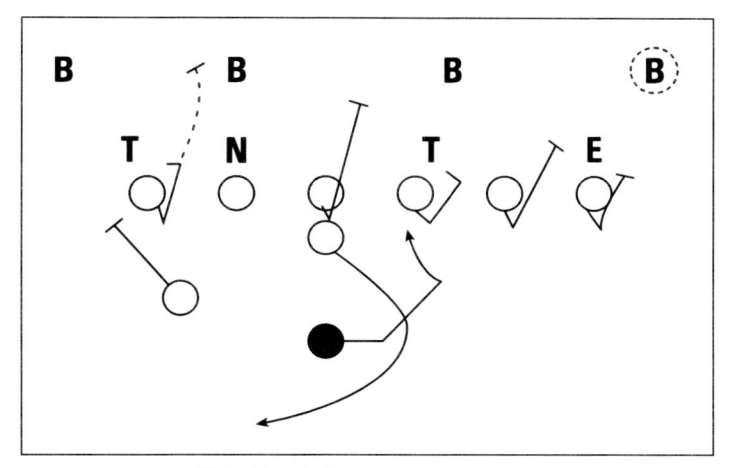

Diagram 3-15: Slide Weak front

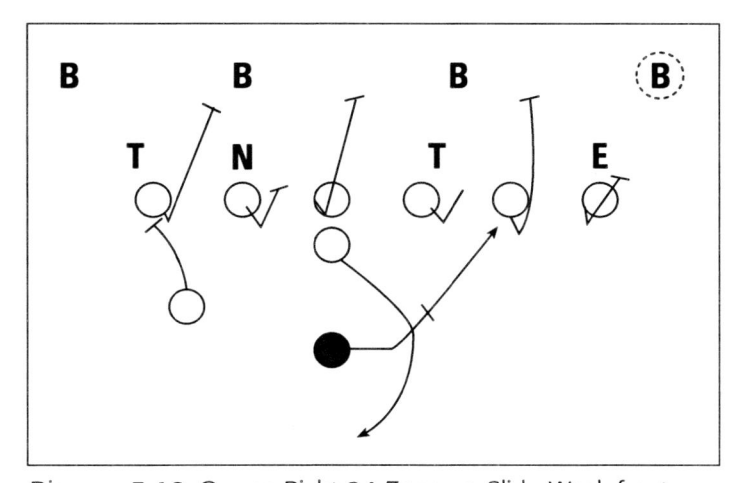

Diagram 3-16: Queen Right 24 Zone vs. Slide Weak front

Against Slide Weak, we want to accomplish three basic objectives:

- Press the line of scrimmage
- Block the foldback defender
- Run at the bubble in the defense

These points can be accomplished while allowing the strong outside linebacker (or the strong safety) to be unblocked. Depending on the alignment of the front, the offensive line could execute a Boss call or a Hawk call to block the Slide Weak front.

Using the King formation for the 24/25 Inside Zone

The 24/25 Inside Zone play can also be run from a King formation. It should be remembered that the King formation puts the fullback on the tight-end side of the formation (Diagram 3-17).

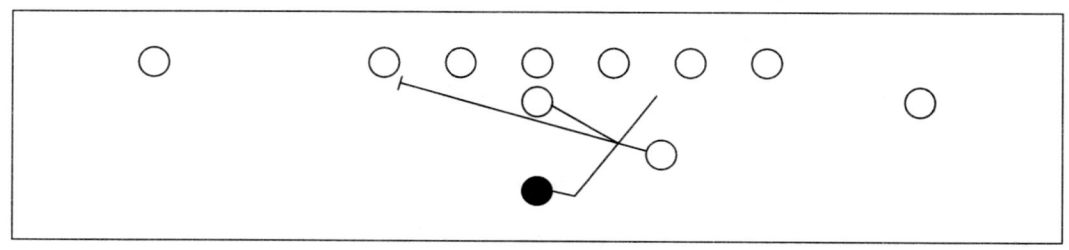

Diagram 3-17: A King Right formation

When running 24/25 Inside Zone out of the King formation, a designation (back) is added to the play call that tells the fullback to go to the backside and do exactly what he does when he is in a Queen formation. This play is shown in Diagram 3-18 against an Eagle Strong alignment. The blocking schemes stay exactly the same, but now the fullback will have to block the edge from the King set. The fullback has to run a path underneath the quarterback and block the backside edge just as he does in the Queen formation. All other blocking assignments remain unchanged.

Another way to break tendencies and alignment keys is by moving the fullback around. For example, when lining up in King Right, the fullback can be motioned into Queen Right, prior to the snap. Diagram 3-19 illustrates this movement.

This motion is accomplished in our system by calling King Right F Liz 24, which looks exactly like Queen Right 24 when the ball is snapped. F Liz tells the fullback to go into Liz motion, which always means to the left (rip motion would mean the fullback would go to the right). 24 tells all players what their blocking assignment is (24 Inside Zone) and indicates to the fullback where he should be when the ball is snapped. The play is shown against a Reduced front in Diagram 3-20.

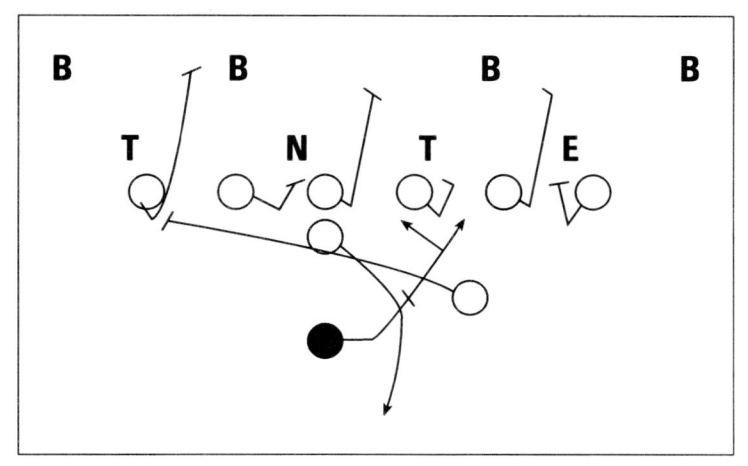

Diagram 3-18: King Right 24 Zone vs. an Eagle Strong front

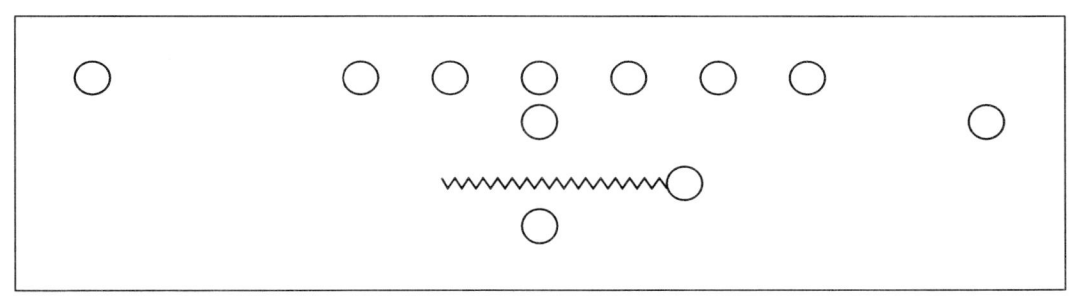

Diagram 3-19: Motion to a Queen Right formation

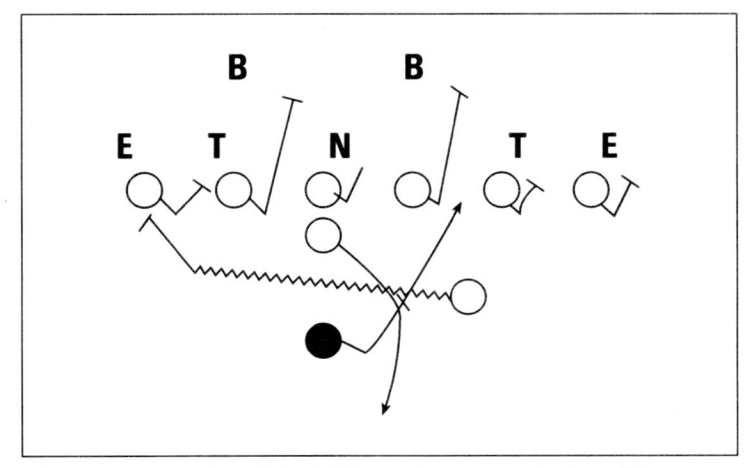

Diagram 3-20: King Right F Liz 24 Zone vs. a Reduced front

The alignments of the wide receivers are varied to help soften up the outside run support that defenses may utilize. Diagram 3-21 illustrates Queen Twins Right against a 4-3 front.

The point was made previously that against a Slide Weak front (or any eight-man front), we could not account for the eighth man, and that we were not going to block the strong outside linebacker. However, when the strong outside linebacker is up on the line of scrimmage and becoming actively involved in stopping the run, the failure to block him is no longer a viable option. Diagram 3-22 illustrates this problem.

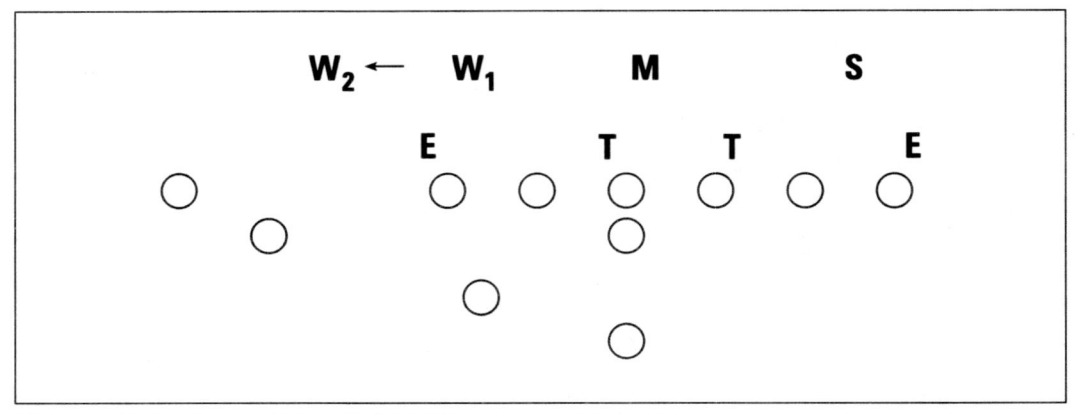

Diagram 3-21: Queen Twins Right 24 Zone vs. a 4-3 front

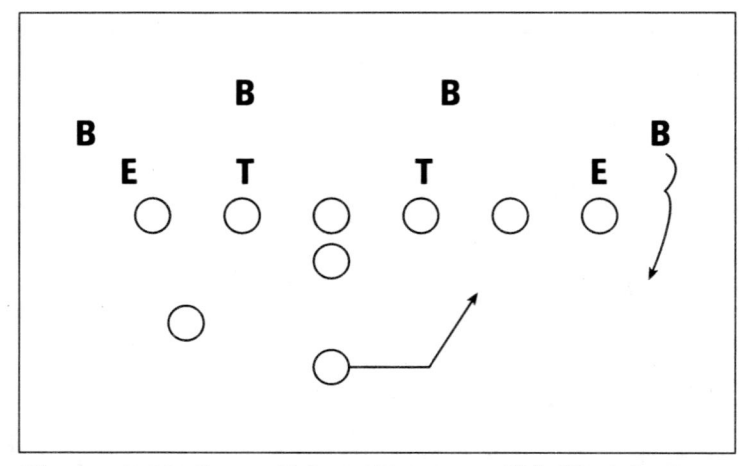

Diagram 3-22: Queen Right 24 Zone vs. a Slide Weak front

One possible answer to this problem is to utilize the flanker to help block a run-support player in order to gain an additional blocker against an eight-man front. This adjustment in scheme is called Smash. Smash tells the flanker to block the strongside edge. We teach this block as a position block only, and tell the flanker that he does not have to achieve a knockdown. The incorporation of a Smash scheme is shown in Diagram 3-23.

Another adjustment that we make to our basic 24/25 Inside Zone blocking scheme is called Wham. Wham allows the fullback to line up in a King formation and trap block a defensive down lineman, thus slowing the lineman's penetration across the line of scrimmage. We especially like to run Wham against a Reduced front. Diagram 3-24 illustrates 24 Wham.

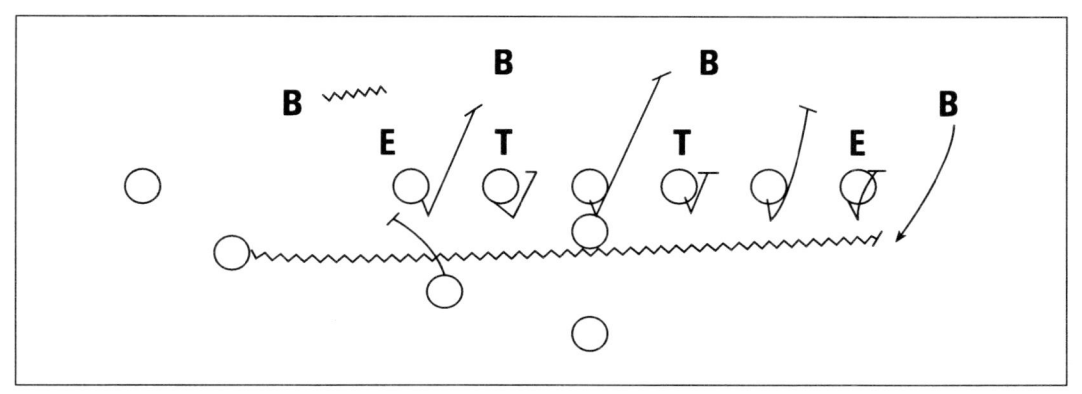

Diagram 3-23: Queen Twins Right Z Rip 24 Smash vs. a Slide Weak front

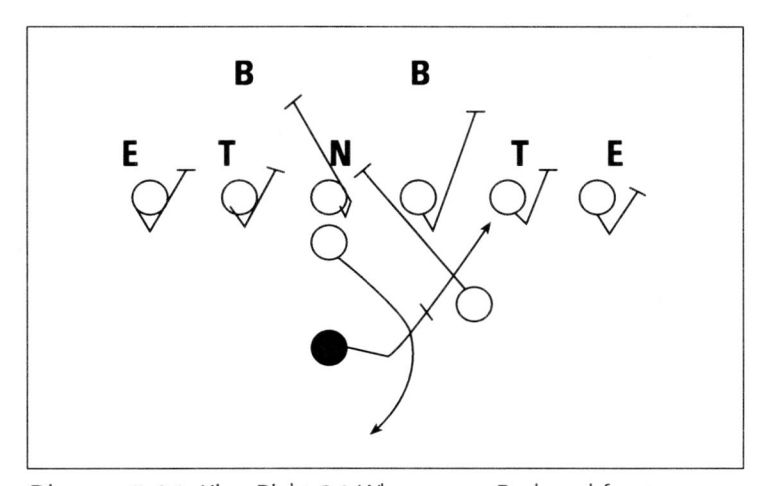

Diagram 3-24: King Right 24 Wham vs. a Reduced front

On the playside, the blocking rules for 24/25 Wham are the same as for 24/25 Inside Zone. An adjustment has to be made on the backside because there is no fullback to account for the edge. As shown in Diagram 3-24, the fullback blocks the shade against a team that plays a Reduced front. The following table summarizes the blocking rules for 24/25 Wham.

Position	Assignment Rules/Coaching Points
Playside Tackle	• Block 24/25 Inside Zone rules. • If uncovered, tightens landmark to the second level.
Playside Guard	• Block 24/25 Inside Zone rules. • If uncovered, tightens landmark to the second level.
Center	• Covered (blunt to first or second level). • Uncovered (block 24/25 Inside Zone rules). • Quick blunt to second level with Bob call.
Backside Guard	• Covered (cut-off 2/3-technique, with shade call). • Uncovered (Bob/Me). • Oversplit to three feet and cut-off 2/3/4I-technique.
Backside Tackle	• Covered (cut-off or Bob numbers 1 and 2 on line of scrimmage).
Tight End	• Block 24/25 Inside Zone rules.
Split End	• Playside (head-up). • Backside (head-up).
Flanker	• Playside (head-up). • Backside (head-up).
Quarterback	• Same as 24/25 Inside Zone.
Halfback	• Same as 24/25 Inside Zone.
Fullback	• Attack line of scrimmages block on line of scrimmage playside A gap to backside using kickout technique.

Table 3-2: The blocking rules for 24/25 Wham

Using a One-Back Formation for the 24/25 Inside Zone

Our basic 24/25 Inside Zone plays can also be run from one-back formations. One season, for example, we averaged over nine yards per rushing attempt when running the one-back Inside Zone. Based on yards per attempt, it was the most effective running play in our entire attack. While an unlimited number of one-back formations exist, we primarily run Inside Zone to the tight-end side from three basic one-back sets—Deuce, Trips, and Trey (Diagrams 3-25 to 3-30).

When one-back zone is run, the fullback is replaced by another wide receiver (Z2). Adding another receiver to the formation forces the defense to cover him, which removes one defensive player from his normal run support position. What we really do is block that defender by alignment. Diagram 3-31 shows our original two-back running play against an Okie front. From this formation, the weak outside linebacker is accounted for by blocking the backside edge with the fullback and the backside tackle.

Diagram 3-25: Deuce Right

Diagram 3-26: Deuce Left

Diagram 3-27: Trips Right

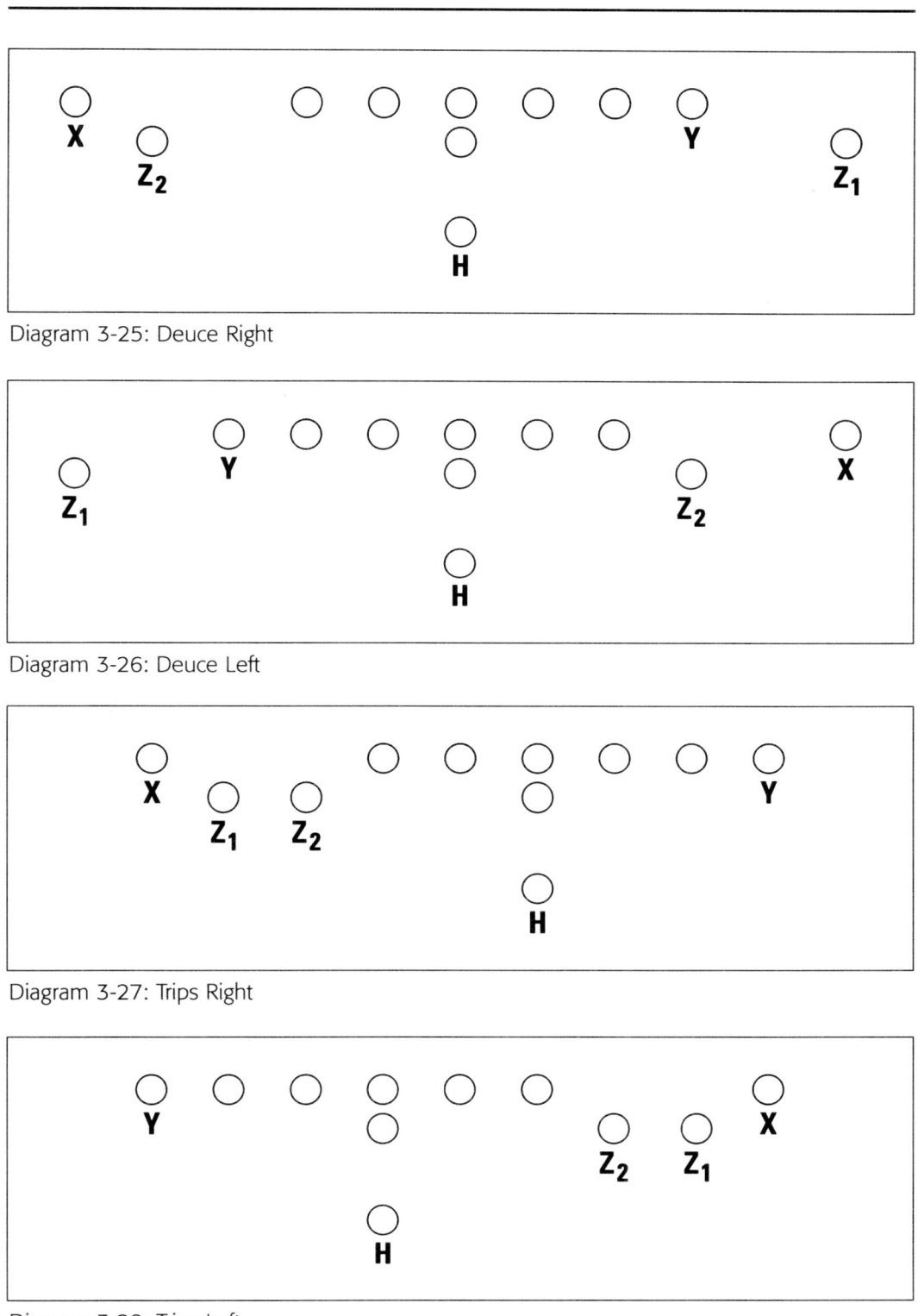

Diagram 3-28: Trips Left

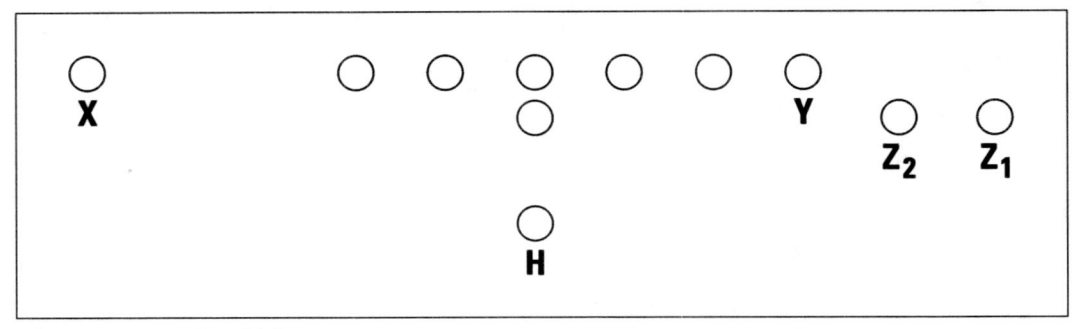

Diagram 3-29: Trey Right

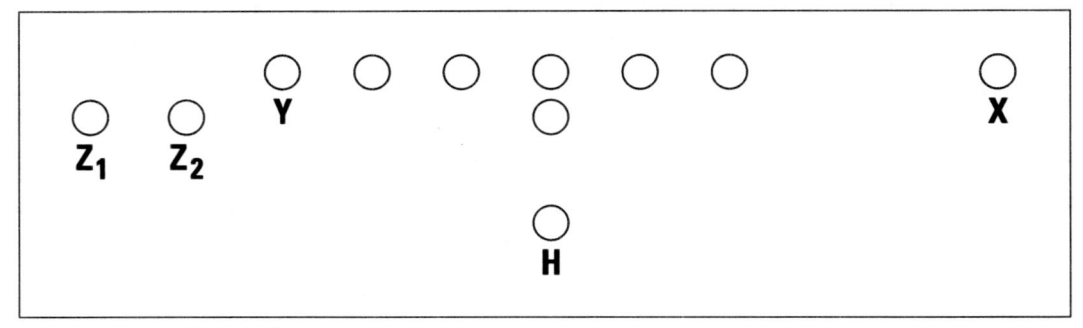

Diagram 3-30: Trey Left

In Diagram 3-32, the weak outside linebacker has removed himself from the defensive structure in order to cover the third receiver. The backside tackle is then allowed to adequately block the edge by himself, without needing help from the fullback. In order to clearly distinguish between one-back and two-back zone schemes, the one-back play Razor is called.

The blocking rules for 24/25 Razor are extremely basic:

- Offensive line:
  - The backside tackle has to know on a Razor call that he stays on a 5-technique.
  - No backside edge is being blocked. The backside edge is accounted for by alignment.
  - The backside tackle has to tighten his landmark and work more vertical.
- Running back:
  - Since the backside edge is not being blocked, he has to think about pressing the landmark first, and then think about cutting back.
  - The player should be aware of what the front is, because the possibility exists of someone coming free on the edge against a blitz or an adjusted front.

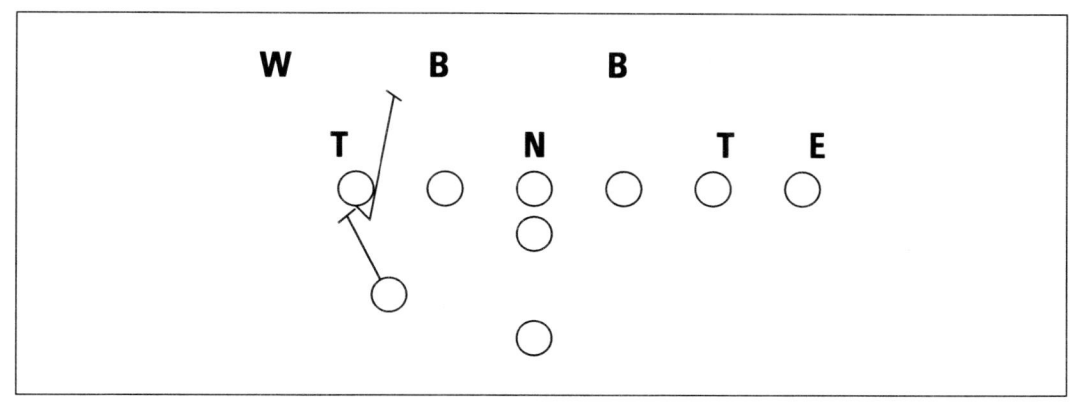

Diagram 3-31: Queen Right 24 Zone vs. an Okie front

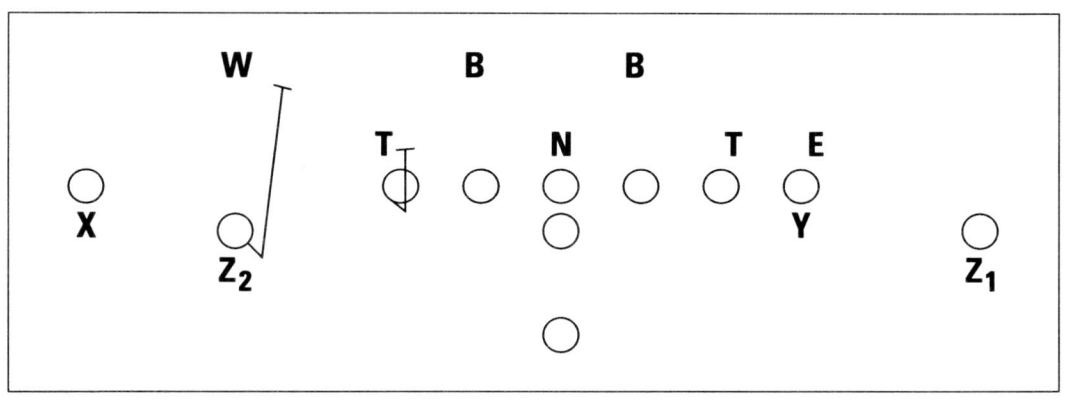

Diagram 3-32: Deuce Right vs. an Okie front

24 Razor is shown against an Okie front in Diagram 3-33. The blocking assignments are as follows:

- The playside tackle covered—reads outside number.
- The playside guard uncovered—bucket steps and zones first level to second level.
- The center covered—reads outside number.
- The backside guard uncovered—zones and does not get flattened out.
- The backside tackle covered—tightens landmark and works vertical.
- The tight end covered—reads outside number.
- The running back (same rules as 24/25 Inside Zone)—watches out for edge.
- The slot—blocks the weak curl defender.

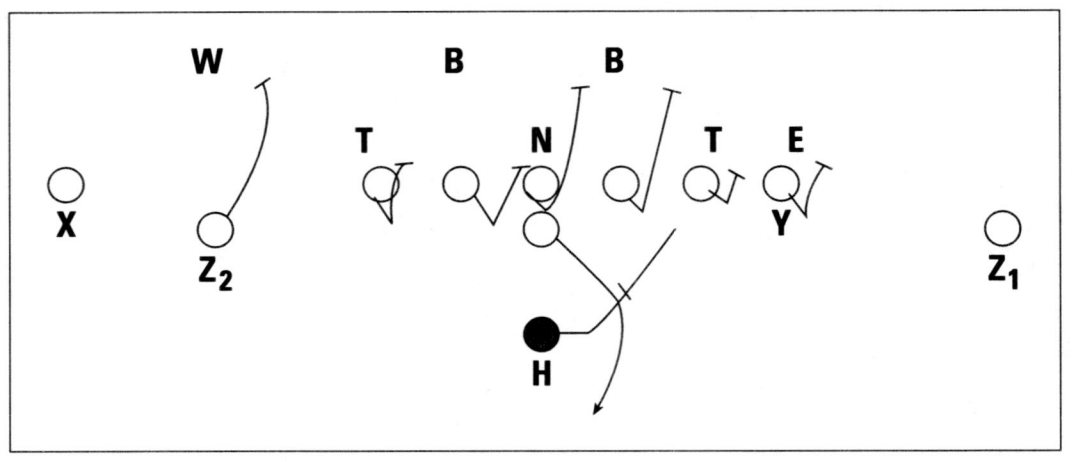

Diagram 3-33: Deuce Right 24 Razor vs. an Okie front

The most important coaching point regarding the one-back zone attack is the incorporation of a check-with-me principle. While we are depending on the defense to remove a defender to cover the third receiver so that we can account for that defender by alignment, the defense may choose not to do this. Some defenses will ignore the third receiver and gang up on the run.

To combat this problem, all of our one-back zone plays are called check-with-me plays, like Deuce Right 24 Razor check-with-me. Check-with-me alerts players to the possibility of the quarterback calling an audible at the line of scrimmage and changing the play. Our quarterbacks are taught to read the alignment of the weak curl/flat defender in order to determine whether to run the called Inside Zone (Razor) play or an available complementary pass play.

Diagram 3-34 shows a defense that refuses to honor the threat of the third receiver. The weak outside linebacker is in a run-support position. This situation requires the quarterback to check out of the one-back Razor run and audible to the corresponding pass play. One possibility in this regard is illustrated in Diagram 3-35.

Obviously, one-back formations give offenses the ability to spread the defense out and make it possible to decrease the number of defenders that have to be blocked at the point of attack. They also provide an additional potential receiving threat—a situation that offers a tremendous advantage against certain run-conscious defensive structures.

While the basic tight-end side Inside Zone run is a very basic play, it is run from a variety of formations and incorporates several different blocking schemes. It is disguised with several types of motions. No matter what defense we face, we are confident in the ability to attack any front with one form or another of the Inside Zone.

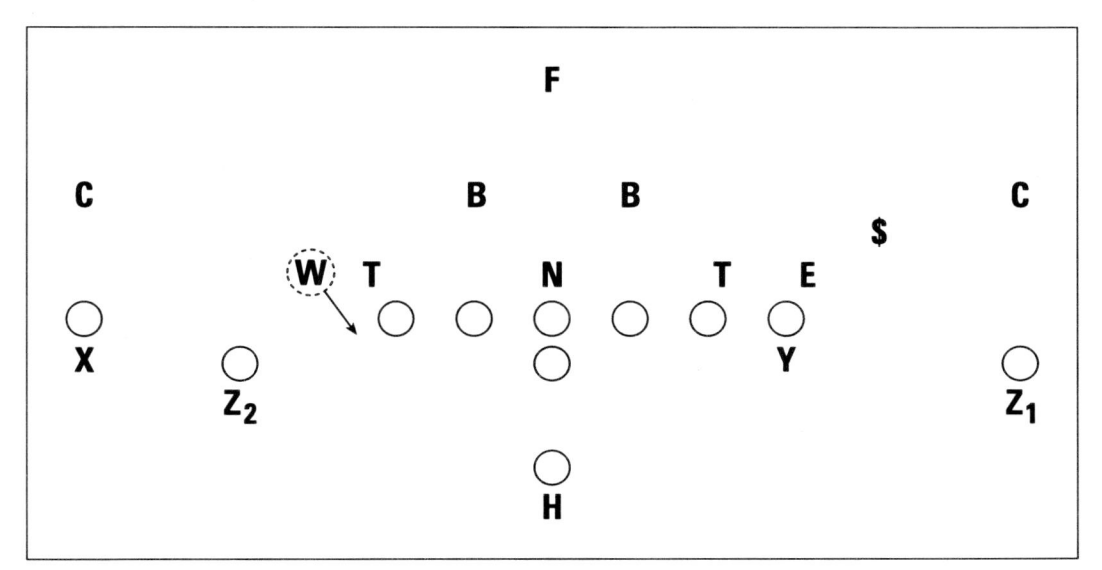

Diagram 3-34: Deuce Right 24 Razor vs. an Okie front

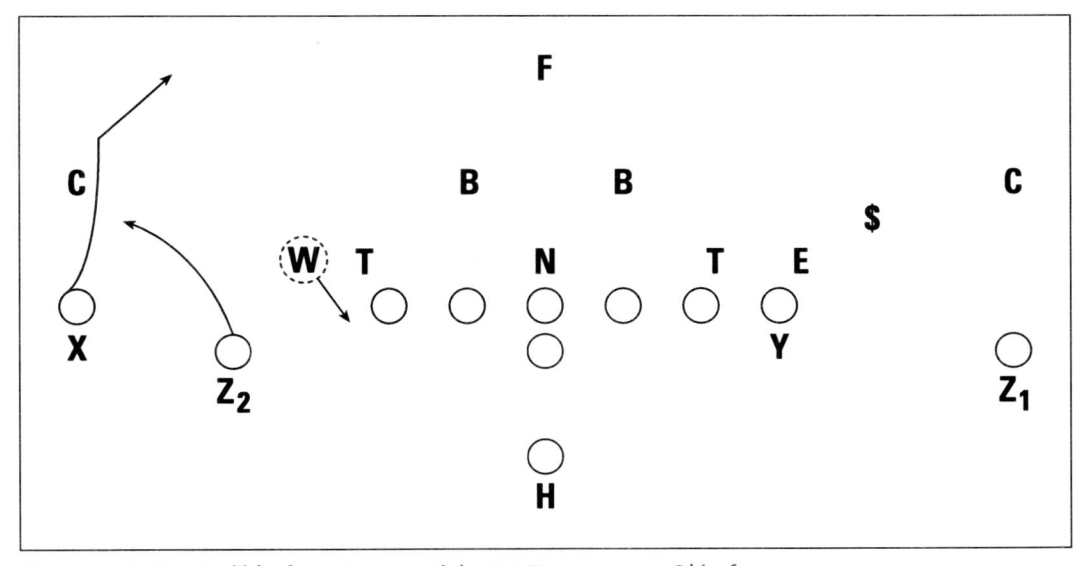

Diagram 3-35: Audible from Deuce Right 24 Razor vs. an Okie front

4

The Inside Zone Play—
Split-End Side

We also run an Inside Zone play to the split-end side of the formation. We add a designation (BOB) to the play title because it is always run away from the tight end to the open side of the formation, and we want to be certain of the changes in the blocking scheme. We call this play 24 BOB (to the right) or 25 BOB (to the left). It is usually run from a Queen formation, but can also be run from a Twins formation.

The approach to this play is exactly the same as the approach regarding the tight end-side play. The only difference in this play is that it is run to the split-end side of the formation. We are somewhat limited in running 24/25 BOB because it can only be run from two-back formations.

The offensive line follows the same covered/uncovered rules discussed in Chapter 3. The offensive line's basic scheme is exactly the same in 24/25 Zone and 24/25 BOB. The BOB designation alerts the fullback that he has a specific blocking assignment on this play. He will block the overhang of the defense. A defense with an overhang player is shown in Diagram 4-1.

Any first or second-level defender aligned on the split-end side of the formation outside of the offensive tackle's alignment is identified as an overhang. We would

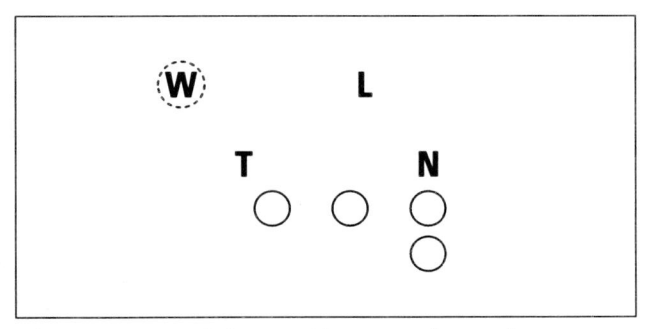

Diagram 4-1: A defense with an overhang player

never treat a rolled cornerback or a half-field safety as an overhang, as shown in Diagram 4-2. If the defensive structure has no overhang, the fullback is responsible for the weak inside linebacker, as shown in Diagram 4-3.

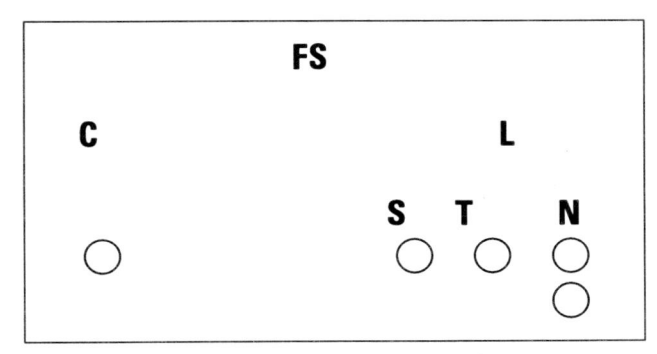

Diagram 4-2: A defense without an overhang

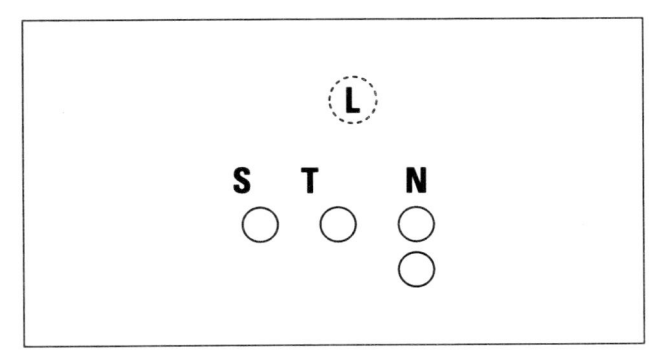

Diagram 4-3: The fullback is responsible for the weak inside linebacker in a defense without overhang

The fullback is also told on 24/25 BOB that his first step will look exactly like it does when the outside zone (Stretch) is run. The fullback will help soften up the defense by preventing them from aggressively attacking the inside play. All of the other offensive players follow the same rules in 24/25 BOB as they do when running 24/25 Zone to the tight-end side, as shown in Chapter 3.

Attacking a 5-2 Okie Front

BOB is illustrated against a standard 5-2 Okie front in Diagram 4-4. Because the Okie defense has an overhang, the fullback will follow his rule and block the overhang. The playside tackle will displace the 5-technique and the playside guard will follow his uncovered rule against the weak inside linebacker. The center and the backside guard will use a double-team/combo scheme against the nose guard and the strong inside linebacker. The backside tackle and the tight end will tighten their landmarks and block the 5-technique and the strong outside linebacker. Tightening the landmark tells an offensive lineman that the football is starting away from him and that he has a defender aligned to his outside, as shown in Diagram 4-5.

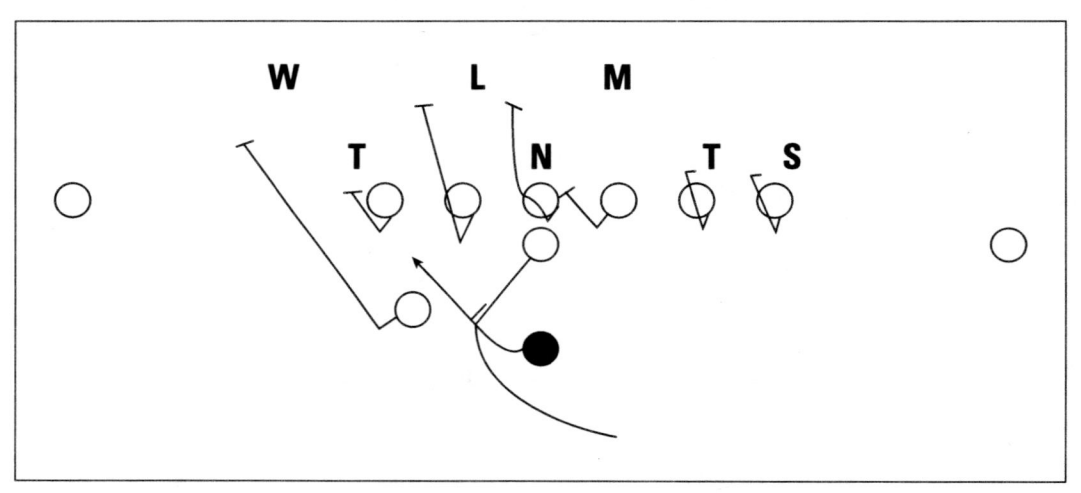

Diagram 4-4: Queen Right 25 BOB vs. an Okie front

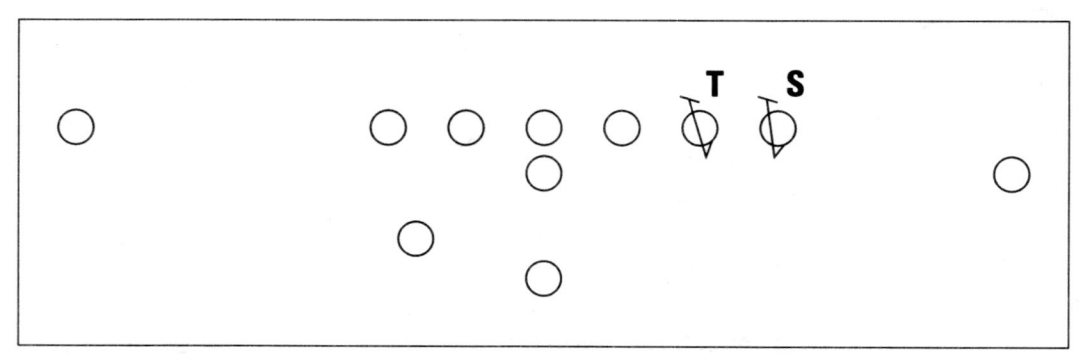

Diagram 4-5: Outside alignments

This alignment tells the blocker to make his first step more vertical in order to prevent the defender from flattening him out along the line of scrimmage. This technique is used to block 24/25 BOB against an Okie front as illustrated in Diagram 4-6. The same play is illustrated against an Eagle Strong front in Diagram 4-7.

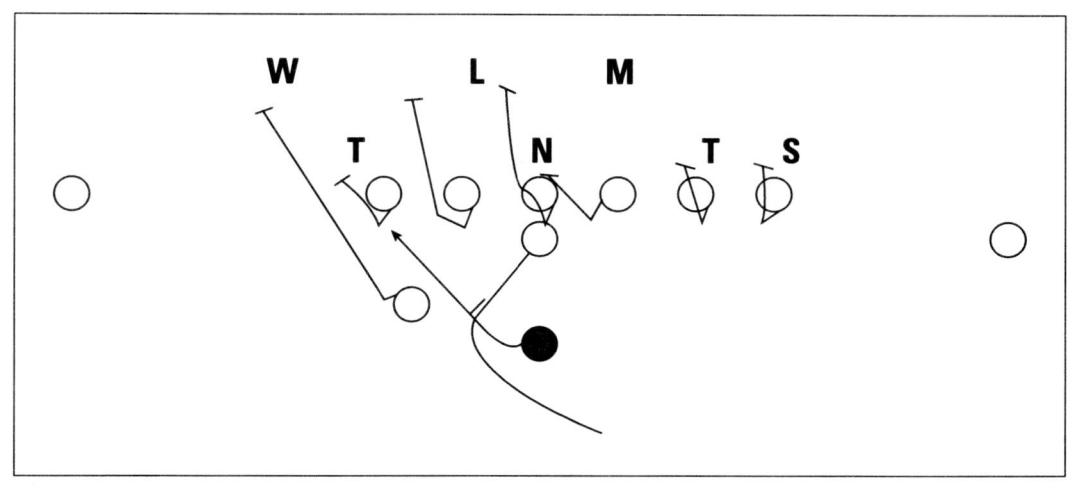

Diagram 4-6: Queen Right 25 BOB vs. an Okie front

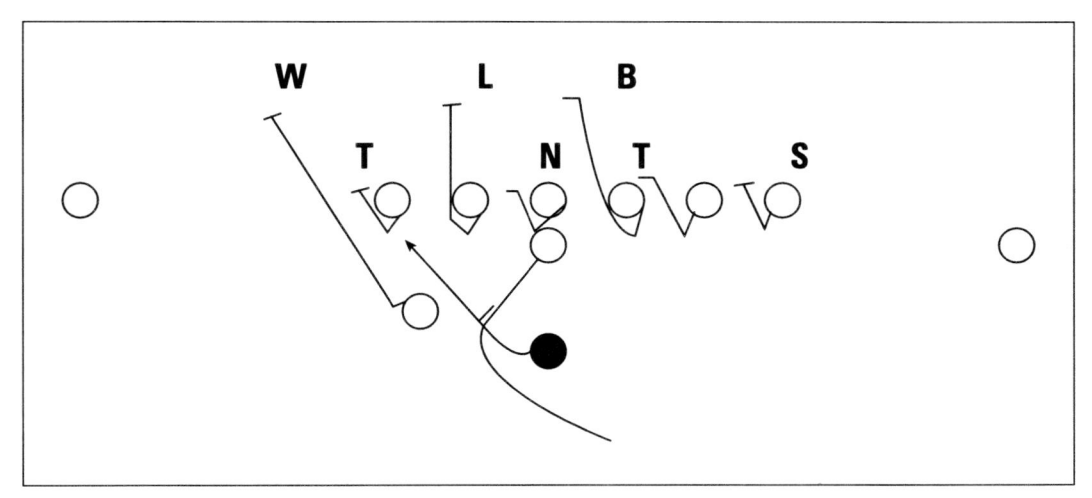

Diagram 4-7: Queen Right 25 BOB vs. an Eagle Strong front

A real advantage of the zone scheme arises from the fact that both the Okie and the Eagle Strong fronts are identical on the split-end side of the formation. This similarity allows offenses to account for these two different fronts in exactly the same way at the point of attack. Against an Eagle Strong front, the fullback, the playside tackle, and the playside guard all block exactly the same way as they do against an Okie structure.

Attacking a 4-3 Front

The 4-3 front (which does not have an overhang) must also be considered. The lack of an overhang changes the assignment of the fullback, as shown in Diagram 4-8. The playside tackle will displace the 5-technique, while the fullback blocks the weak outside linebacker. As discussed in Chapter 3, the left guard makes a Boss call, allowing him to wrong step with his right foot, and then work with the center to double team/combo the shade to the Mike linebacker. When this combo block is taught, the center steps with his left foot and the left guard steps with his right foot. They will secure movement along the line of scrimmage to the second-level linebacker. The right guard executes the same Boss call with the right tackle—the right guard wrong steps with his right foot, and the right tackle steps with his left foot to combo block the 3-technique to the same linebacker.

The tight end blocks the 7-technique, employing what is called a backside rip. The tight end takes a deeper drop step with his left foot and then shoots his hip and his arm past the 7-technique. The tight end gets as vertical as he can without allowing the 7-technique to cross his face. The running back presses the line of scrimmage hard because of the Boss scheme that is being executed on the shade.

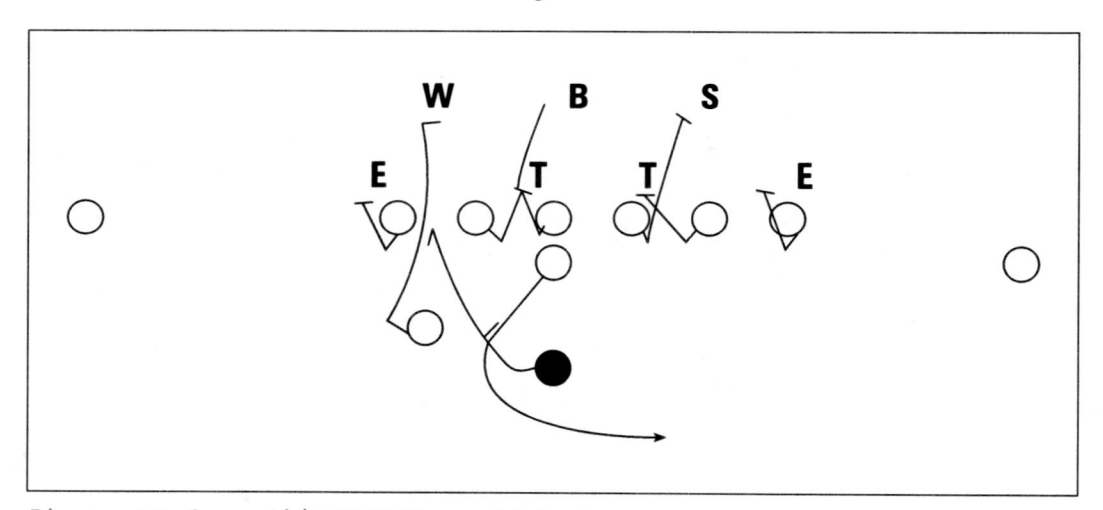

Diagram 4-8: Queen Right 25 BOB vs. a 4-3 front

Attacking a Stack Front

Another defensive structure without an overhang is the Stack front. Against this alignment, the fullback blocks the playside inside linebacker (Diagram 4-9). The playside tackle blocks the 5-technique, and the playside guard blocks the 3- technique. The fullback blocks the playside inside linebacker, taking an outside lead step to soften up the inside linebacker and then running to daylight as if he is carrying the football. If the fullback has been properly coached, the inside linebacker will follow him.

The center makes an IN call to the backside guard, telling the guard that the center is going to wrong step with his right foot and, along with the right guard, combo block the nose guard to the backside inside linebacker. The right tackle and the tight end tighten their landmarks and execute blocks on the 5-technique and the 9-technique, respectively. The halfback reads the playside guard's block on the 3-technique and presses the line of scrimmage to the feet of his offensive linemen before making a decision on where to run the football.

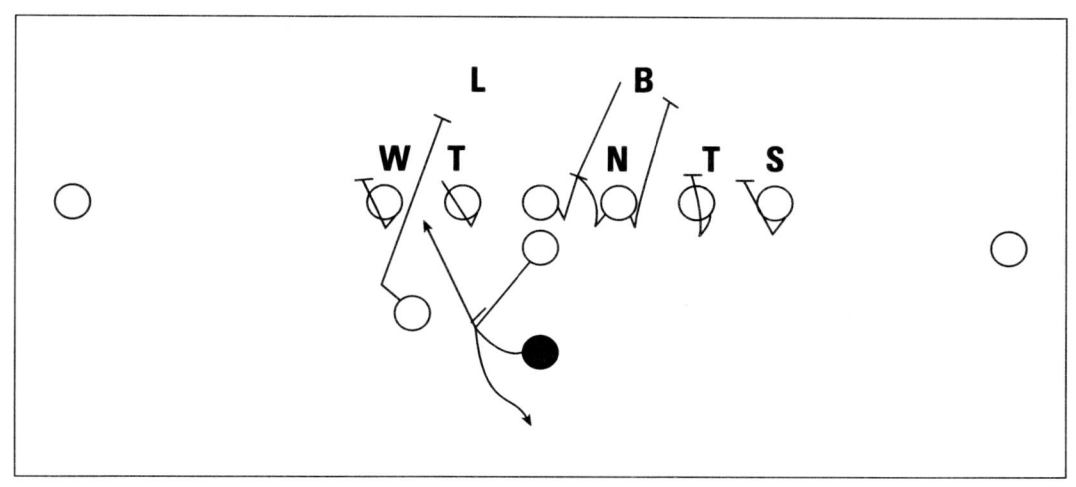

Diagram 4-9: Queen Right 25 BOB vs. a Stack front

Attacking a Reduced Front

A Reduced front resembles a Stack front, except that the nose guard becomes a strongside shade on the center, making this one of the greatest assets that the zone attack possesses. The basic blocking scheme, with the exception of the center and the backside guard, remains exactly the same. As a result, a team that practices against a Reduced front is also getting reps against a Stack front.

Against a Reduced front, the center and the backside guard work a double-team/combo block on the shade and the backside inside linebacker. The playside tackle blocks the 5-technique, the playside guard blocks the 3-technique, and the fullback blocks the playside inside linebacker. The backside tackle and the tight end tighten their landmarks on the 5- and 9-techniques.

Attacking a Slide Weak Front

Another defensive front that must be considered is Slide Weak, a true eight-man front. A Slide Weak front forces offenses to make decisions regarding their blocking schemes. Because only seven offensive linemen are available to block the defense's

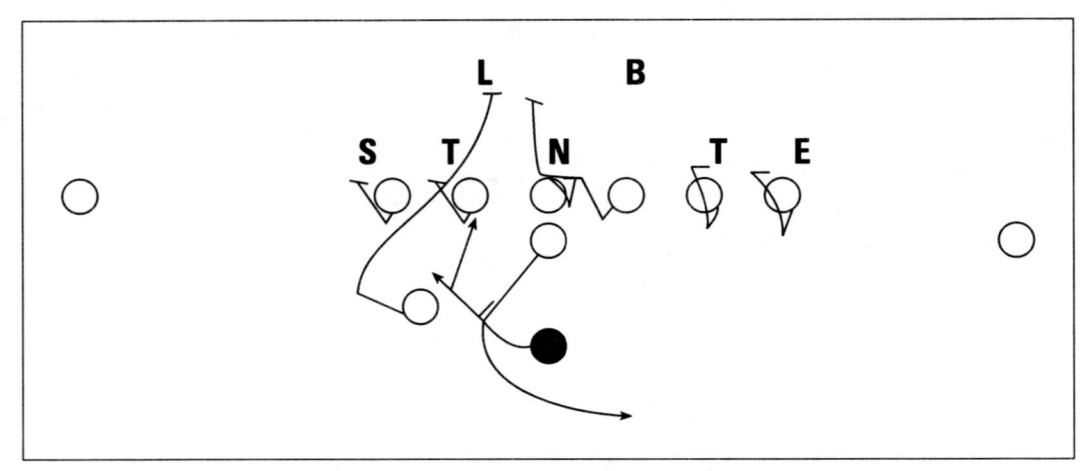

Diagram 4-10: Queen Right 25 BOB vs. a Reduced front

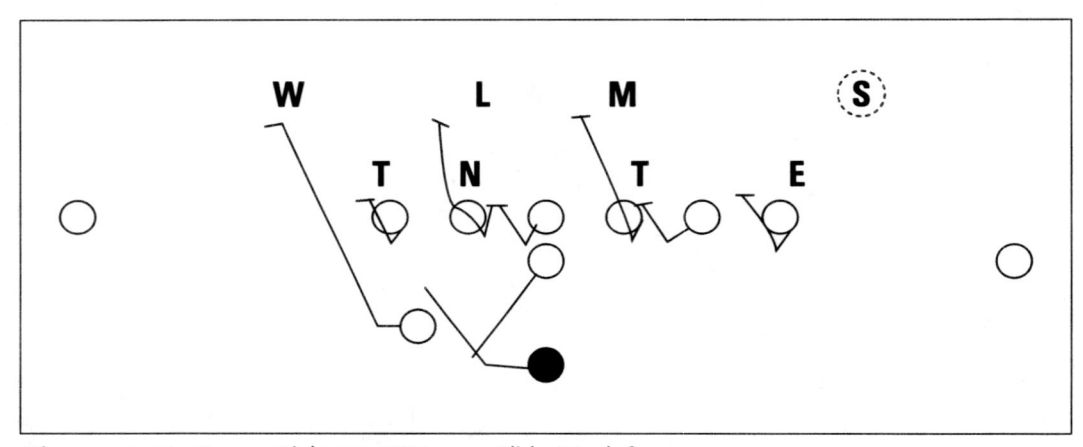

Diagram 4-11: Queen Right 25 BOB vs. a Slide Weak front

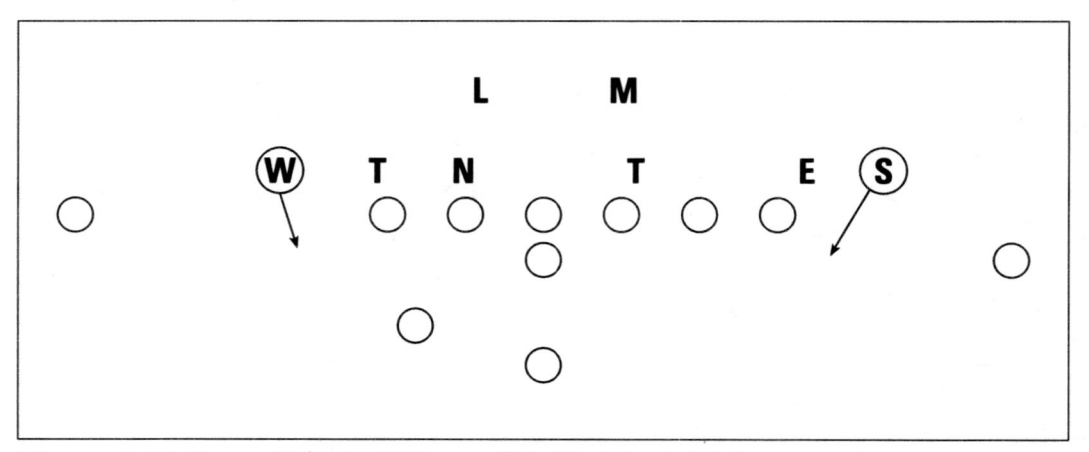

Diagram 4-12: Queen Right 25 BOB vs. a Slide Weak front (blitz)

eight linemen, the defensive player farthest away from the point of attack is always left unblocked, as shown in Diagram 4-11. If the player that is not accounted for aligns himself in a blitz position, then the offense has to make an adjustment, as shown in Diagram 4-12.

The quarterback has to decide whether to audible to the quick passing game to take advantage of the resulting coverage, or to audible to an Outside Zone (Stretch) play to run away from the blitzer. We also game plan the cadence in order for players to get off the ball quickly or to make the blitzer jump offsides. BOB can still be run against a blitz, but the halfback has to know there will probably not be any chance for a cutback. The bootleg action of the quarterback following the Inside Zone play should slow down the blitzer (Diagram 4-13). The scheme shown in Diagram 4-14 is used to block a Slide Weak front.

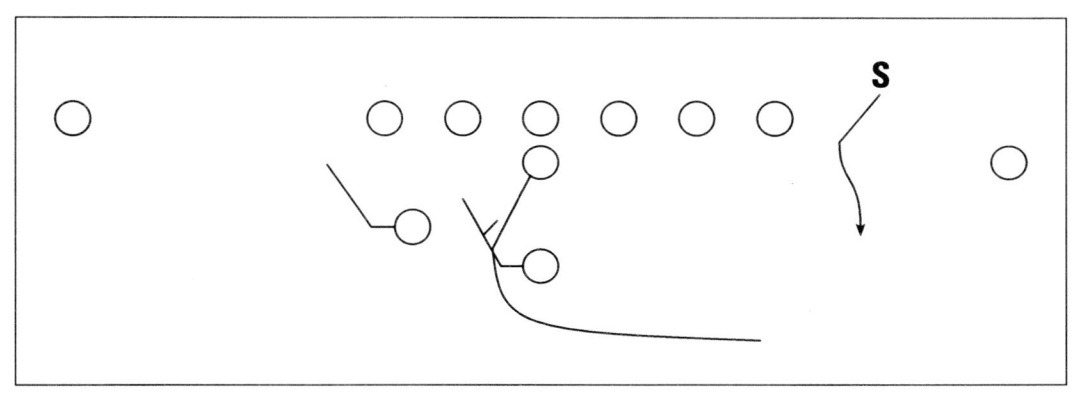

Diagram 4-13: Quarterback bootleg/naked action vs. an edge blitz

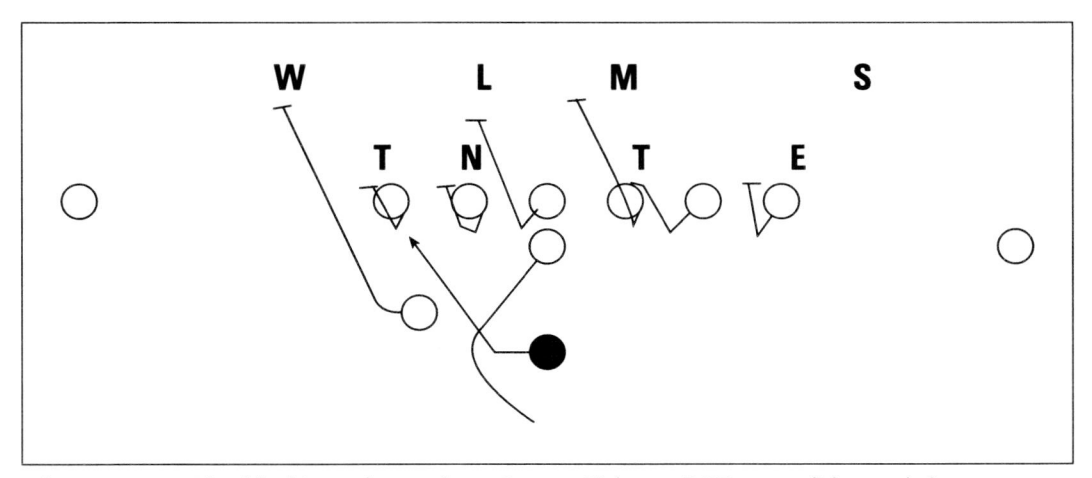

Diagram 4-14: The blocking scheme for a Queen Right 25 BOB vs. a slide weak front

The Slide Weak structure has an overhang, and the fullback will block the overhang—the weak outside linebacker. The playside tackle blocks the 5-technique, the playside guard and the center will double-team/combo block the 2i or the 2-technique. If it is a 3-technique, the guard blocks the 3-technique by himself. The various possibilities are illustrated in Diagrams 4-15, 4-16, and 4-17.

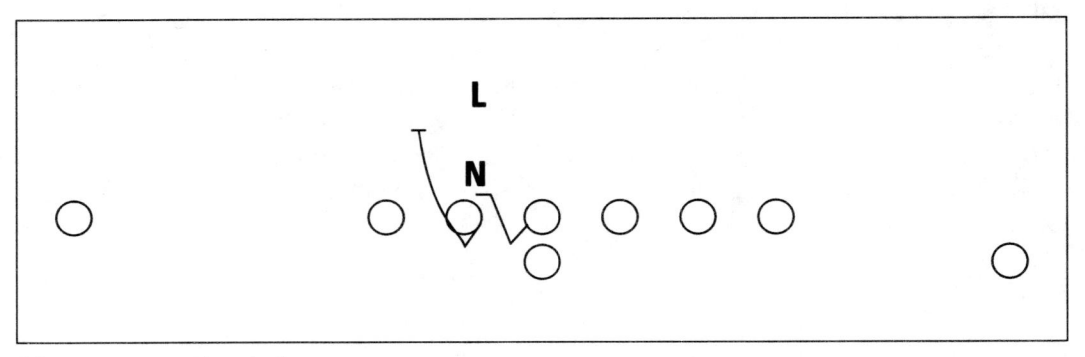

Diagram 4-15: 2i-technique

Diagram 4-16: 2-technique

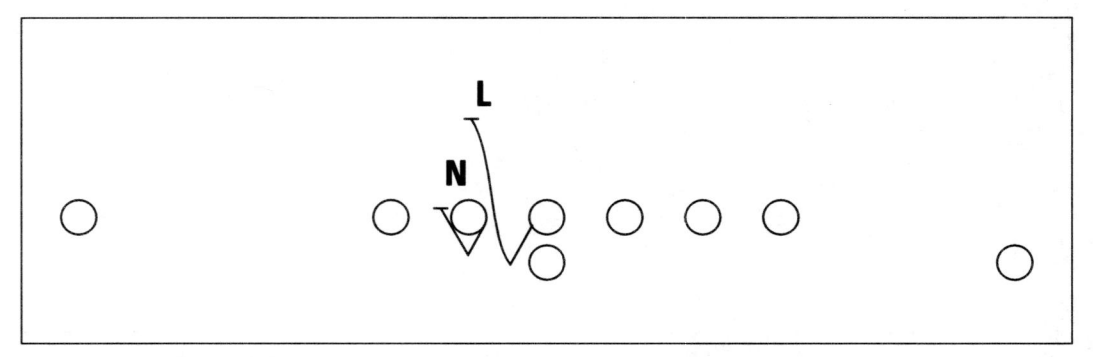

Diagram 4-17: 3-technique

The center makes a Mate call, telling the playside guard what is shown in Diagrams 4-15, 4-16, and 4-17. The center will help the playside guard on a 2- or a 2i-technique. If there is a 3-technique, the center will step playside and work up to a second-level linebacker. The backside guard and the backside tackle work a double-team/combo scheme on the defensive lineman and the strong inside linebacker. The tight end tightens his landmark, blocking the strong outside linebacker and letting the eighth man go free.

Blocking Assignments for the Receivers

The blocking assignments for receivers in Inside Zone should stay as simple as possible. Wideouts should still be aggressive, because a downfield block is usually the difference between a 10-yard gain and a 20-yard gain, or the difference between a 20-yard gain and a touchdown. Receivers have to recognize three different looks that indicate the secondary coverage. The receivers have a different blocking assignment on each of the three different coverages. Their assignments against Cover 3 are shown in Diagram 4-18.

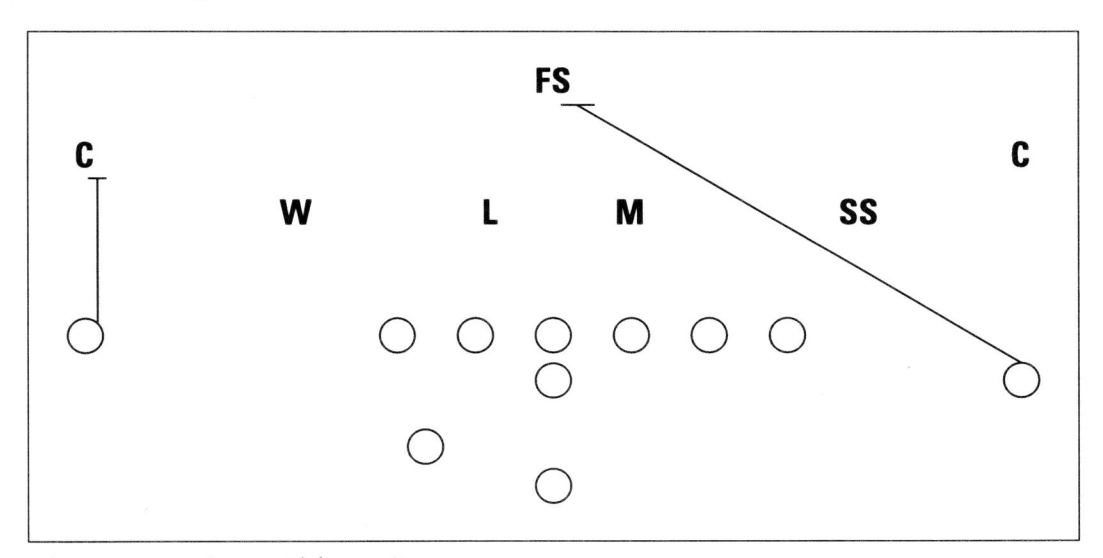

Diagram 4-18: Queen Right vs. Cover 3

Against three-deep coverage, receivers block the deep-outside third player (usually a cornerback) when the ball is run toward them. When the ball is run away from them, receivers block the deep-middle third player in the coverage (usually a safety). This assignment is shown in Diagram 4-19.

When receivers read Cover 2, they block the half-field safety aligned to their side of the field, regardless of where the ball is being run. This assignment is illustrated in Diagram 4-21.

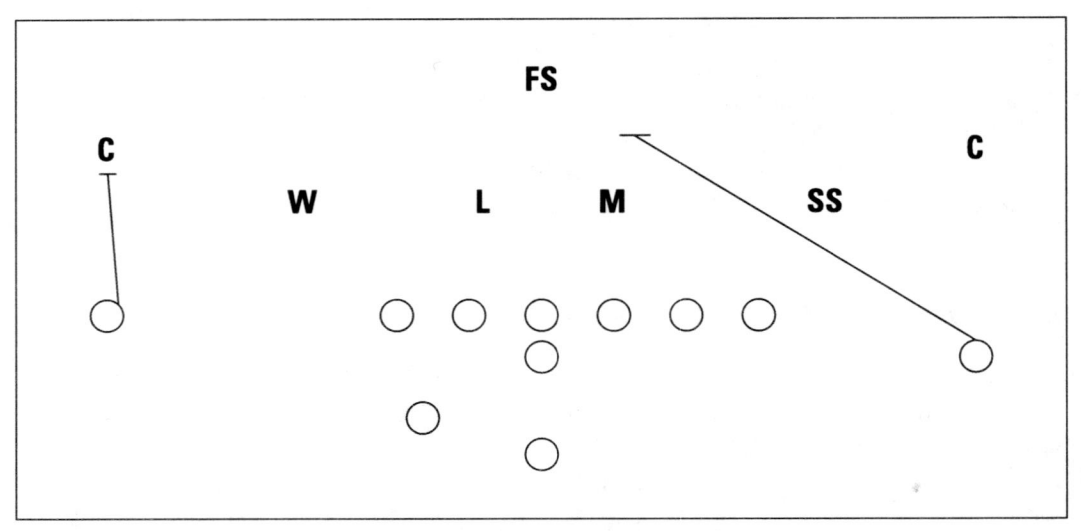

Diagram 4-19: Split-end block in Queen Right 24 Zone

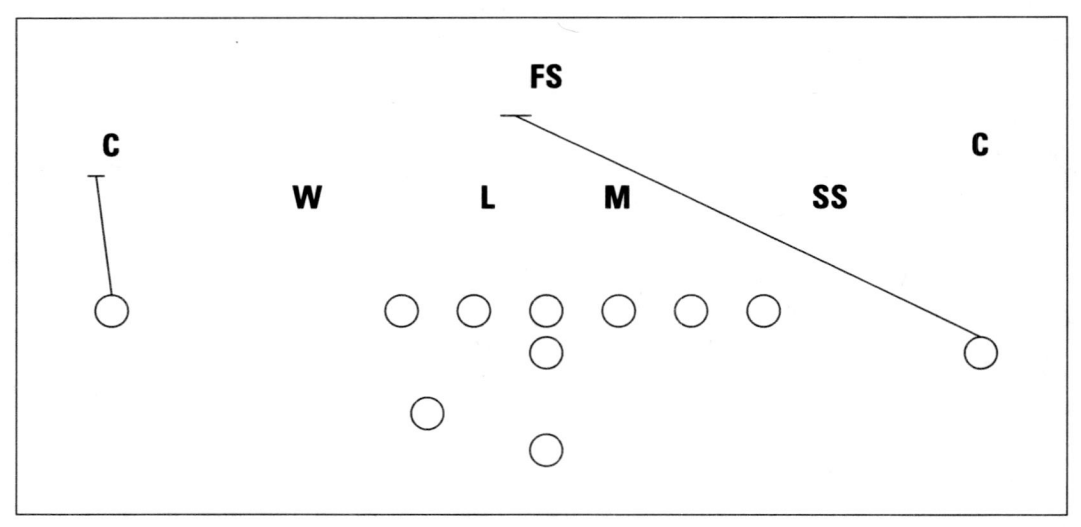

Diagram 4-20: Split-end block in Queen Right 25 BOB

Against any man-to-man coverage, whether there is a free safety or Cover 2 over the top, receivers block the man responsible for covering them on a pass play. The only other rule is that if the defender is playing any type of bump technique, the receiver runs a take-off route instead of blocking the defender, as shown in Diagrams 4-22 and 4-23.

In a man-to-man coverage situation, receivers will use a stalk block and a cut block. Their importance should be stressed in the run game. They should fully understand that they are an integral part of the offensive running attack.

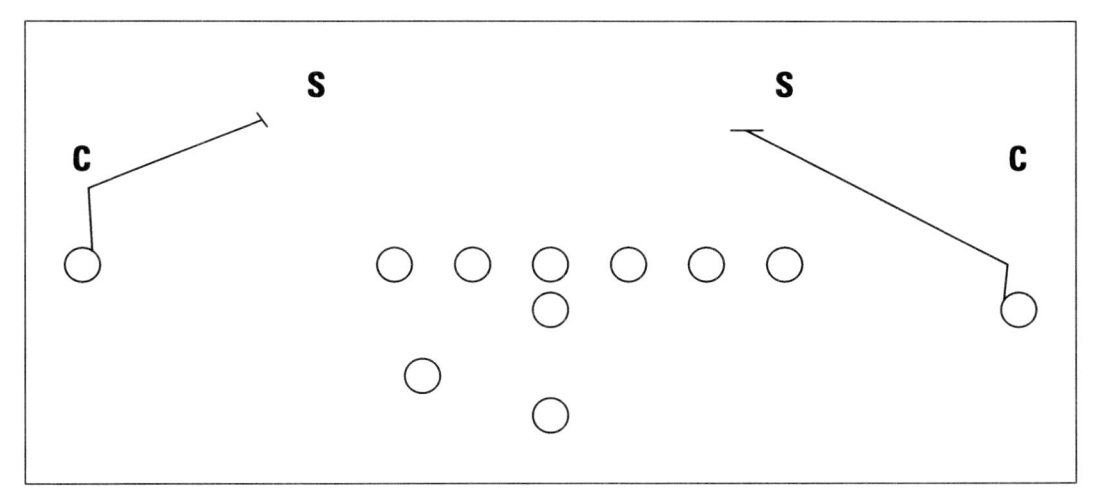

Diagram 4-21: Queen Right vs. Cover 2

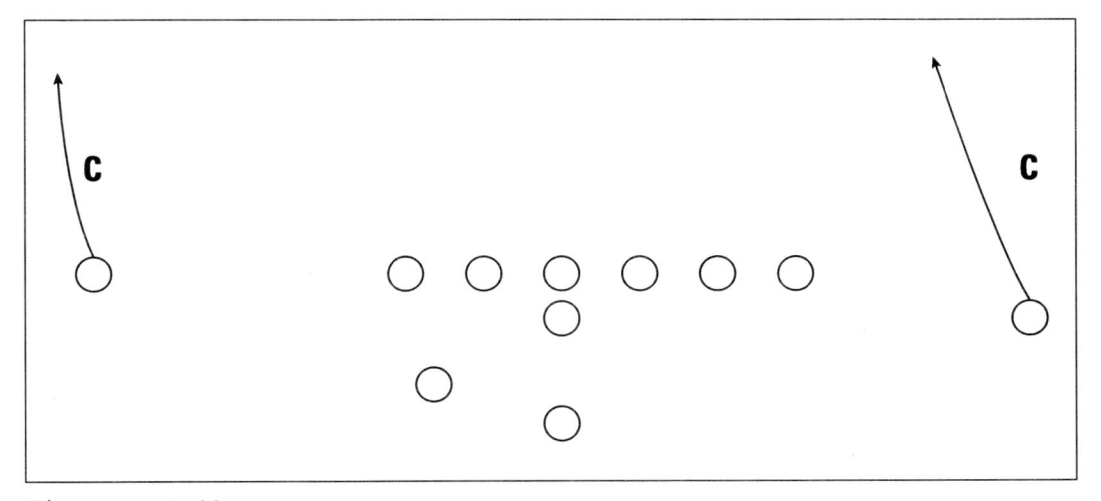

Diagram 4-22: Man coverage

One-Back Formation

One final factor that must be considered involving the Inside Zone scheme is a one-back Inside Zone play to the split-end side of the formation. We do not call this play BOB because BOB is strictly a two-back formation play. The designation "Blade" is added when we run Inside Zone to the split-end side from one-back formations. Accordingly, 24/25 Blade is the one-back Inside Zone play to the split-end side.

24/25 Blade can be run from any one-back formation. It is exactly like 24/25 Razor, except that it is run to the open side of the formation. When Blade is run, we want to spread the defense out and force them to defend the entire field horizontally,

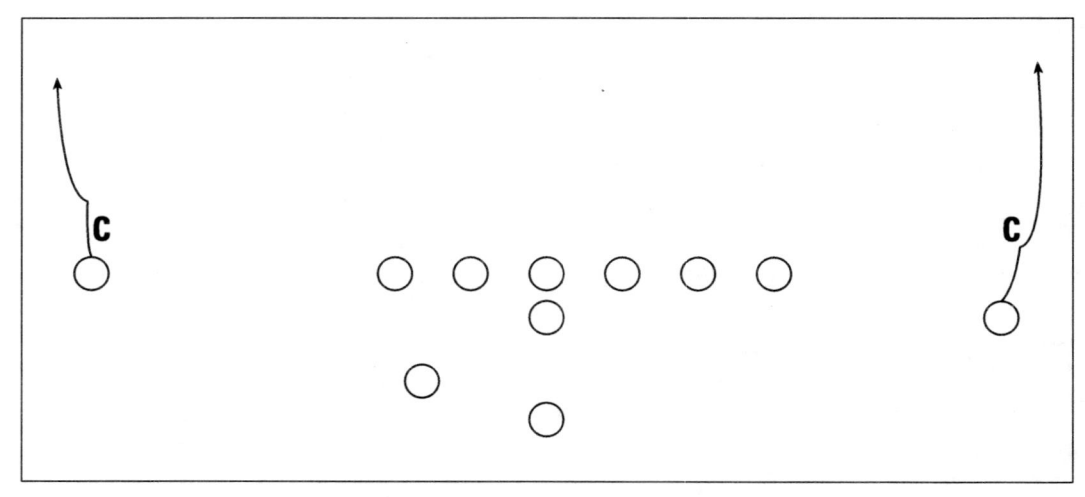

Diagram 4-23: Bump man coverage

thereby opening up the Inside Zone running lanes, as shown in Diagram 4-24. The Blade play is blocked exactly like BOB, except that there is no fullback to block the stacked linebacker, as illustrated in Diagram 4-25.

24/25 Blade is always used as a check-with-me play. If the defense plays an Eagle Strong or a Stack look to the split-end side, the play will be checked to a pass. We like to use 24/25 Blade in a hurry-up situation or in a situation where we want to get three receivers into our formation and force the defense to defend the entire field.

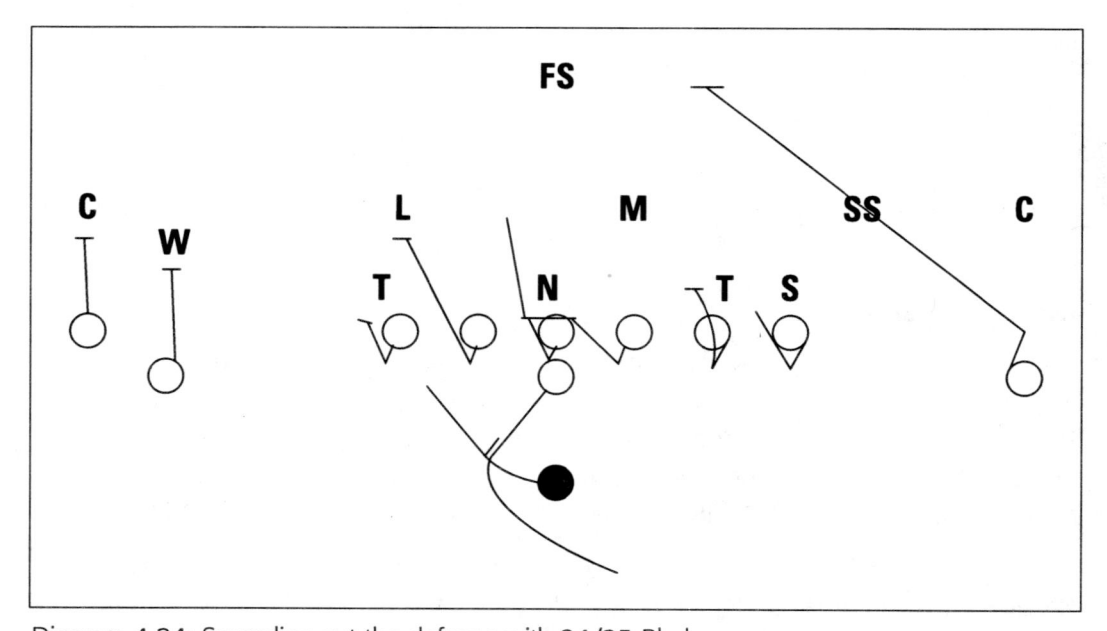

Diagram 4-24: Spreading out the defense with 24/25 Blade

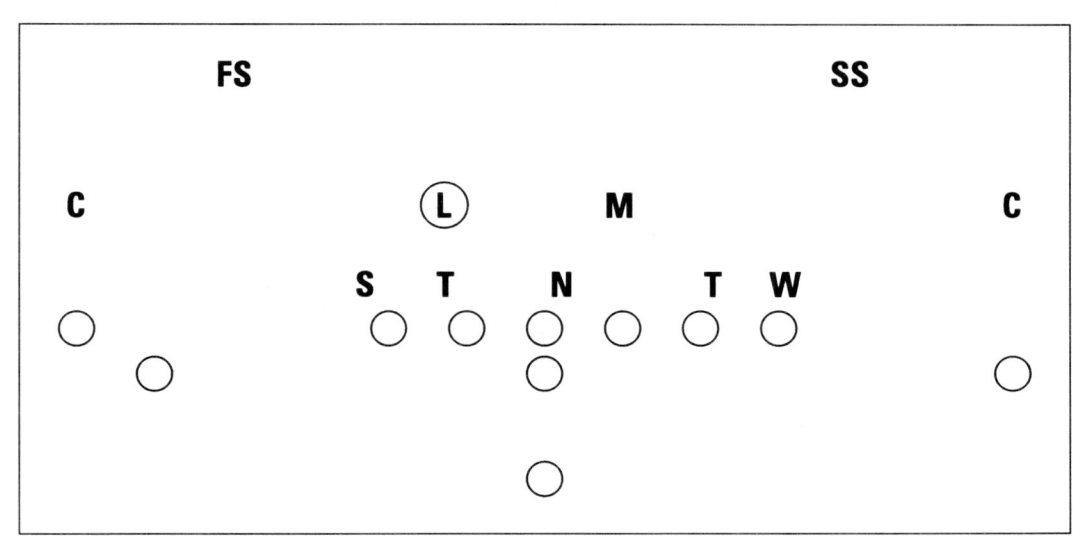

Diagram 4-25: Accounting for the stacked linebacker

5

The Outside Zone Play—
Tight-End Side

The Outside Zone, or Stretch play, is the basic zone running play to attack the edge of the defensive structure. It is to our zone attack as the Toss Sweep is to I-formation running teams. When we run Stretch, we want the halfback to press a landmark one yard behind and three yards outside of the tight end's alignment. The halfback will stay on this course until a wrong-colored jersey crosses his face, and then he will make an immediate and abrupt north-south cut, never cutting back across the field.

The goal is to always confuse the defender on the edge of the line of scrimmage. The quarterback will hand the ball off to the halfback by opening up to 10 o'clock and sprinting the ball to the halfback, who is farther away because of the wider point of attack. After handing the ball off, the quarterback continues on his bootleg/naked path.

A significant difference between the Stretch play and the Inside Zone play is that the fullback, in a two-back formation, should always be aligned to the side that the Stretch play is being run. In a tight-end side Stretch play, the fullback will always be aligned to the tight-end side in a King formation (Diagram 5-1). An overview of how to break this obvious formation tendency will be discussed in a later chapter.

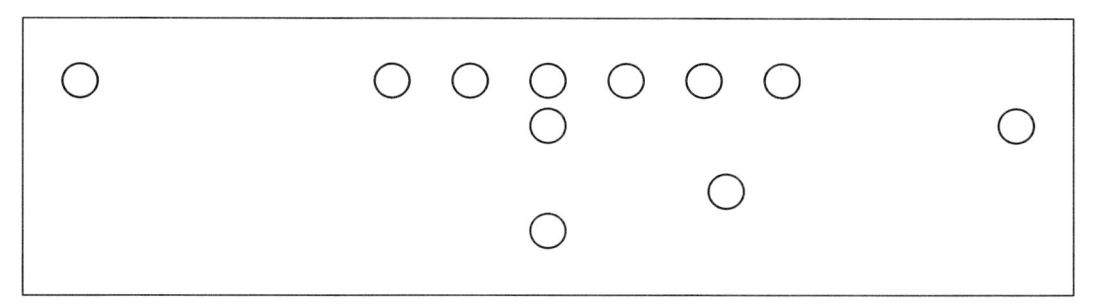

Diagram 5-1: King Right formation

Blocking Fundamentals and Rules for the Outside Zone

The Outside Zone, or Stretch play, incorporates a very simple blocking scheme that all offensive linemen, from tackle to tight end, use to overtake an adjacent defensive player. To an offensive lineman, overtake means if a lineman is covered by an outside technique defender (a 3- or 5-, for example), he has to reach block that defender. If the offensive lineman is uncovered, he will execute a three-step bucket progression in which he will bucket step, perform a crossover step, and on his third step make a decision about overtaking a down lineman or moving off to a second- or third-level defensive player.

The offensive line's blocking rules for 28 and 29 Stretch to the tight-end side are fairly simple and always the same. The playside tackle is the key to the play. He cannot get flattened out. He will reach block a 5-technique. On the other hand, if there is a 6- or 7-technique, he will not bucket step, but instead attempt to overtake the adjacent player. If he misses the 6- or 7-technique, he has to miss to the inside and keep his outside perspective. The rules for the playside tackle are shown in Diagram 5-2 and Diagram 5-3.

The playside guard has to reach a 3-technique, but treat a 2 or a 2i-technique as uncovered, and use the three-step bucket progression. This three-step bucket progression for uncovered offensive linemen is illustrated in Diagrams 5-4, 5-5, and 5-6.

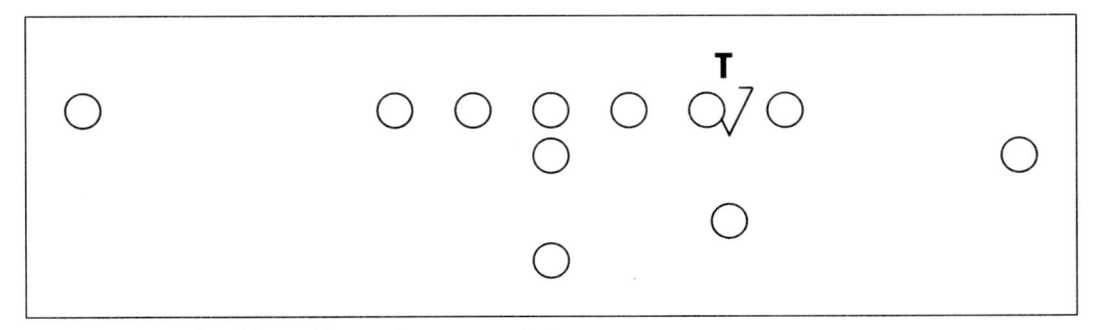

Diagram 5-2: Playside tackle reaches a 5-technique

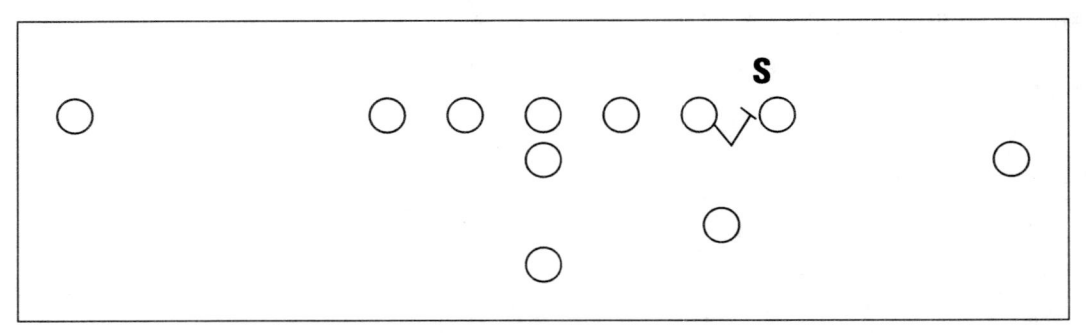

Diagram 5-3: Playside tackle overtakes a 7-technique

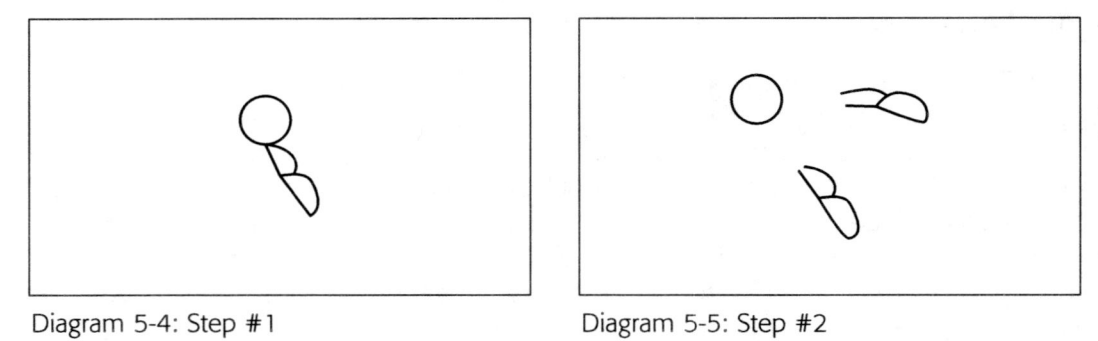

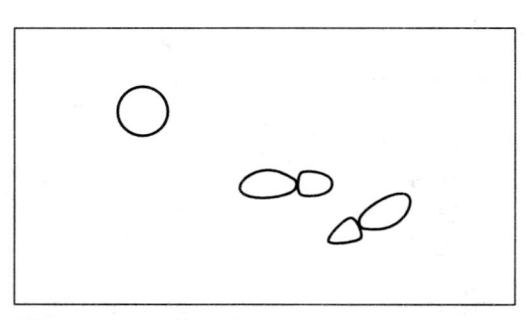

Diagram 5-4: Step #1

Diagram 5-5: Step #2

Diagram 5-6: Step #3

Step #1 is a deep bucket step with the blocker's shoulders almost square to the sidelines, while step #2 is a crossover step with the blocker's back foot almost parallel to the line of scrimmage.

Step #3 is the decision step. If the offensive lineman can overtake the adjacent defensive lineman, he should do so. If he cannot overtake the adjacent defensive lineman, he turns upfield and works to the second or third level. This decision is always helped by recognizing what technique the defender is playing. We always expect to overtake an inside-shaded player or a head-up defensive player. The bucket step allows the offensive lineman to gain an angle to either overtake a down lineman or to cutoff a second-level defensive player.

The offensive center will reach block a strongside shade, and treat a weakside shade as uncovered and use the three step-bucket progression. The backside guard will drop step and cut block a weakside shade or a 2i-technique, and drop step and overtake a 2-technique. He will treat a 3-technique as uncovered and use the three-step bucket progression.

The backside tackle will overtake a 4-technique or a 4i-technique, and treat a 5-technique as uncovered and use the three-step bucket progression. The tight end will drop step and overtake a 9-technique. Against a 6- or a 7-technique, the tight end should drop step and hold off the defender until an overtake occurs, at which point he will work off to the second level.

The defense needs to be softened up at the point of attack (i.e., addressing the 5-technique). The playside tackle has to knock the 5-technique off the ball in order to have a successful play. 28 and 29 Stretch require a zone scoop on the backside, while the playside linemen should get to where they are going against defensive line movement. The basic rules are simple—if playside and covered, then reach block; if playside and uncovered, then use the three-step bucket progression.

Attacking an Okie Front

Diagram 5-7 illustrates the Stretch play to the tight-end side against an Okie front. Attacking an Okie front, the tight end has a 9-technique, and his assignment is to overtake the 9-technique, while the playside tackle should overtake the 5-technique. The playside guard is uncovered and uses the three-step bucket progression. The playside guard will bucket step, crossover on his second step, and make a decision on his third step. If he can overtake the 5-technique, then he does. If he cannot, then he will work up to the second level. The center has an 0-technique, that he treats as uncovered. The center drop steps and tries to work off to the second level. If the nose guard latches on, the center blocks him. If the nose guard lags behind, then the center works up to the second level. The center and the backside guard have a zone scoop-combination block on the nose guard and the weak inside linebacker, as shown in Diagrams 5-8 and 5-9.

The center and the backside guard have to account for the nose guard and the weak inside linebacker. The backside guard will execute a combination block with the center, using the three-step bucket progression—step #1, the bucket step; step #2, the crossover step; and step #3, the decision step.

The backside tackle has a 5-technique that he treats as uncovered. He uses the three-step bucket progression to work up to the second level. The fullback always blocks the force element of the defense on the Stretch play, and in the Okie defense, the strong safety provides is the force element. The fullback should be taught to recognize the different types of force that he will see from different defensive structures. Some of the various possibilities are shown in Diagrams 5-10, 5-11, 5-12, and 5-13.

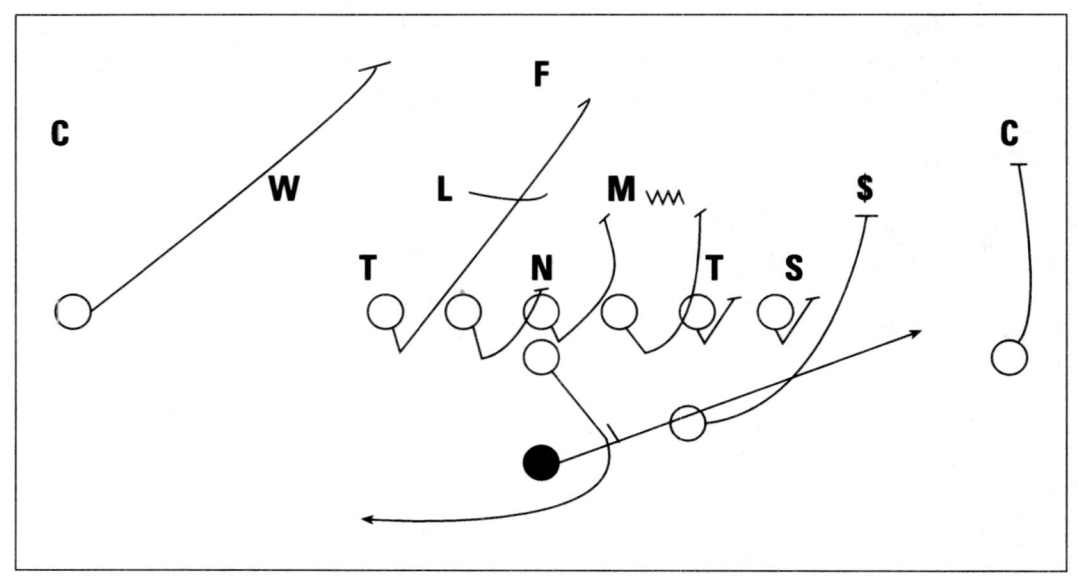

Diagram 5-7: King Right 28 Stretch vs. an Okie front

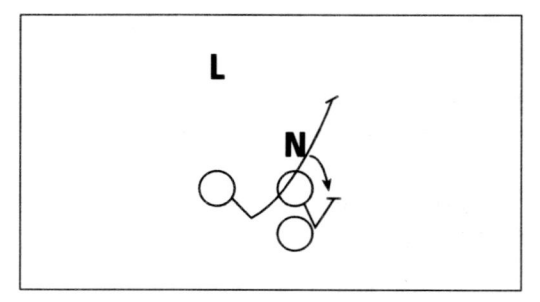

Diagram 5-8: Nose slant strong

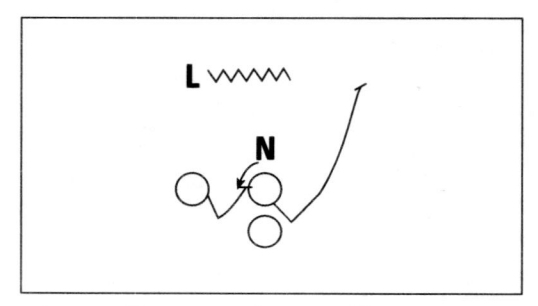

Diagram 5-9: Nose slant weak

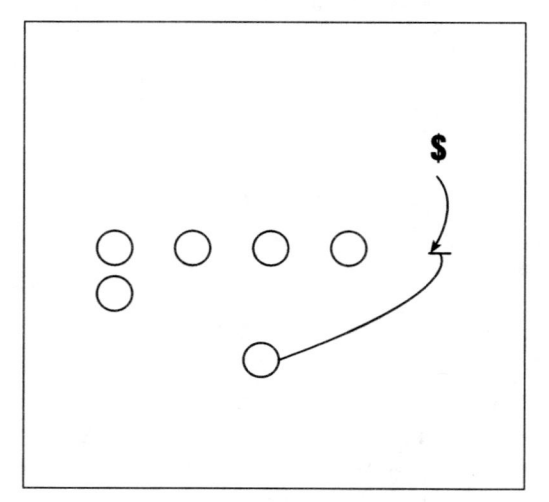

Diagram 5-10: Strong safety or invert force

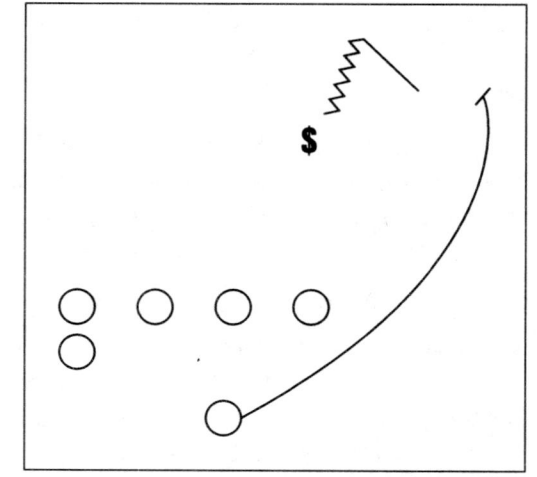

Diagram 5-11: quarter coverage force

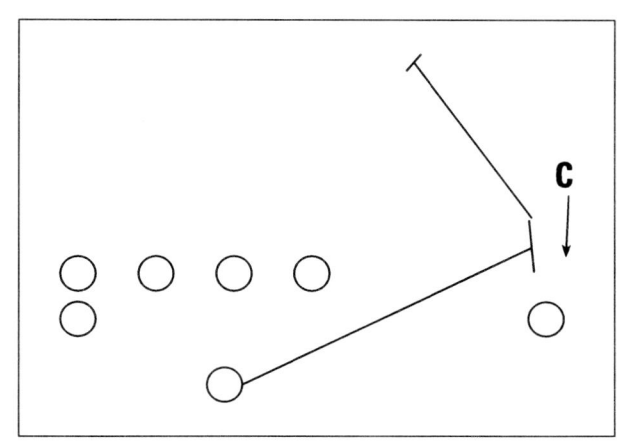

Diagram 5-12: Roller corner force

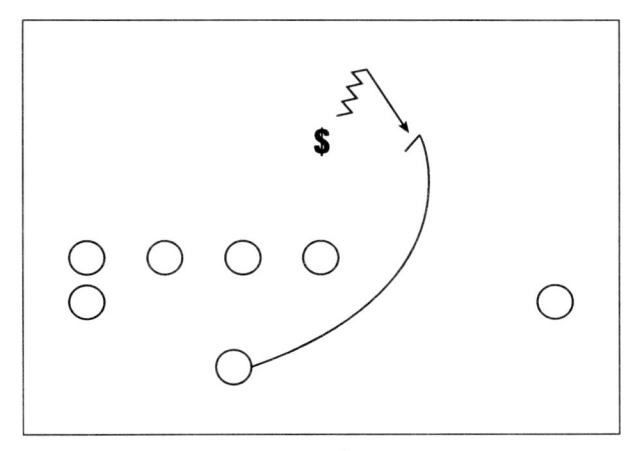

Diagram 5-13: Man-to-man force

An explanation of how the wide receivers and the fullback can account for a variety of different types of forces is provided in a later chapter. At this point, it is only necessary to understand that the fullback attacks the force by blocking the outside half of the force with the inside half of the fullback's own body, while trying to maintain outside leverage. If the force defender flows outside, the fullback will drive him out of bounds.

The halfback's technique is to press the point of attack, a position one-yard deep and three-yards outside of the tight end's alignment. The halfback stays on this course until a wrong-colored jersey crosses the halfback's face. If someone crosses his face, he will make a north-south break. The quarterback opens up to two o'clock on 28 Stretch and to 10 o'clock on 29 Stretch, sprinting the ball to the halfback because of the halfback's wide landmark. After executing the hand-off, the quarterback continues on his bootleg/naked play-action pass course.

Attacking the Eagle Strong Front

When facing the Eagle Strong front, the Stretch is blocked as shown in Diagram 5-14. The tight end should drop step and hold off the 7-technique until the playside tackle can overtake that player. The tight end keeps an eye on the strong inside linebacker because that player is his second-level assignment. The playside tackle is uncovered and the tight end has a 7-technique, so the tackle's assignment is to overtake the 7-technique, while the playside guard has to reach block a 3-technique. The center will treat a weakside shade as uncovered, while executing the three-step bucket progression to the second level.

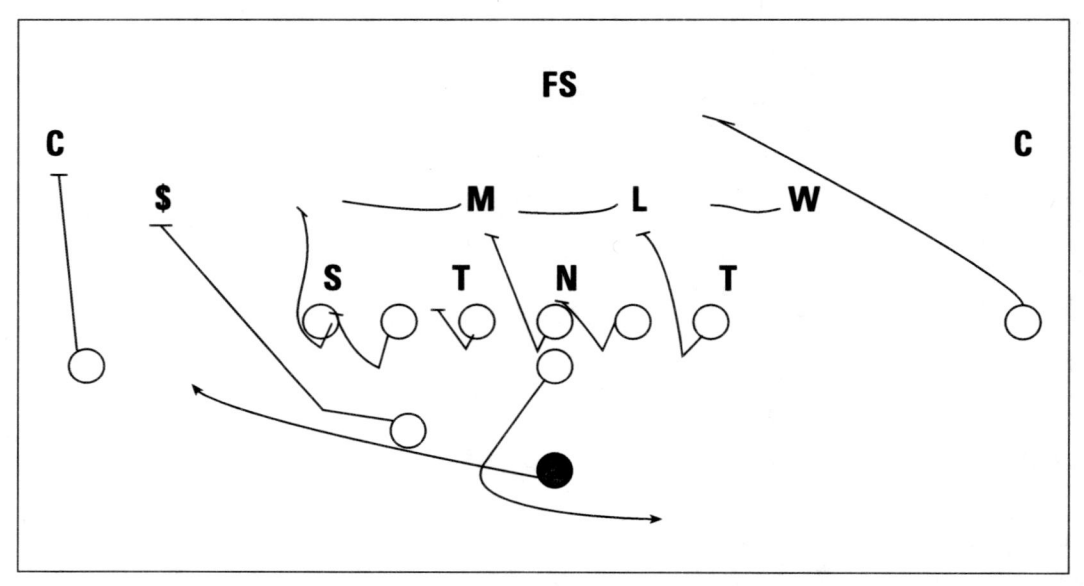

Diagram 5-14: King Left 29 Stretch vs. an Eagle Strong front

The backside guard is uncovered, but the center has a weakside shade. The guard's job is to cut block the weakside shade. The backside tackle has a 5-technique that he treats as uncovered, and uses the three-step bucket progression to advance up to the second level. The fullback blocks the force, which will be is the strong safety in this defense. The halfback runs his usual course, and the quarterback runs a bootleg/naked play action route after handing off the ball.

Attacking a 4-3 Front

Stretch is blocked against a 4-3 defense, as shown in Diagram 5-15. The tight end has a 9-technique (i.e., his assignment is to reach block that player). The playside tackle is uncovered. Accordingly, he should use the three-step bucket progression. Against 4-3 fronts, the playside tackle should be aware of a possible strong outside linebacker run-through, or a blitz, as shown in Diagram 5-16.

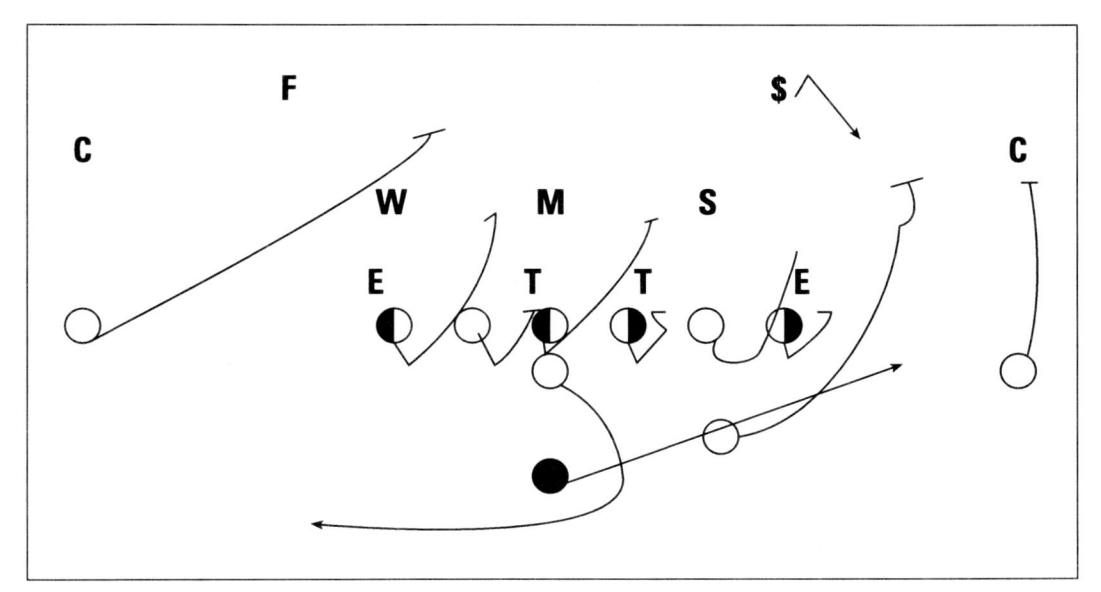

Diagram 5-15: King Right 28 Stretch vs. a 4-3 front

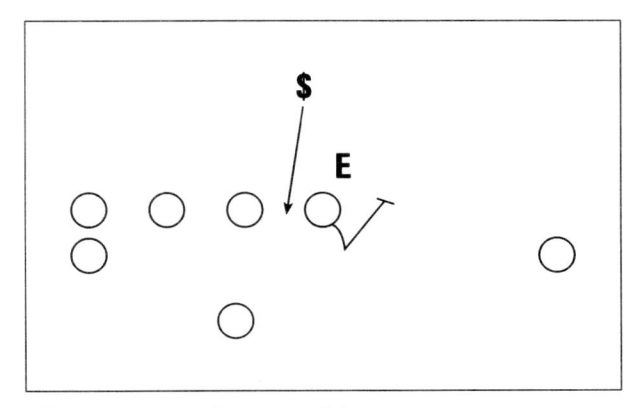

Diagram 5-16: Blitz potential

If the strong outside linebacker tries to run through the C gap, the playside tackle would have to redirect from his normal path and block that player. The playside guard reach blocks the 3-technique. The center treats a weakside shade as uncovered, and uses the three-step bucket progression to work off to the second level or to overtake the 3-technique covering the playside guard. The uncovered backside guard uses the three-step bucket progression to work off to the second level. The fullback blocks the force, a player coming from a quarter-field position in this front. The fullback has to identify the angle of the force and block that player's outside half. The quarterback and the halfback carry out their usual Stretch assignments.

Attacking a Stack Front

The Stack defense is attacked with the Stretch play, as shown in Diagram 5-17. The only uncovered offensive lineman in a Stack front is the center. The tight end could face either a 9-technique or a 6-technique. He should reach block either one of those players. The playside tackle could reach block a 5-technique, or bucket step against a 4-technique and work up to the second level. The playside guard has a 2-technique, or possibly a 2i-technique, and uses the three-step bucket progression against either player to work up the field. The uncovered center also uses the three-step bucket progression. Diagram 5-18 illustrates the Stretch against a Stack front with a 6-technique, a 4-technique, and a 2-technique.

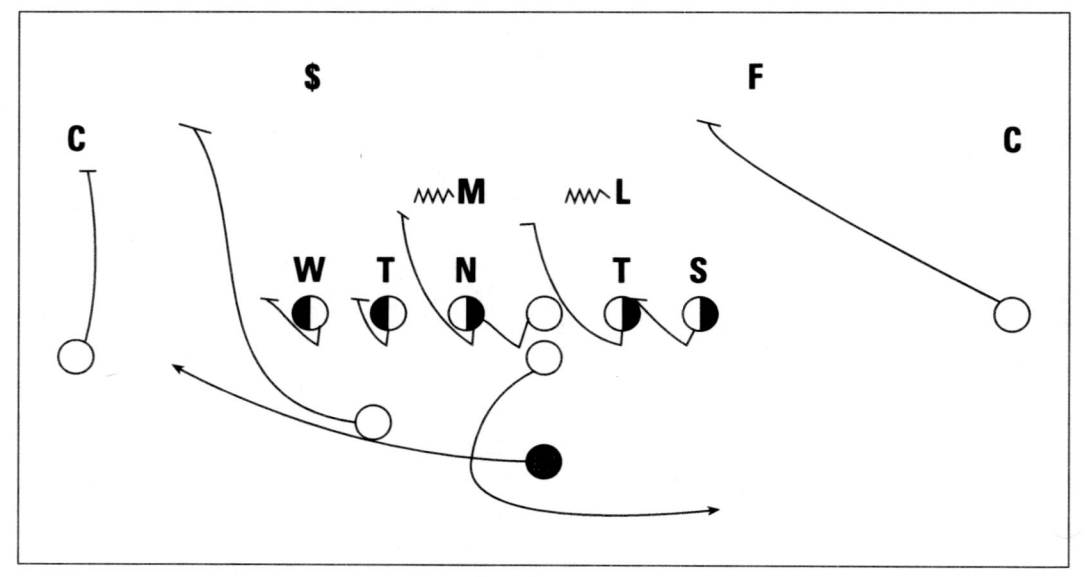

Diagram 5-17: King Left 29 Stretch vs. a Stack front

If all three of the down linemen are slanted inside, the tight end would come off to the linebacker. In Diagram 5-19, the defense is playing a Stack front with a 9-technique, a 5-technique, and a 2i-technique.

The 9-technique and the 5-technique are reach blocked by the tight end and the playside tackle, respectively. The playside guard and the center zone block the 2i-technique and the weak inside linebacker. In Diagram 5-20, the defense is still playing a Stack front, in this situation with a 9-technique, a 4-technique, and a 2-technique.

The play illustrated in Diagram 5-20 shows that the playside tackle could be the player working off to the Lou linebacker. No matter what the playside defensive alignments of the front actually are, the Outside Zone scheme can handle every look. On the backside, the guard has a 2-technique that he treats as uncovered, and works the three-step bucket progression up to the second level. The backside tackle has a 5-technique that he also treats as uncovered, and works up to the second level with a three-step bucket progression. The fullback blocks the cornerback in this structure. The cornerback will have a wider alignment and will be more difficult to gain outside leverage against. This type of force sometimes requires the fullback to make a kickout block, allowing the halfback to run the alley inside of the kickout block. The halfback and the quarterback follow their same assignments.

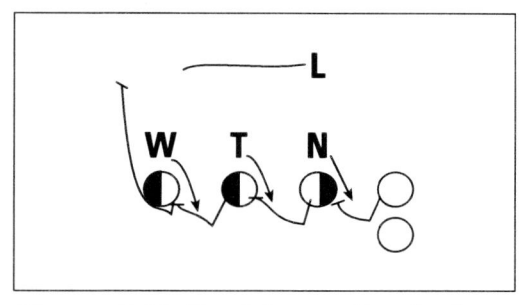

Diagram 5-18: The defense with a Stack front playing 2/4/6-techniques

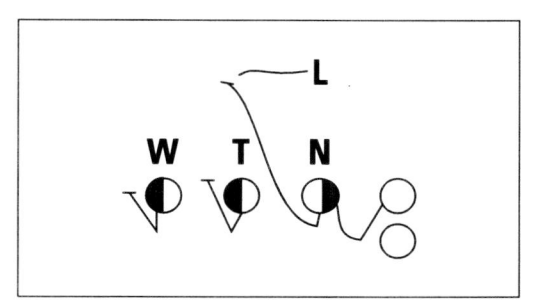

Diagram 5-19: The defense with a Stack front playing 2i-/5-/9-techniques

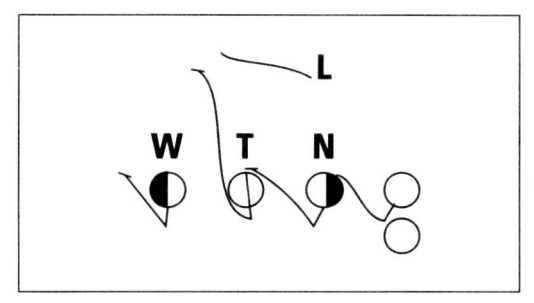

Diagram 5-20: The defense with a Stack front playing 2-/4-/9-techniques

Attacking a Reduced Front

The way to block the Reduced front is shown in Diagram 5-21. We like to run Stretch against Reduced fronts because it matches up the tight end against the weak outside linebacker, who is aligned to the strongside of the formation. The tight end and the playside tackle will reach block the 9-technique and the 5-technique, respectively. Concurrently, the playside guard uses the three-step bucket progression to attempt reach blocking the 5-technique, while keeping an eye on the strong inside linebacker. The center has a strongside shade and has to reach block that player. The backside guard has a 3-technique that he treats as uncovered, and uses the three-step bucket progression to work up to the second level. Reduced defensive structures normally utilize some form of rolled-up coverage to support the run. The standard way to block this type of force with the fullback is shown in Diagram 5-22. The alley player is blocked by the wide receiver, and the flat force defender is blocked by the fullback. The halfback should run the alley.

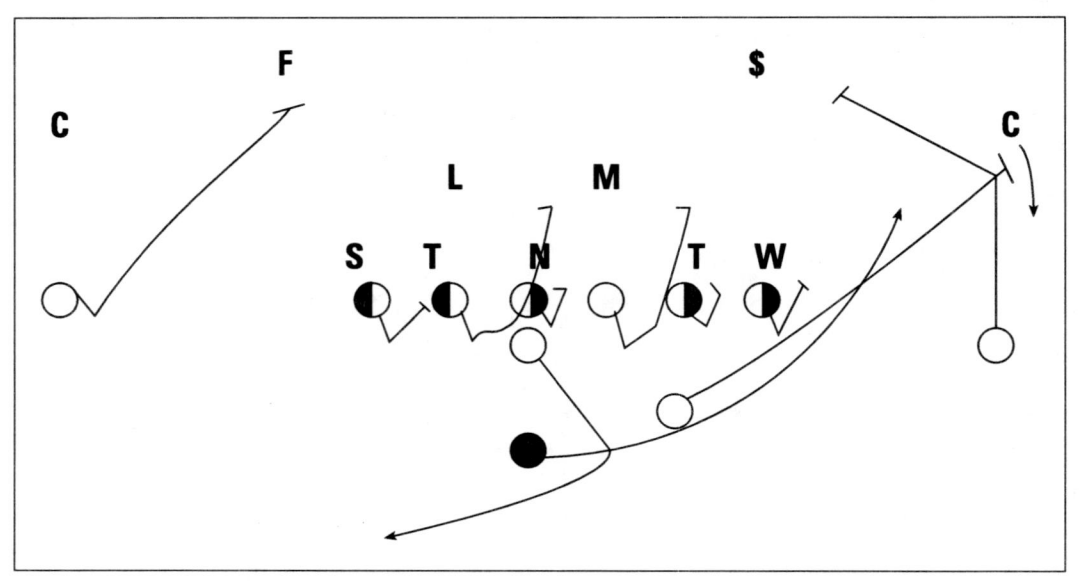

Diagram 5-21: King Right 28 Stretch vs. a Reduced front

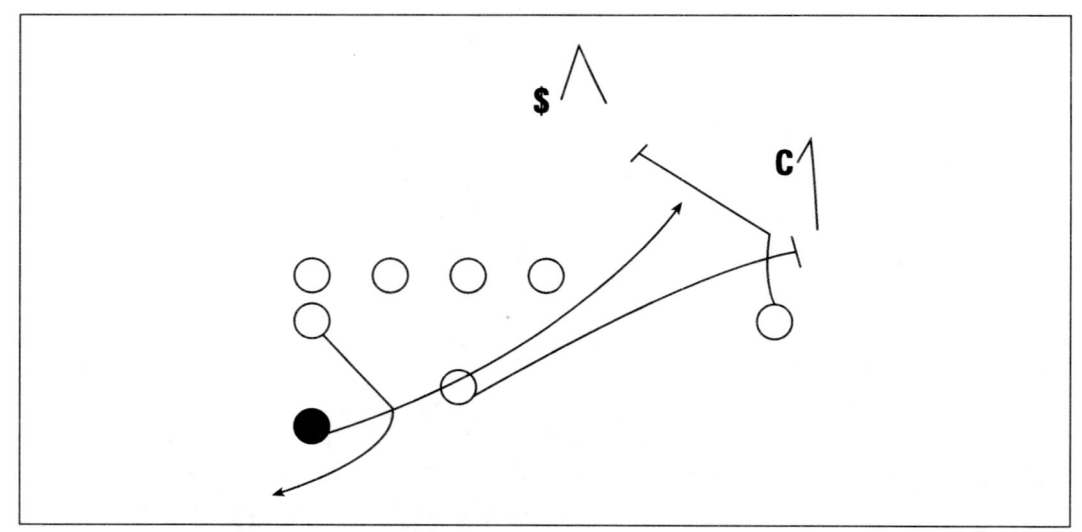

Diagram 5-22: Using the fullback to block rolled corner force

Attacking the Slide Weak Front

The blocking for the tight-end side Stretch against a Slide Weak front is shown in Diagram 5-23. Because Slide Weak is a true eight-man front, it can be difficult to handle up front. Zone blocking principles, however, simplify the blocking scheme. The tight end and the playside tackle use their zone combination rules to block the 6-technique and the strong inside linebacker. Several of the various blocking possibilities are illustrated in Diagrams 5-24, 5-25, and 5-26.

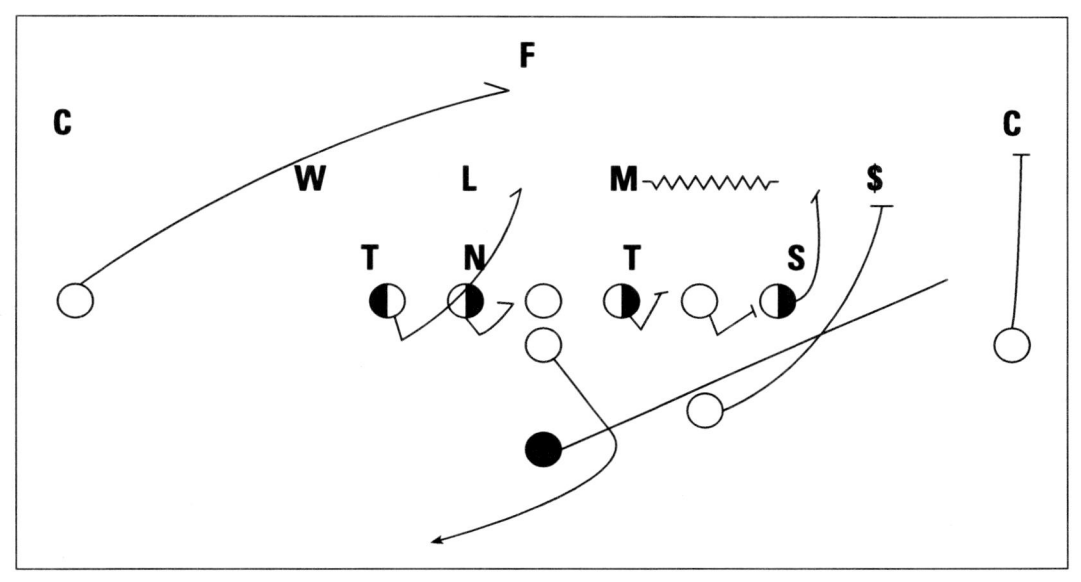

Diagram 5-23: King Right 28 Stretch vs. a Slide Weak front

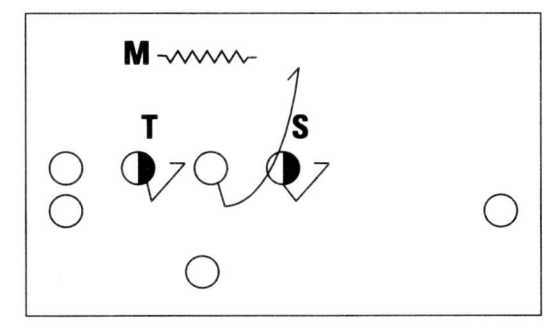

Diagram 5-24: Blocking the 9-technique and the stacked linebacker

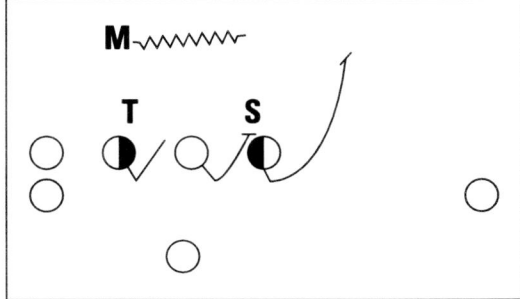

Diagram 5-25: Blocking the 7-technique and the stacked linebacker

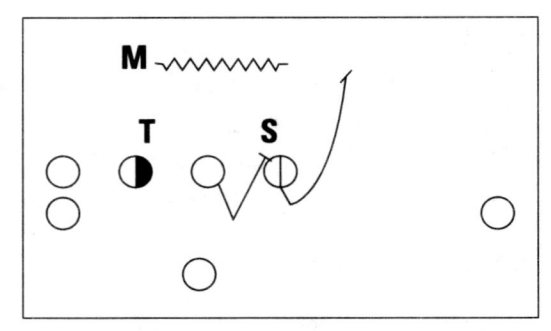

Diagram 5-26: Blocking the 6-technique and the stacked linebacker

The tight end keeps an eye on the strong inside linebacker, while holding off the 7-technique until the playside tackle can overtake that player (Diagram 5-25). The 6-technique is treated exactly like a 7-technique because the 6-technique is a C-gap player. The tight end holds off the 6-technique until the playside tackle can overtake him (Diagram 5-26). If the 6-technique fights outside, the tight end would reach block him, and the tackle would work upfield to the strong inside linebacker. The playside guard and the center use the identical technique to block their defenders. In Diagram 5-27, the playside guard has a 3-technique, and the center is uncovered. The playside guard reach blocks the 3-technique, and the center uses the three-step bucket progression to work up to the weak inside linebacker.

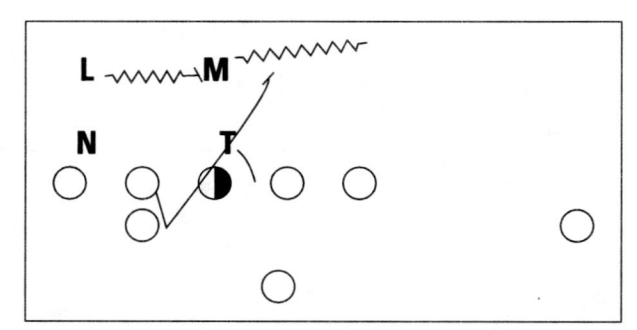

Diagram 5-27: Blocking the 3-technique and the stacked linebacker

In Diagram 5-28, the playside guard has a 2-technique and will hold off that player until the center can overtake him. The guard will then come off to the weak inside linebacker. We coach the two offensive linemen to keep three hands on the down lineman (the inside lineman keeps both hands and the outside lineman uses his inside hand) and four eyes on the linebacker.

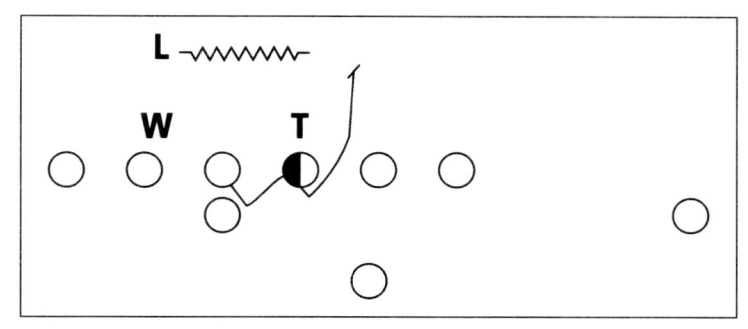

Diagram 5-28: Blocking the 2-technique and the stacked linebacker

Diagram 5-29 illustrates the point that the exact same scheme is used to block a 2i-technique. When the backside guard in a Slide Weak front has a 2i-technique, his assignment is to cut block that player. The backside tackle has a 5-technique and uses the three-step bucket progression to work up to the second level. In a Slide Weak front, he would cut-off a 4-technique or a 4i-technique. The fullback blocks the force (the strong safety in a Slide Weak front), and the halfback runs his usual Stretch course.

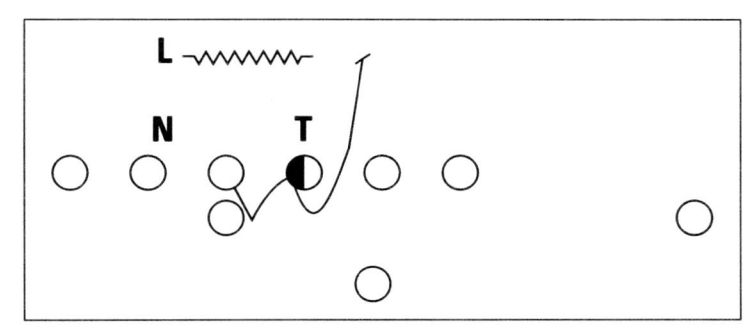

Diagram 5-29: Blocking the 2i-technique and the stacked linebacker

Seal Block

Several ways exist to present different looks to the defense when running the Stretch play to the tight-end side. The first variation is what we call the Seal play. The play calls 28 and 29 Seal tell the offensive line that they are going to help the tight end on the edge by getting an extra blocker to the point of attack, as shown in Diagram 5-30. In Diagram 5-30, a wide receiver is used to execute the Seal block. Another way to run Seal is to get into a two-tight end formation and bring a tight end across the formation to seal the edge, as shown in Diagram 5-31. The Seal block is used to make sure the edge gets softened up.

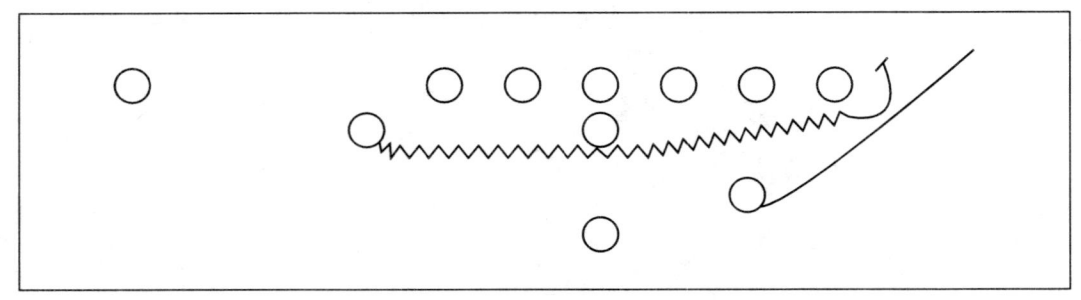

Diagram 5-30: 28 Seal (one tight end)

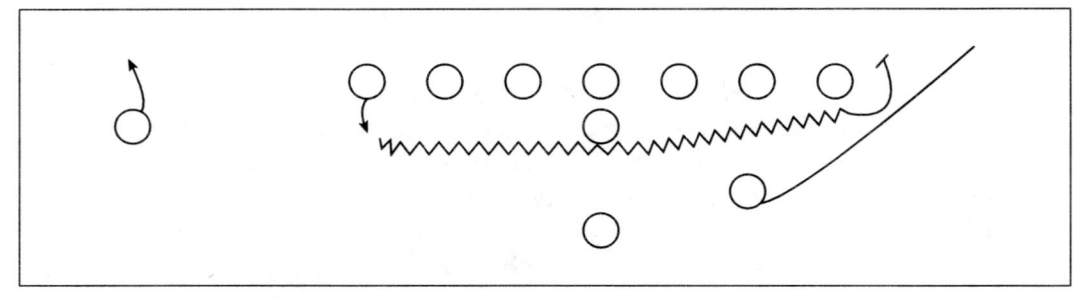

Diagram 5-31: 28 Seal (two tight ends)

Crack Scheme

Another option is the use of a Crack scheme. Crack refers to a wide receiver blocking the force for the fullback, and the fullback blocking the outside third defender or the secondary run-support defender, as shown in Diagram 5-32. The crack scheme is used against a Cover 3 look.

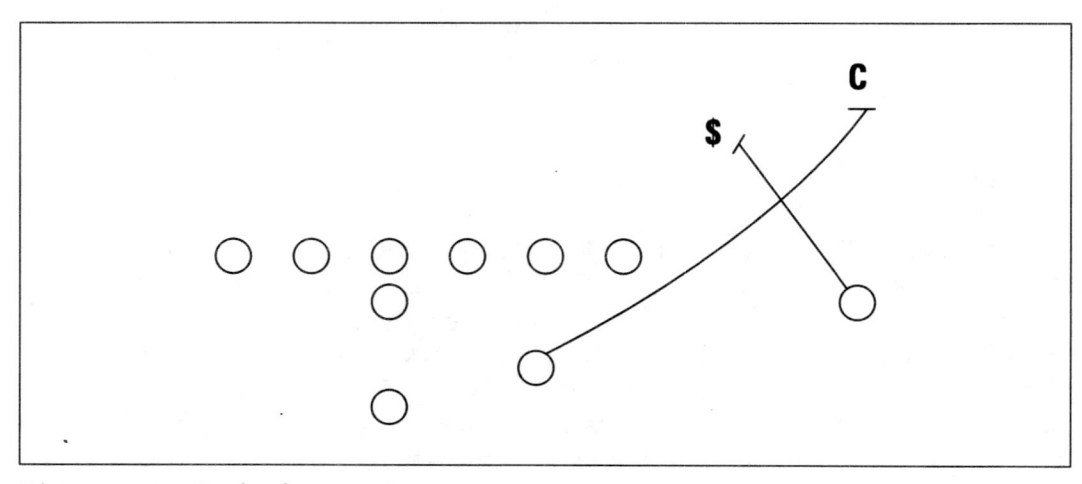

Diagram 5-32: Crack scheme

The tight-end side Stretch can also be run from one-back formations. This play is called 28/29 Edge. Edge tells offensive linemen that no fullback is in the game, and one of the wide receivers has to be assigned to block the force element of the defense, as shown in Diagram 5-33. Obviously, offenses will be trying to exploit any opportunity for a play-action pass in one-back sets. Teams want to stretch the defense horizontally and vertically in order to run the ball.

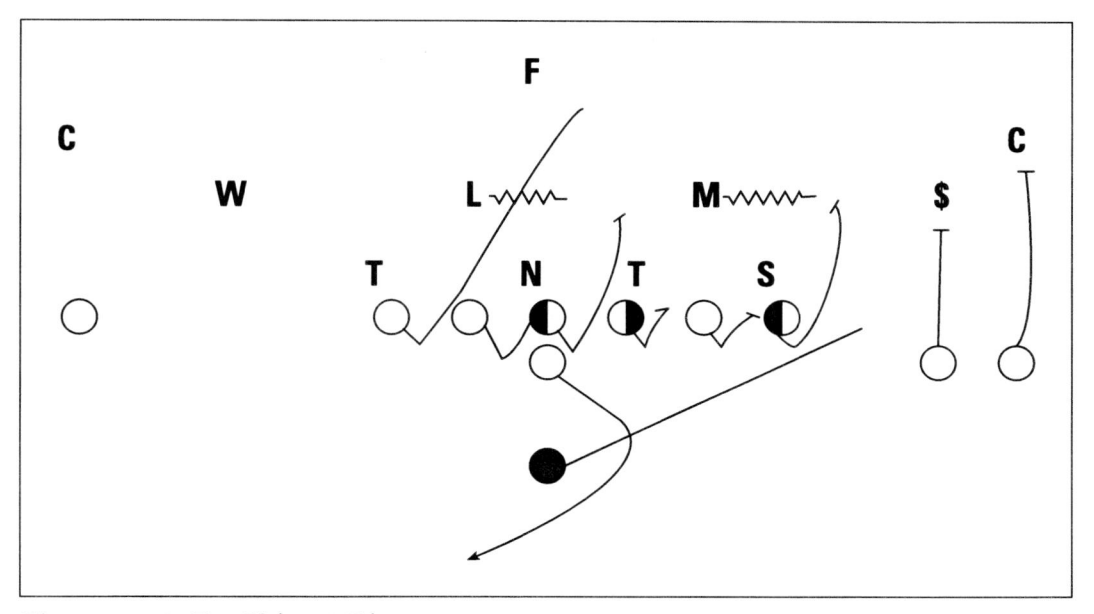

Diagram 5-33: Trey Right 28 Edge

6

The Outside Zone Play— Split-End Side

In our terminology, the split-end side Outside Zone play is also called 28 Stretch (when run to the right) or 29 Stretch (when it is run to the left). We do not add a designation to the play when running Stretch to the split-end side out of a two-back formation.

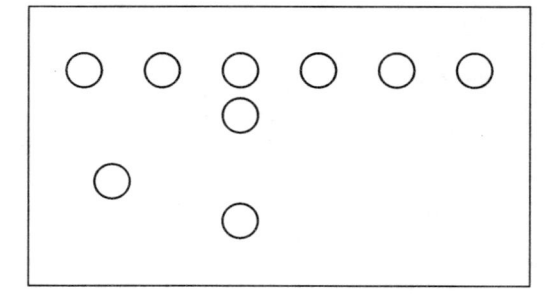

Diagram 6-1: Queen Right formation

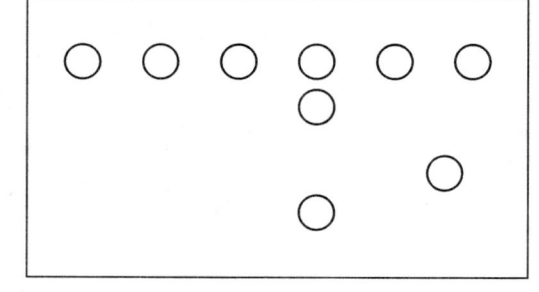

Diagram 6-2: Queen Left formation

The play is run and coached exactly the same as 28/29 Stretch to the tight-end side, even though it is run away from the strength of the formation and toward the split end. The only significant change is in the halfback's landmark, which is now at a point one yard behind and three yards outside the alignment of a ghost tight end on the split-end side of the formation. This change means the halfback is supposed to envision a tight end in normal alignment outside of the weakside tackle, and then find a point one yard behind and three yards outside where this ghost tight end would be. The halfback will stay on this course until a wrong-colored jersey crosses his path, and then this player should make a north-south cut up the field.

The split-end side Stretch play gets to the point of attack much faster than the tight-end side Stretch play due to the fact that the weakside edge of the formation is one man closer to the quarterback than the edge on the strongside. To account for this alignment, fullbacks are taught a technique called Bongo. Bongo is a technique used exclusively by fullbacks when running the split-end side Stretch. The fullback helps the weakside tackle block the edge of the defense, as long as the overhang or the force of the defensive structure plays soft.

Attacking an Okie Front

On the split-end side 28/29 Stretch against an Okie defensive front, the playside (split-end side) tackle reaches and displaces the 5-technique defensive tackle. The uncovered playside guard executes the three-step bucket progression. The guard is hoping to overtake the 5-technique, but if he can't, he will block the weak inside linebacker. The center has a head-up 0-technique and will consider himself uncovered. The center drop steps and holds off the 0-technique for the backside guard. If the 0-technique fights hard and slants playside, the center will lock onto that player, and the backside guard will execute a three-step bucket progression and continue on to the second level. These two possibilities are shown in Diagrams 6-4 and 6-5.

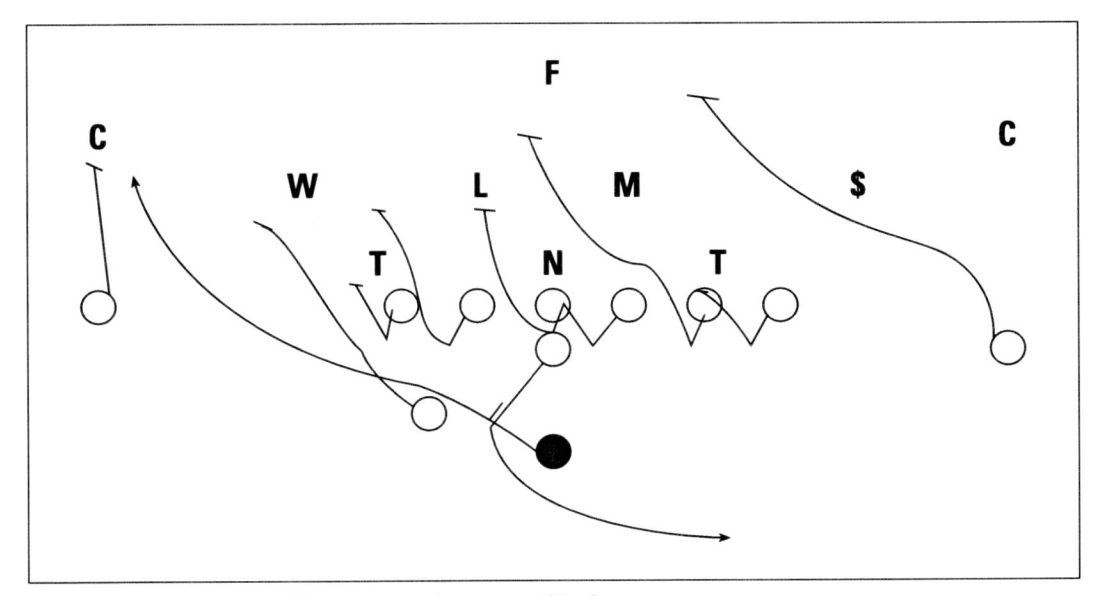

Diagram 6-3: Queen Right 29 Stretch vs. an Okie front

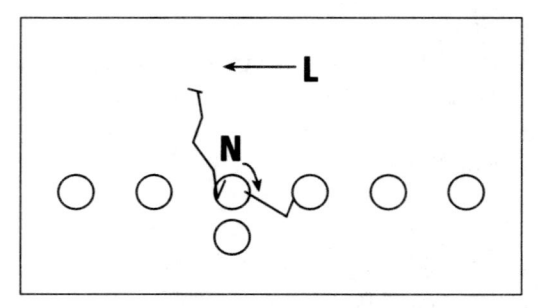

Diagram 6-4: The center holds off the 0-technique for the backside guard

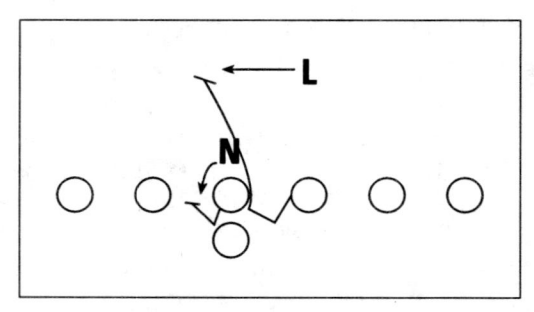

Diagram 6-5: The center locks onto the 0-technique

The backside guard executes a three-step bucket progression, to reach the nose guard or work up to the second level. The backside tackle has a 5-technique. With the Stretch play being run away from him, the backside tackle considers himself uncovered and executes a three-step bucket progression to the second level. It is possible that, because of the uncovered guard, the tackle may end up blocking the third level. The tight end treats the 9-technique as uncovered and cut blocks the 5-technique for the tackle. The fullback executes his Bongo technique after determining whether the defensive structure has an overhang. The two possibilities are illustrated in Diagrams 6-6 and 6-7.

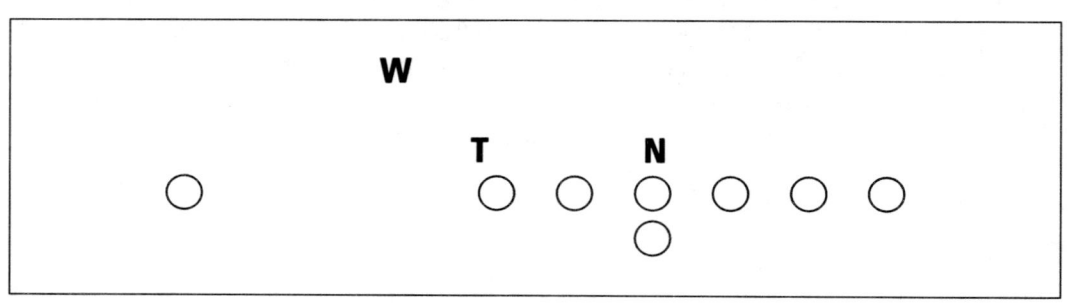

Diagram 6-6: Defensive structure with an overhang

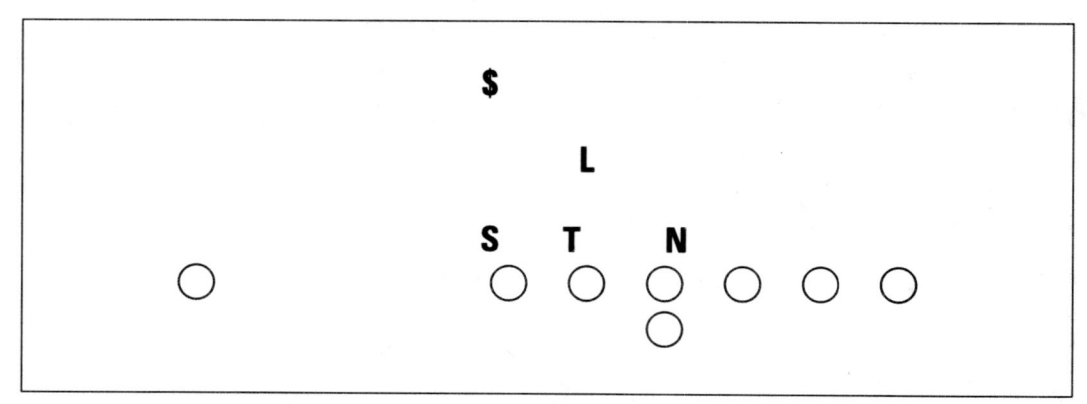

Diagram 6-7: Defensive structure without an overhang

Any defensive force player on the second level is in an overhang position. A weak outside linebacker in an invert position is considered to be an overhang. A rolled cornerback or a half-field safety with alley run-support responsibility is not considered an overhang.

If the fullback identifies an overhang in the defensive structure, he should realize that the overhang is his responsibility. If the overhang player stays soft, the fullback will Bongo and help the offensive tackle. The Bongo technique involves helping the offensive tackle with the 5-technique by knocking the 5-technique back onto the block of the tackle. The fullback simply executes a one-armed punch and stabs the outside armpit of the 5-technique with his own inside arm. The fullback has to recognize an overhang in hard run support, and then block the overhang without being concerned about one-arm punching the 5-technique. The fullback should understand that against some defensive fronts without overhang players in their structure, he will still utilize a Bongo technique and wait to engage his inside linebacker key, as shown in Diagram 6-10.

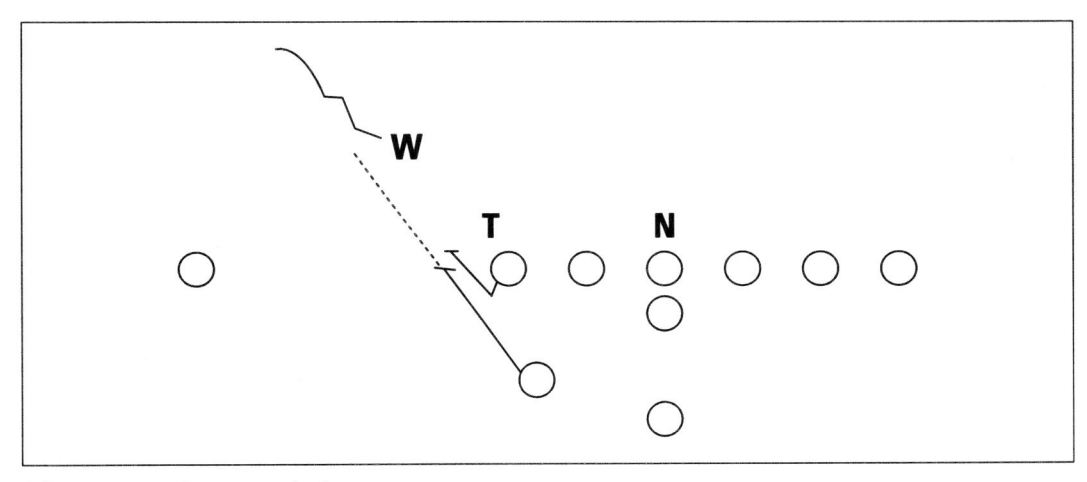

Diagram 6-8: Bongo technique

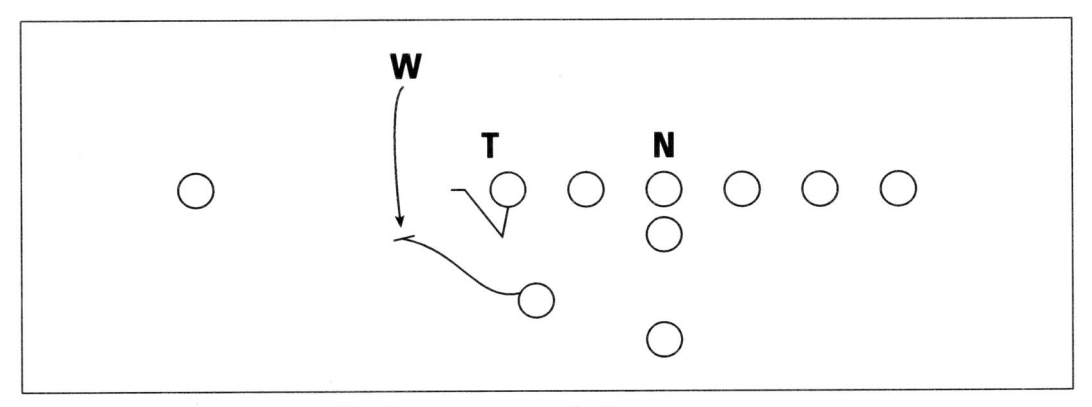

Diagram 6-9: Engage immediately—no Bongo technique

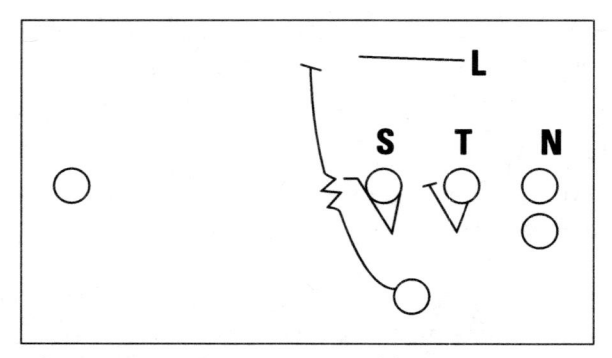

Diagram 6-10: Bongo vs. no overhang

The halfback's landmark really remains exactly the same as it is in the tight-end side Stretch, except in this instance his one-yard deep and three-yard wide aiming point is outside of a ghost tight end rather than a real tight end. He has to stay on that path until a wrong-colored jersey crosses his face, and then he should make an immediate north-south cut up the field. After handing off the ball, the quarterback continues with his bootleg/naked play-action pass footwork toward the tight-end side.

Attacking an Eagle Strong Front

On the split-end side Stretch against an Eagle Strong front, the playside tackle will reach block the 5-technique and knock that player off the ball, while the uncovered playside guard uses the three-step bucket progression to try and overtake the 5-technique. If the guard cannot overtake the 5-technique, then he will work up to the second level and look for a linebacker. The center treats the 0-technique as uncovered. He will one-arm punch the 0-technique and work up to the second level to cut off the strong inside linebacker. The backside guard and the center are really utilizing a zone-combination scheme on the 0-technique and the strong inside linebacker. Diagrams 6-12, 6-13, and 6-14 show the possible situations for which the zone combination scheme has to be utilized effectively.

The backside tackle has a 5-technique. Because the play is being run away from him, he treats the 5-technique as if he is uncovered and uses the three-step bucket progression to work up to the second or even the third level. The tight end is always on the backside of the split end Stretch, and against an Eagle Strong front, the tight end will ignore the 9-technique and instead cut block the 5-technique. If the tight end has a 7-technique (a distinct possibility against some teams), he should use a backside-rip technique to cross that defender's face.

The fullback is responsible for the force player in the defense, which is the weak outside linebacker in an Eagle Strong structure. The fullback uses the Bongo technique as long as the weak outside linebacker stays loose. The fullback, however, will block the weak outside linebacker as soon as that player steps up toward the play.

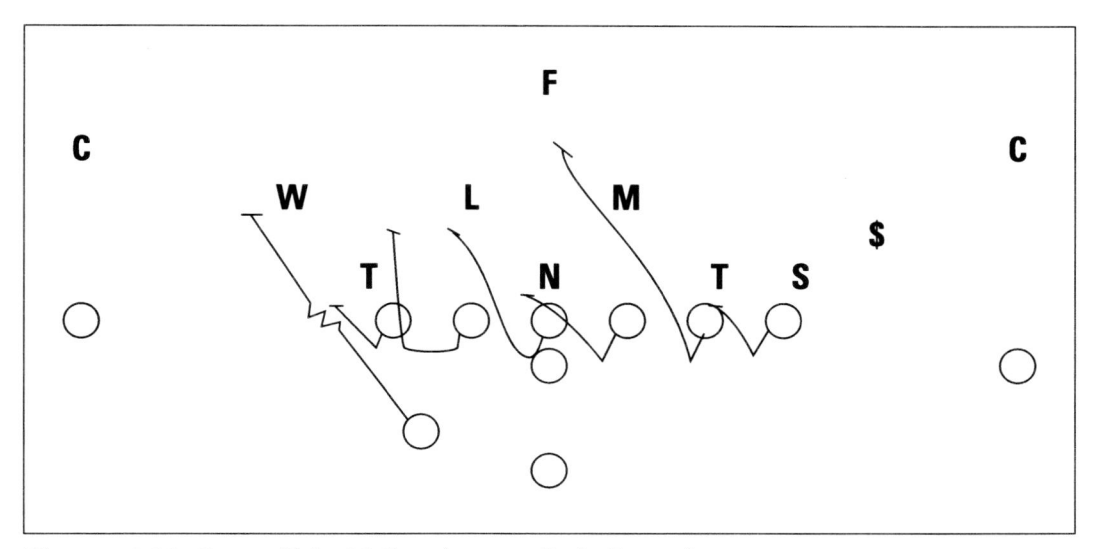

Diagram 6-11: Queen Right 29 Stretch vs. an Eagle Strong front

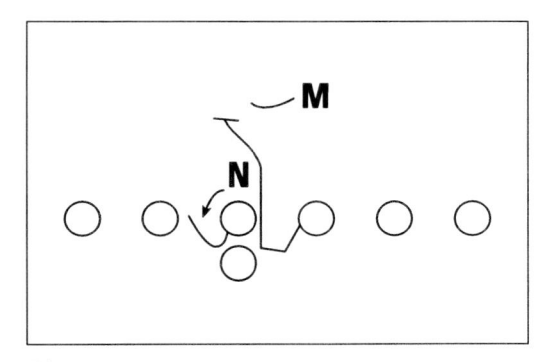

Diagram 6-12

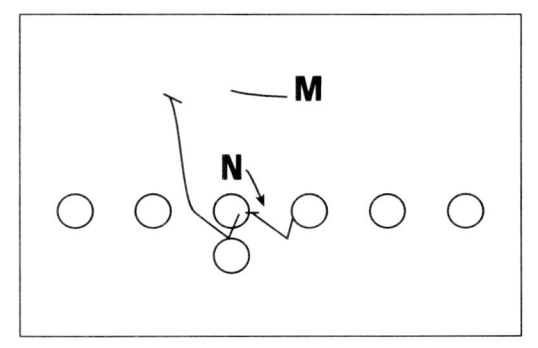

Diagram 6-13

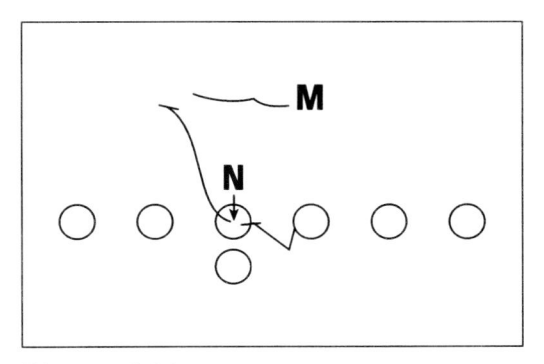

Diagram 6-14

The halfback accepts the ball from the quarterback and runs his Stretch path one yard deep and three yards outside of the alignment of a ghost tight end. He will stay on this path until a wrong-colored jersey crosses his face, and then he will make an immediate north-south cut up the field, finding a seam and getting whatever yardage he can. The quarterback hands off the ball and runs his bootleg/naked path to hold the backside edge (it should be noted that this movement is not accounting for the backside 9-technique).

It is extremely important for the wide receivers to be able to block in this offensive system. If a receiver cannot block and help make the run game successful, then that player will have difficulty finding playing time. In the split-end side Stretch, the split end is the playside receiver. The split end might see three possible looks. The split end has be able to identify the secondary coverage and block his assignment accordingly. Against Cover 3 (three-deep zone coverage), the split end will block the cornerback, as shown in Diagram 6-15.

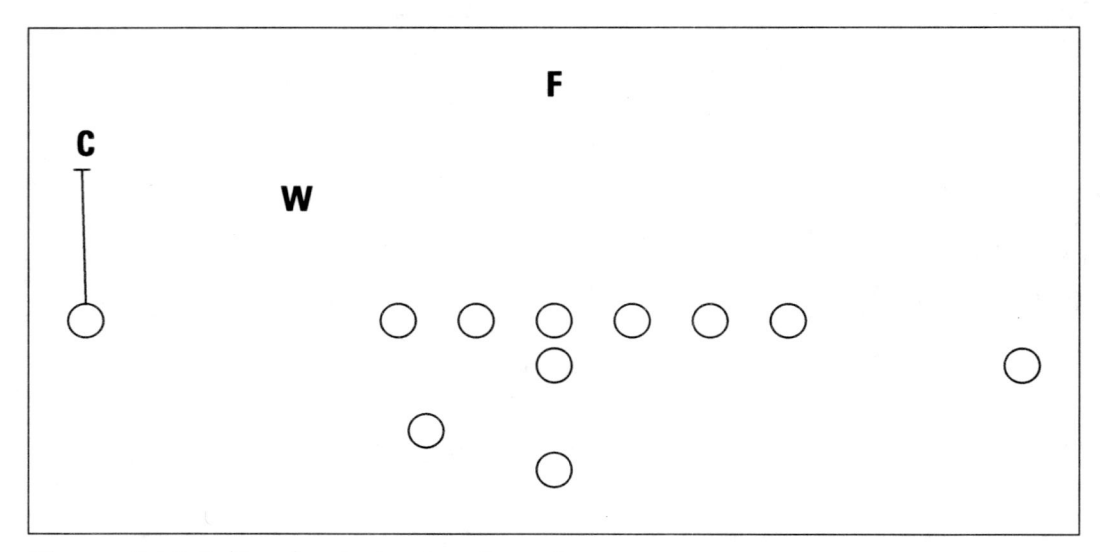

Diagram 6-15: Split end assignment vs. Cover 3

The split end drives off the line of scrimmage and stalk blocks the outside third defender. Against teams that like to play Cover 2, there are two possible schemes that might be utilized. The first possibility is shown in Diagram 6-16. The split end blocks the cornerback, who is the force player in the structure. The fullback blocks the weak inside linebacker or the strong safety, whatever player shows up at the point of attack first.

Against Cover 2, the halfback would run the alley inside of the cornerback instead of trying to get to the sideline. Another scheme that can be used against Cover 2 teams is shown in Diagram 6-17. In this situation, the split end jams the cornerback and then releases inside to block the half-field safety. Again, the halfback should run the alley

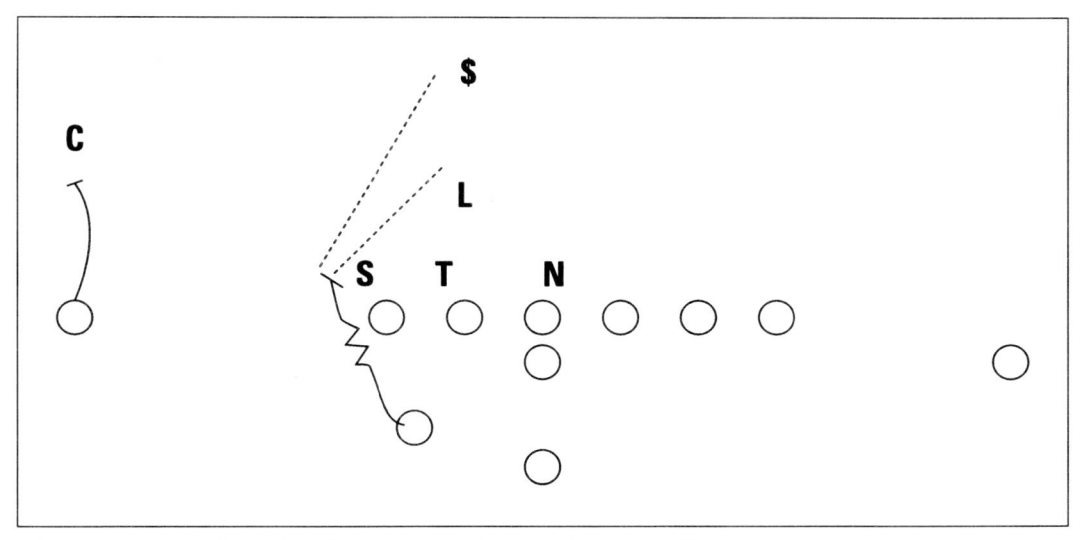

Diagram 6-16: Split end assignment vs. Cover 2 (cornerback)

rather than getting wide and running to where the cornerback is being blocked. The final possibility that the split end should be aware of is a form of man-to-man coverage, which is illustrated in Diagram 6-18.

If the secondary is playing what is referred to as Loose Man coverage, a stalk block will be used. If the coverage technique is more aggressive (bump man or man underneath with Cover 2 over the top), the split end will run a take-off route, as shown in Diagram 6-19.

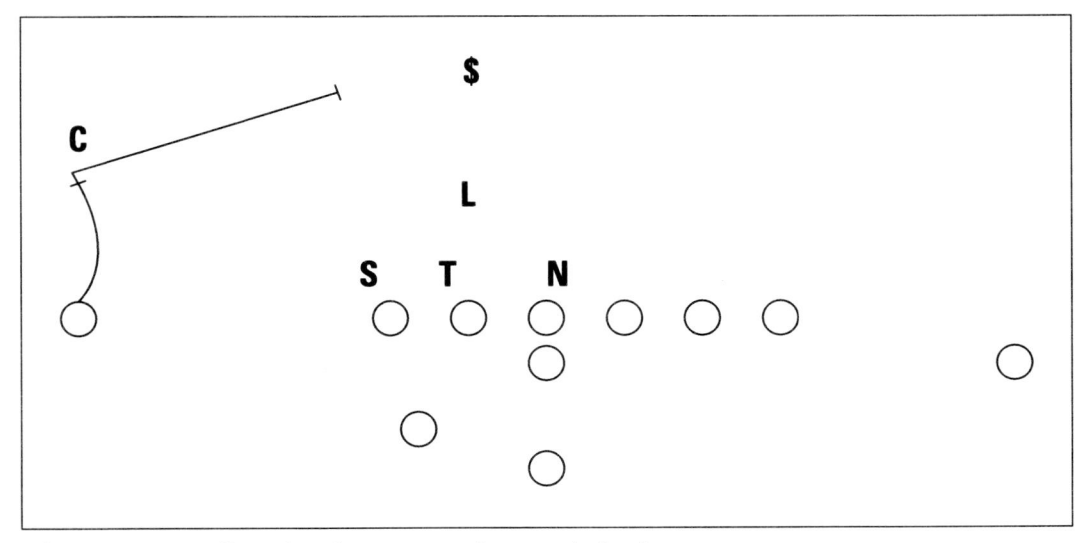

Diagram 6-17: Split-end assignment vs. Cover 2 (safety)

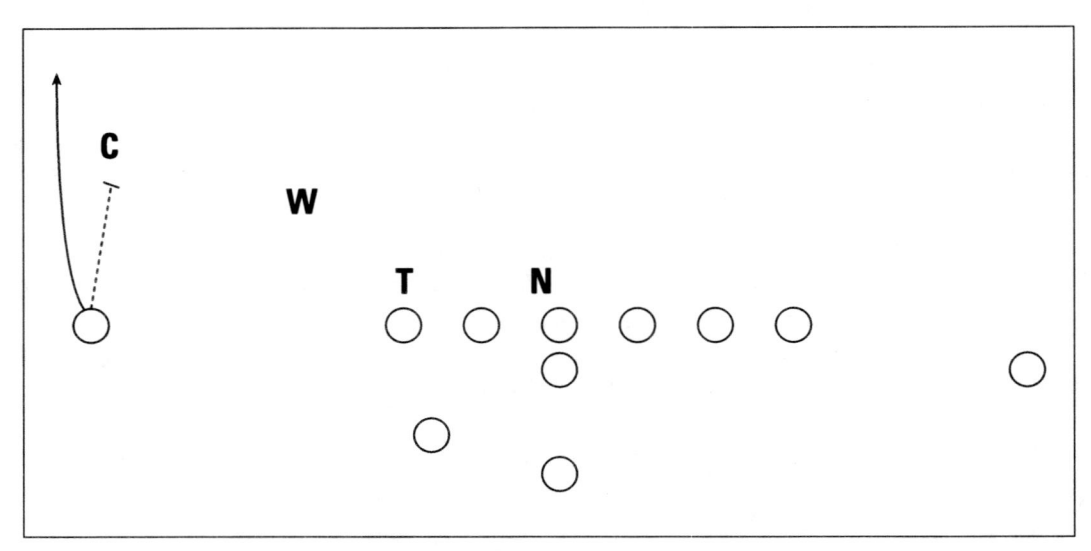

Diagram 6-18: Split-end assignment vs. man coverage

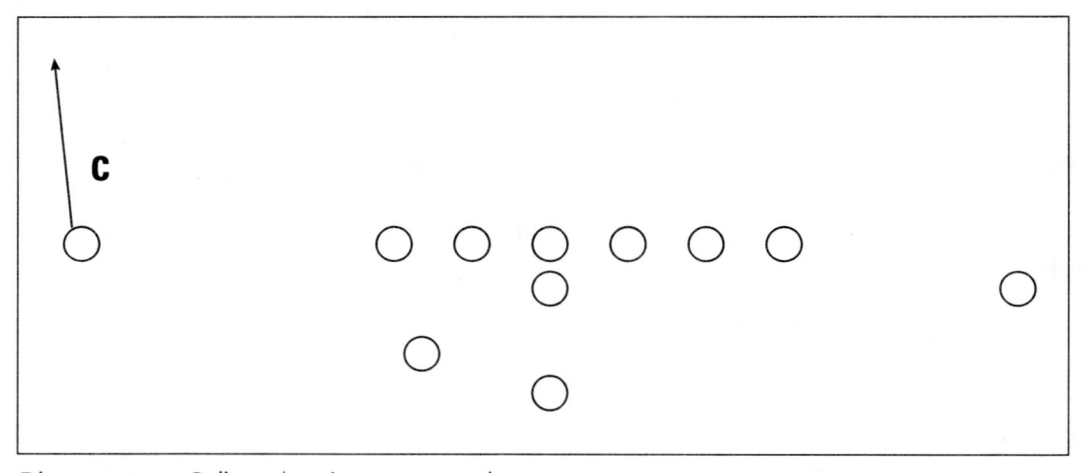

Diagram 6-19: Split-end assignment vs. a bump-man coverage

Some other adjustments exist that can be made to the wide receiver blocking schemes that will be discussed later in this chapter. The role of the flanker on the backside of the play will be considered first. The flanker has one basic rule of thumb—get to the middle third of the field and block whatever player shows up there first. The flanker will stalk block any wrong-colored jersey that crosses his face. The three looks the flanker will have to block are shown in Diagrams 6-20, 6-21, and 6-22.

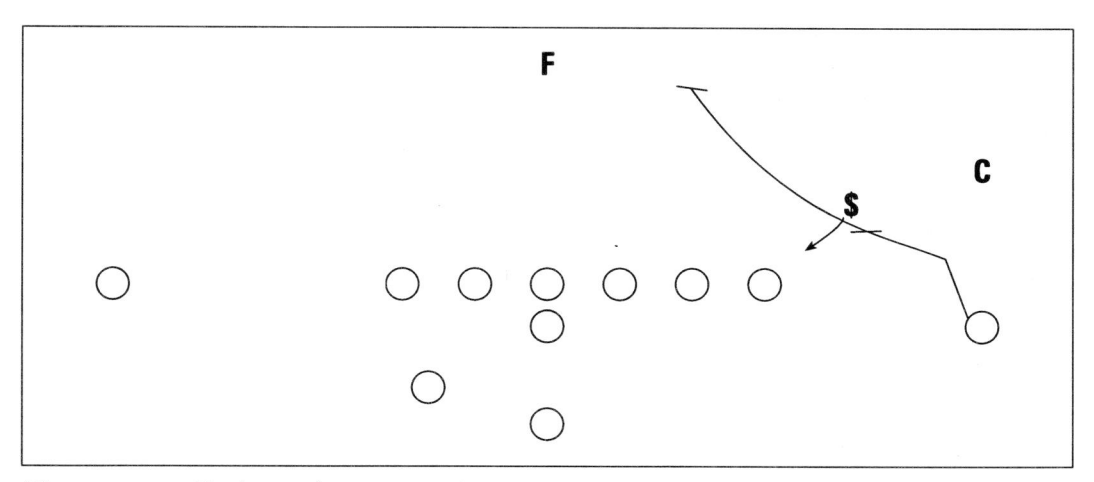

Diagram 6-20: Flanker assignment vs. Cover 3

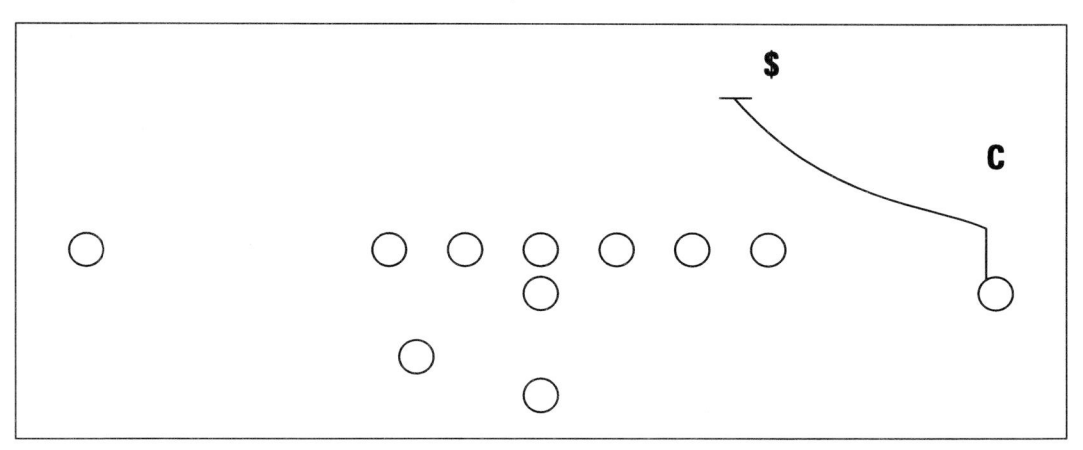

Diagram 6-21: Flanker assignment vs. Cover 2

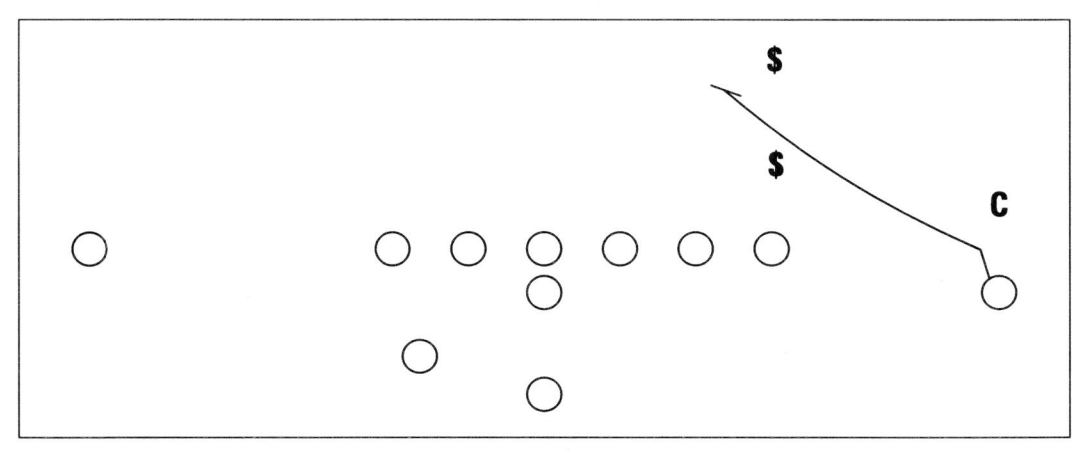

Diagram 6-22: Flanker assignment vs. man coverage

Attacking a 4-3 Front

The 4-3 front is attacked, as shown in Diagram 6-23. The playside tackle has a 5-technique and will reach block that player. The playside guard is uncovered and will use the three-step bucket progression to work up to the second level. The center has a weak-shaded defensive tackle and will reach block the shade. The uncovered backside guard will use the three-step bucket progression in an attempt to cut-off the strong inside (middle) linebacker. The backside tackle is uncovered, but has to cut block the 3-technique playing over the adjacent guard. The tight end has a 9-technique and will attempt to use the three-step bucket progression to cut-off the strong outside linebacker. The fullback has to identify this as a structure without an overhang player, and realize that he will probably not have a second-level assignment because of the technique the playside guard is using, as shown in Diagram 6-24.

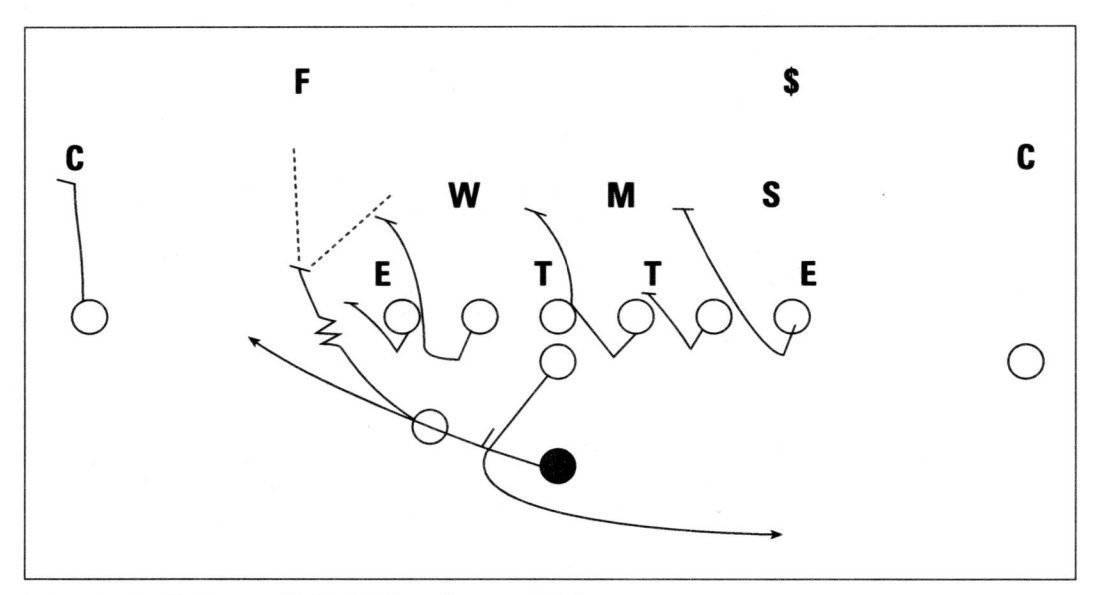

Diagram 6-23: Queen Right 29 Stretch vs. a 4-3 front

Against a 4-3 front, the fullback will use the Bongo technique to help the playside tackle. He then will continue upfield, waiting for a wrong-colored jersey to appear. If no second-level player appears from the middle of the field, he will look for the force player in the structure coming out of the deep half. This progression is illustrated in Diagram 6-25.

Attacking a Stack Front

Diagram 6-26 shows how to attack the Stack front. The playside tackle has a 5-technique. He has to reach block that player, while the playside guard has a 2-technique that could possibly be a 2i or a 3-technique. The playside guard and the center use a

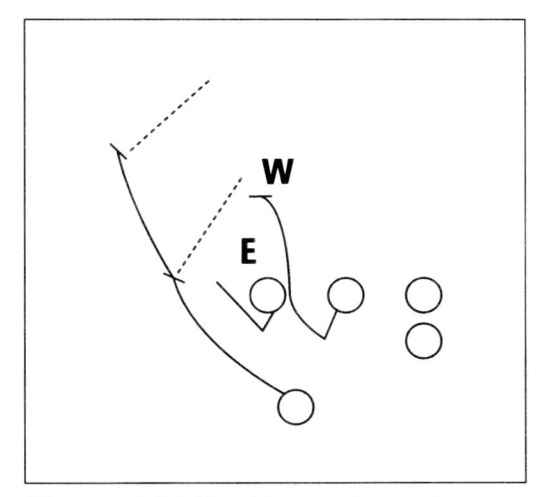

Diagram 6-24: Playside guard overtake

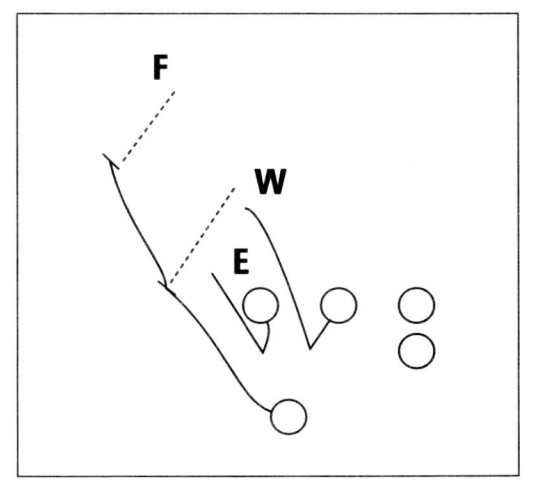

Diagram 6-25: Fullback progression against a 4-3 front

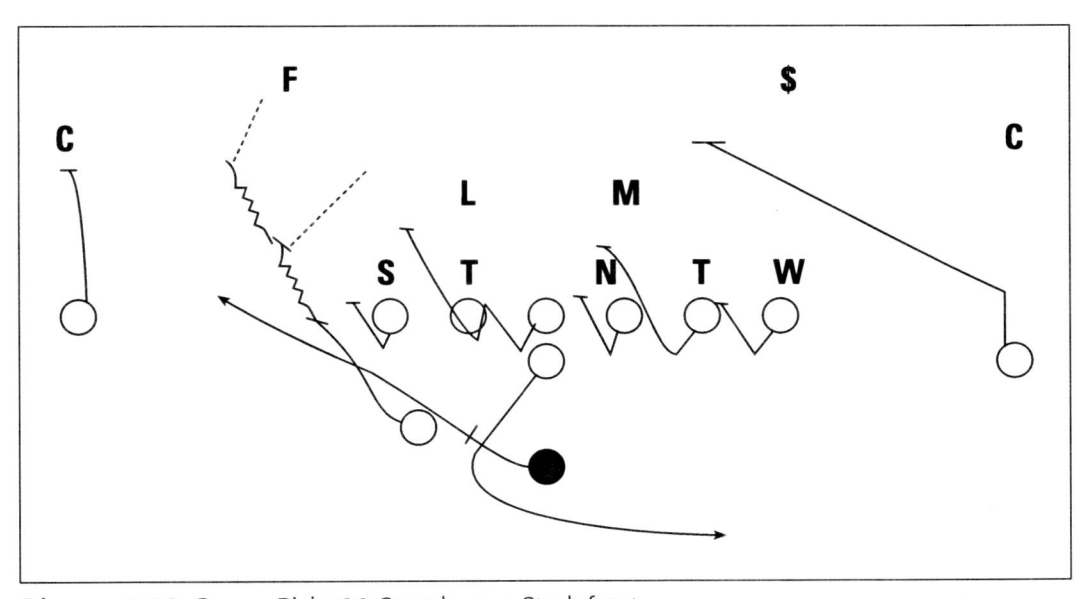

Diagram 6-26: Queen Right 29 Stretch vs. a Stack front

zone-combination scheme to block the 2-technique and the weak inside linebacker, regardless of their alignments, as shown in Diagrams 6-27, 6-28, and 6-29. The blocker working off the zone-combination scheme will probably not get to the weak inside linebacker if the weak inside linebacker has flowed to the perimeter. The blocker should then locate the strong inside linebacker and cut that player off.

    The backside guard will also face one of three possible alignments. If the backside guard sees a 2- or a 2i-technique, then the guard will block that player. If the defender is playing a 3-technique, then the guard will use a three-step bucket progression, and the backside tackle will cut block the 3-technique. Against a Stack front, the tackle would have to block a 4- or a 4i-technique, and the tight end would block a 5-technique. The tight end will block a 6-technique or a 7-technique, but let a 9-technique go and use the three-step bucket progression, along with the adjacent tackle, to work off to the second level.

The fullback uses a Bongo technique to help the playside tackle, while keeping an eye on the weak inside linebacker. If the weak inside linebacker flows free over the top, then the fullback will come off and block him. If either the guard or the center blocks the weak inside linebacker, then the fullback will focus his attention on the playside half-field safety. The wide receivers apply their normal rules, and the halfback runs his normal path. The quarterback stays on the bootleg/naked course after the hand-off to help freeze the edge players.

One point regarding the Stretch play has to be emphasized. As we have become successful, it appears that most of our opponents have come up with their own plan to stop the Stretch. The zone principles on which our entire running game is based would dictate blocking any defensive front with a hard-slanting, playside 2-technique, a hard-slanting, playside 4-technique, and a weak inside linebacker flowing free over the top, as shown in Diagram 6-30.

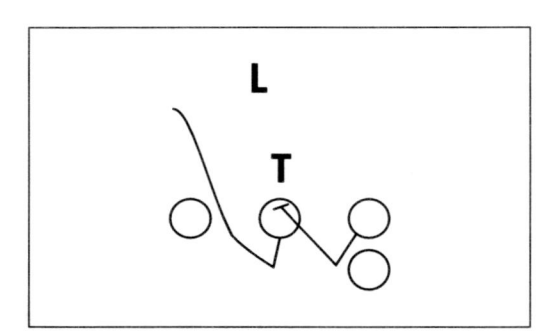

Diagram 6-27: 2-technique

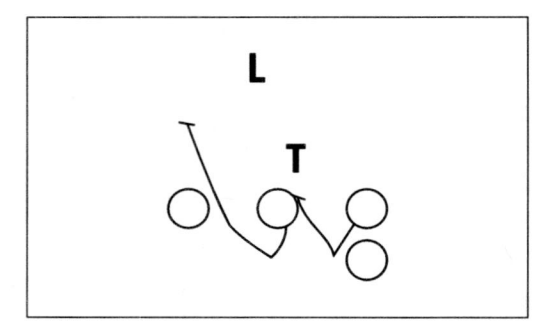

Diagram 6-28: 2i-technique

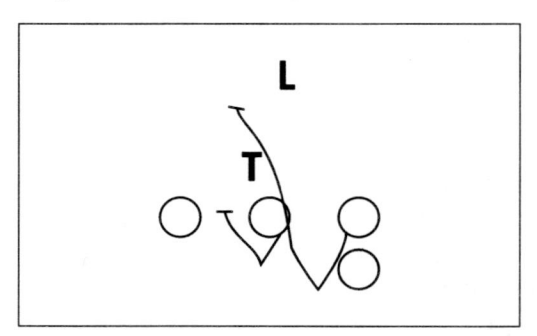

Diagram 6-29: 3-technique

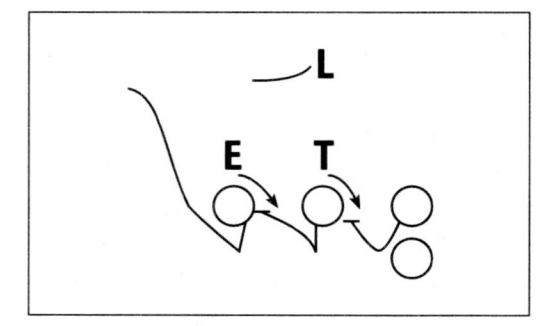

Diagram 6-30: Blocking a 2-technique and a 4-technique

Attacking a Reduced Front

The front we refer to as Reduced is actually a 50-based front, with an Eagle look on the weakside. Against a Reduced front, the playside tackle and the playside guard will reach the 5-technique and the 3-technique (Diagram 6-31). The center has a strong shade on the backside of the play, so the center utilizes the three-step bucket progression to overtake the playside 3-technique and works off to the second level, trying to cut-off the weak inside linebacker. The uncovered backside guard reacts to the shaded nose guard over the center and cut blocks that player. The backside tackle will treat the 5-technique as uncovered and use the three-step bucket progression footwork to step playside and work off to the second or third level. The tight end will ignore the 9-technique and cut block the 5-technique.

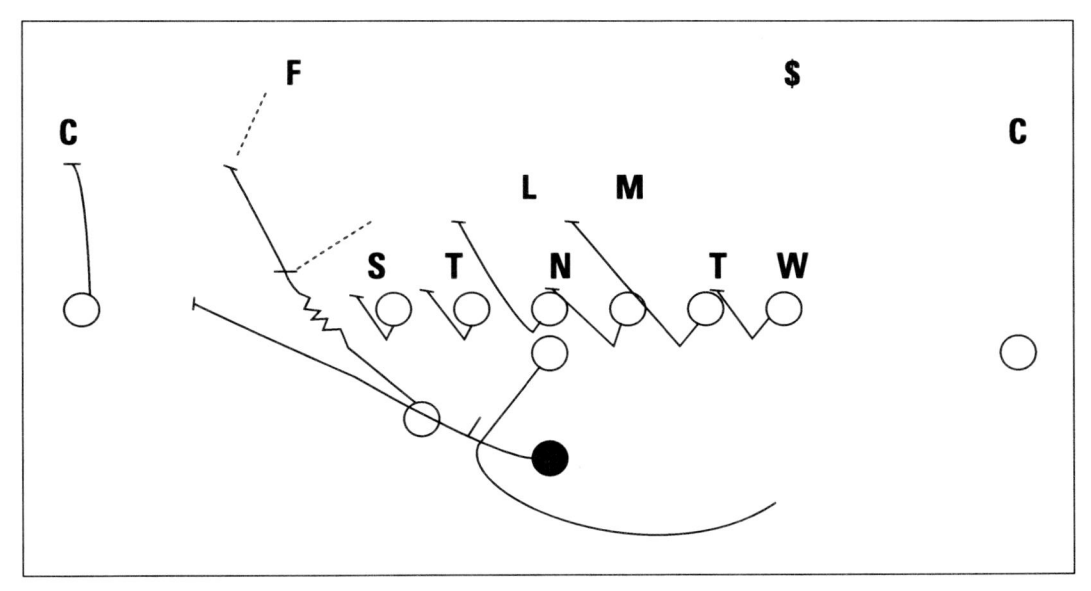

Diagram 6-31: Queen Right 29 Stretch vs. a Reduced front

Attacking a Slide Weak Front

Because the Slide Weak is an eight-man front, a defender will be unaccounted for in this defensive alignment. The playside tackle is going to reach block the 5-technique. The playside guard is going to treat the 2i-technique as uncovered and use the three-step bucket progression footwork to try and overtake the 5-technique and work up to the second level. The center will reach block the 2i-technique. The backside guard will one-arm punch the backside 2-technique and work off to the second level, as the adjacent uncovered backside tackle tries to overtake the 2-technique. Against an eight-man front, like Slide Weak, the backside guard and the tackle can see a multitude of looks. Diagrams 6-33, 6-34, and 6-35 illustrate some of the various possibilities.

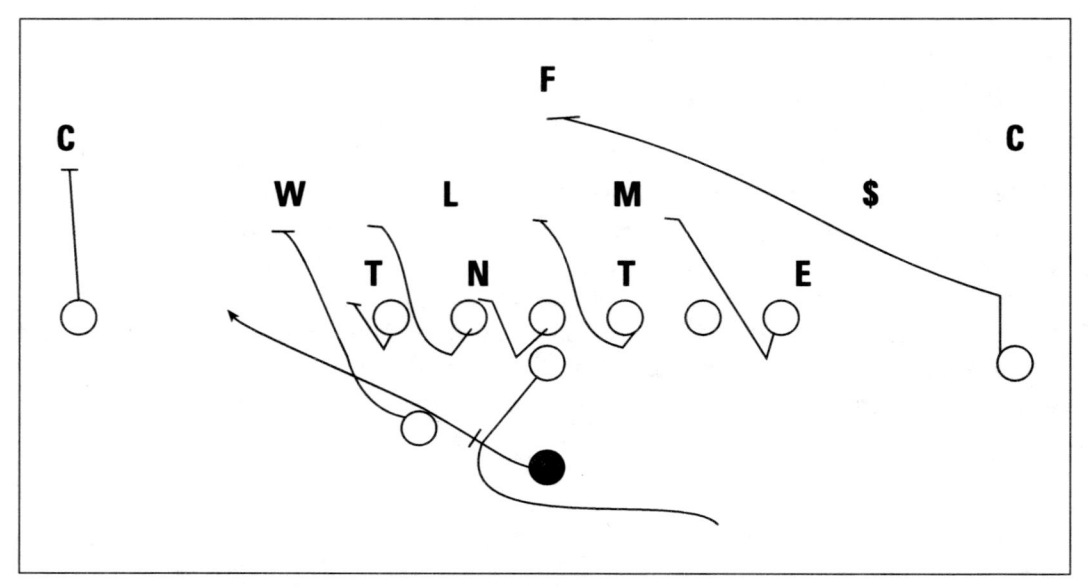

Diagram 6-32: Queen Right 29 Stretch vs. a Slide Weak front

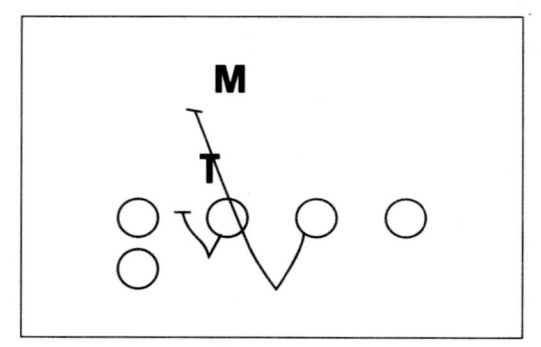

Diagram 6-33: 2i-technique

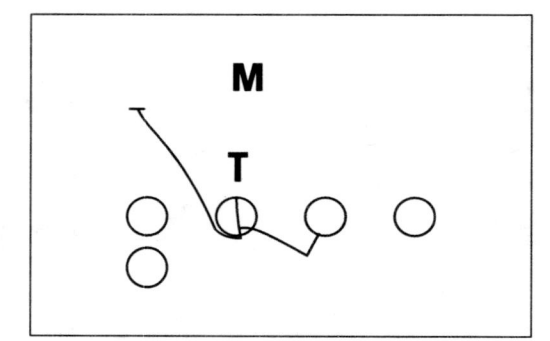

Diagram 6-34: 2-technique

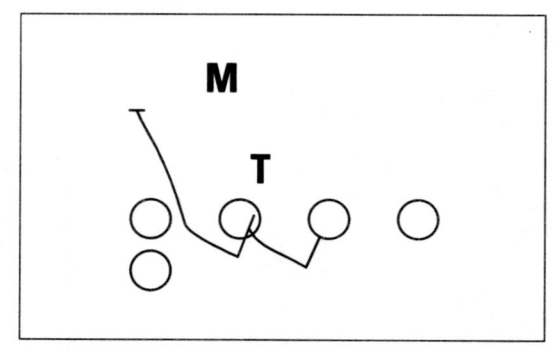

Diagram 6-35: 3-technique

84

Against Slide Weak, the tight end will cut block a head-up 6-technique responsible for the C gap. Because the Slide Weak front has an overhang, the fullback will use his normal Bongo technique, helping the playside tackle as long as the weak outside linebacker plays soft. The receivers apply their blocking rules to the coverage they read, and the quarterback continues on his bootleg/naked path after handing the ball off to the halfback. Several adjustments can be made to the normal split-end side Stretch play, but the one that is used most involves a formation adjustment in which a Twins look is utilized to block the edge, as shown in Diagram 6-36.

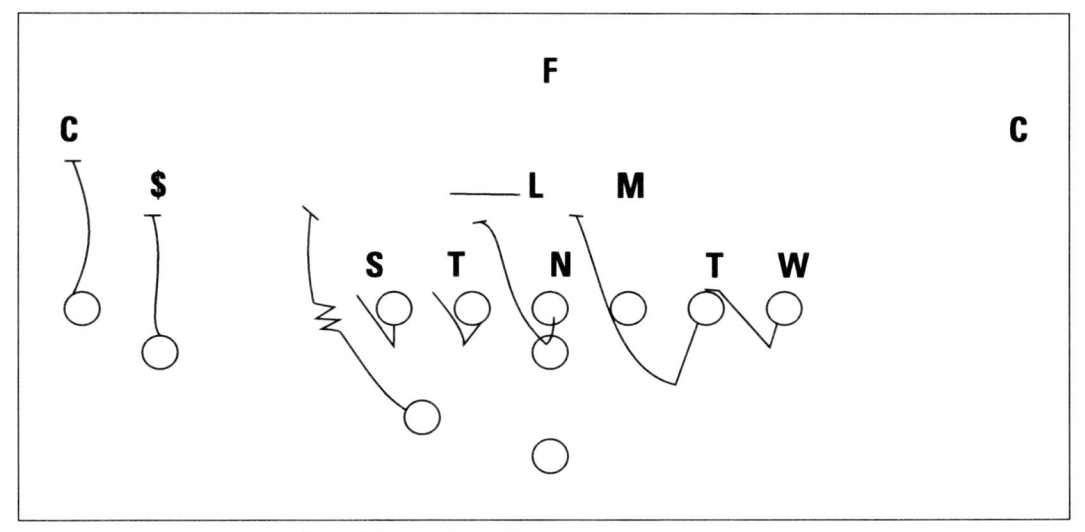

Diagram 6-36: Queen Twins Right 29 Stretch

In this situation, the flanker can block the force player in the defensive structure, and the fullback can stay with his Bongo technique longer to help the tackle, before working all the way up to the third level. Another possibility from Twins is some sort of Crack scheme that is shown in Diagram 6-37. A Crack scheme could assign the flanker to block a linebacker and assign the fullback to block the force of the defense. A double Crack scheme could also be used, in which both wide receivers would execute crack blocks, while the fullback would block the outside third defender or other secondary run support, as shown in Diagram 6-38.

Another variation that can be used is to start in a King formation, motion the fullback to a Queen formation, and snap the ball while the fullback is on the move. This variation provides an excellent way to attack defensive structures that attempt to mirror two-back formations with their linebackers. Diagram 6-39 shows the fullback-motion version of the split-end Stretch play. On this play, the quarterback is instructed to snap the ball when the fullback is aligned at the position he would assume in a Queen formation.

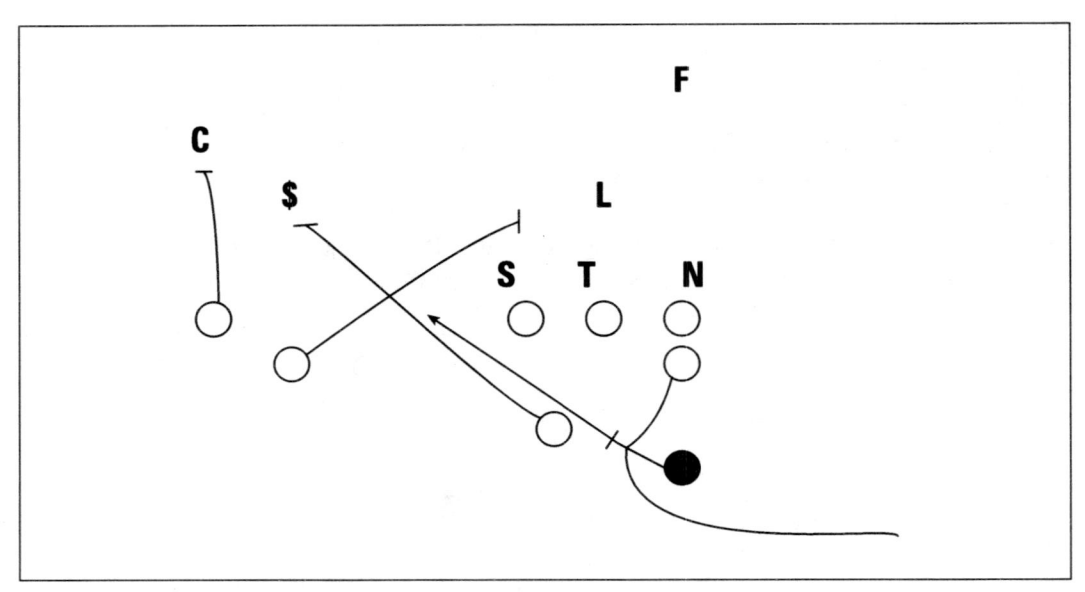

Diagram 6-37: Queen Twins Right Z Crack 29 Stretch

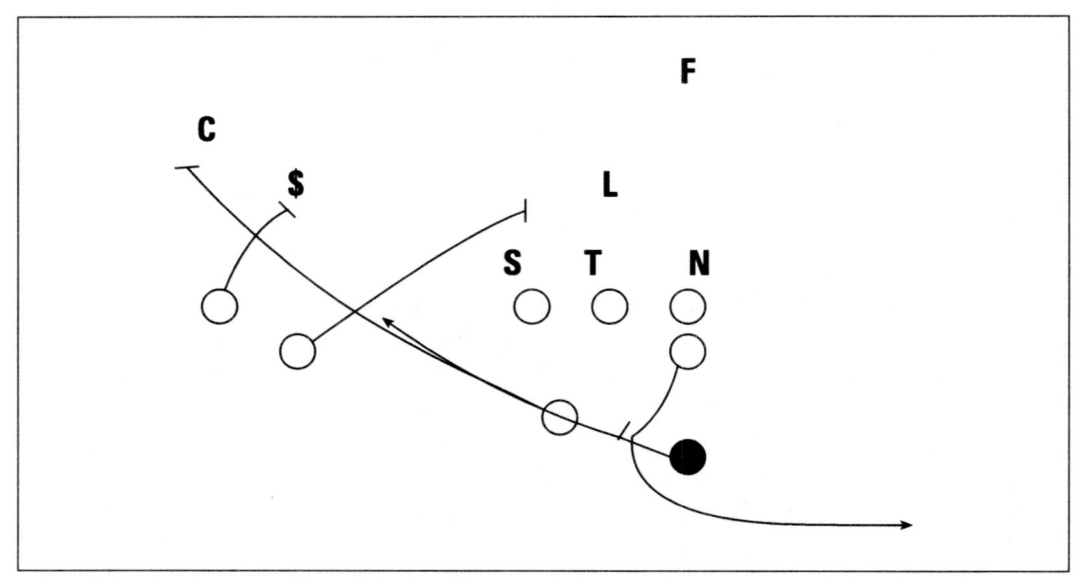

Diagram 6-38: Queen Twins Right Double Crack 29 Stretch

Another highly successful variation involves what we refer to as tight-end Trade—a formation shift in which the tight end moves from the one side of the formation to the other, thereby changing the strength of the formation. This shift by the tight end causes defenses to make both a front adjustment and a secondary adjustment. As such, it can help determine what type of structure the defense is actually playing. Diagrams 6-40 and 6-41 show the formation both before and after the tight-end Trade.

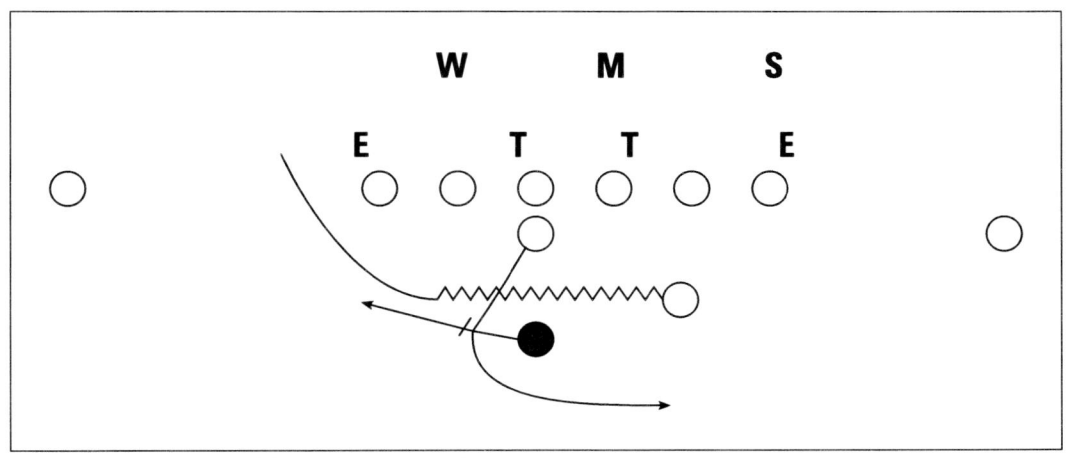

Diagram 6-39: King Right F Liz 29 Stretch

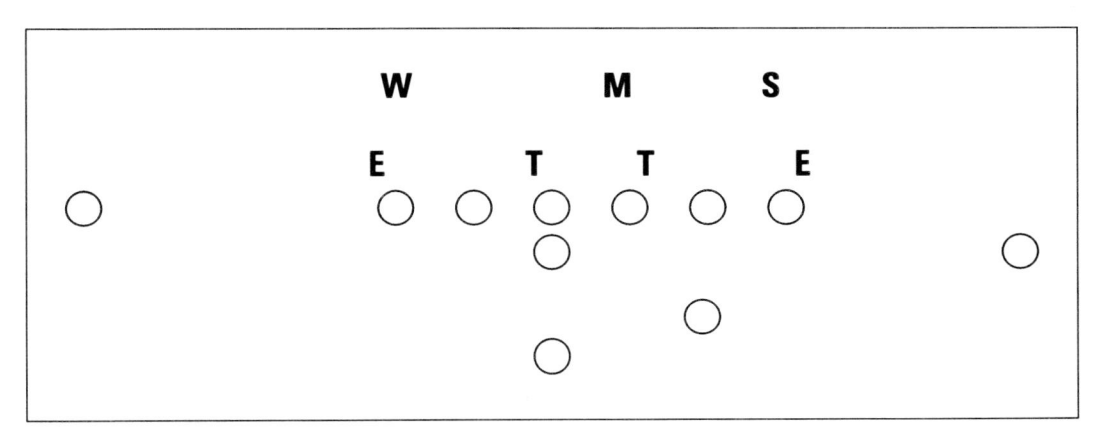

Diagram 6-40: King Right

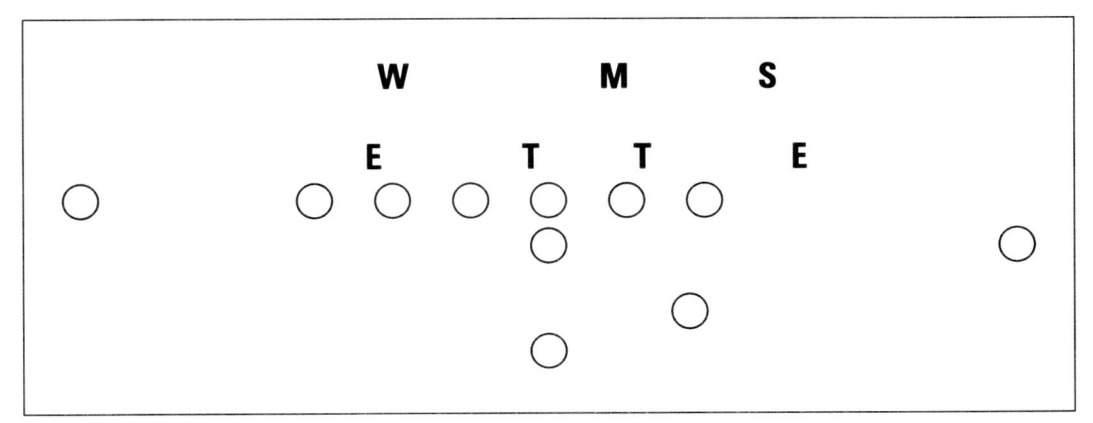

Diagram 6-41: Trade to Queen Left

The tight-end Trade is especially effective because it forces defensive linemen to play different techniques than they are accustomed to playing, and it may force personnel to play in positions they have not practiced. It is beneficial to the offense to have defensive players being forced to use techniques at which they are not very proficient. We want defenses to have to react to what the offense does in the heat of battle, rather than having the offense react to the defense's pressure or what they do.

A final adjustment involves snapping the ball while the tight end is in motion, as shown in Diagram 6-42. This adjustment would be used against defenses that are trying to adjust to motion by moving their personnel from one side of the center to the other side, as shown in Diagram 6-43.

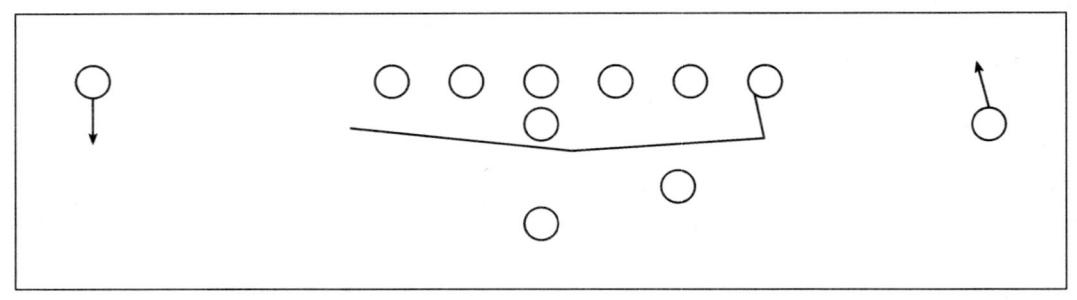

Diagram 6-42: King Right Y Liz

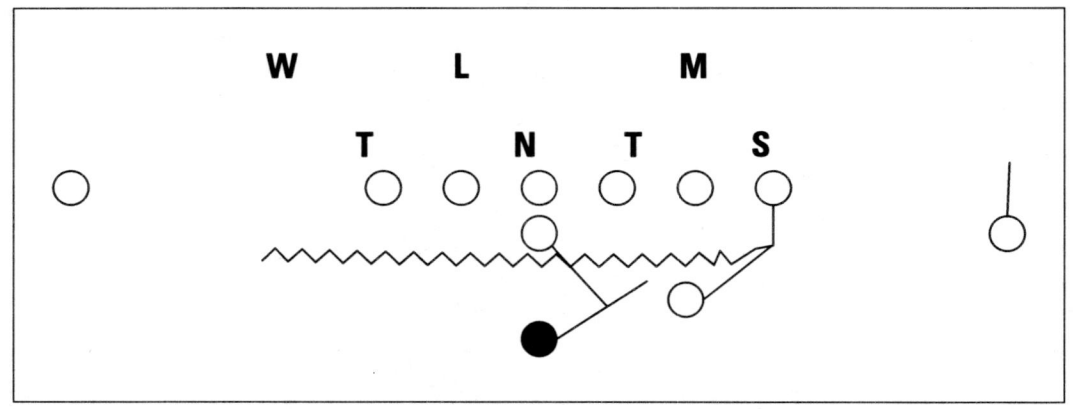

Diagram 6-43: King Right Y Liz 28 Stretch

We also run split-end side Stretch from one-back formations. We change the name of the play, however, to 28/29 Open to indicate that the ball is run to the split-end side, and that no fullback is in the game to block the force player. This play forces one of the receivers to assume the fullback's assignment and block the force element of the defense. The goal is to spread the defense out as much as possible horizontally and try to create a running lane for the halfback. One of the important changes in one-back Stretch to the split-end side involves the path of the halfback. The halfback in 28/29 Open should take a running lane if one opens up inside of the tackle's reach block. This point is emphasized in Diagrams 6-44 and 6-45.

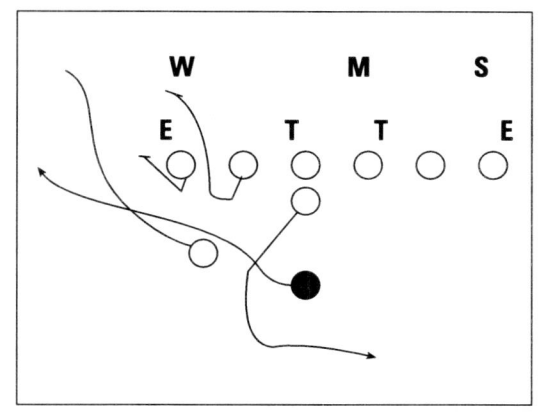

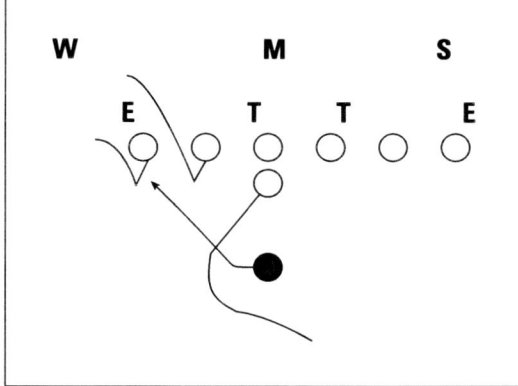

Diagram 6-44: Two-back Stretch

Diagram 6-45: One-back Open

A variety of formations and motions are used in the one-back Stretch attack. It is necessary to emphasize the importance of the check-with-me package in putting together the play-action passing attack and the quick-passing game with the one-back running game. Diagrams 6-46, 6-47, and 6-48 show three situations, which offenses can counter effectively with check-with-me plays. Like every aspect of the zone running attack, no matter how much experimentation is done with formations, motion, shifts, or trades, the basic offensive line blocking schemes remain exactly the same.

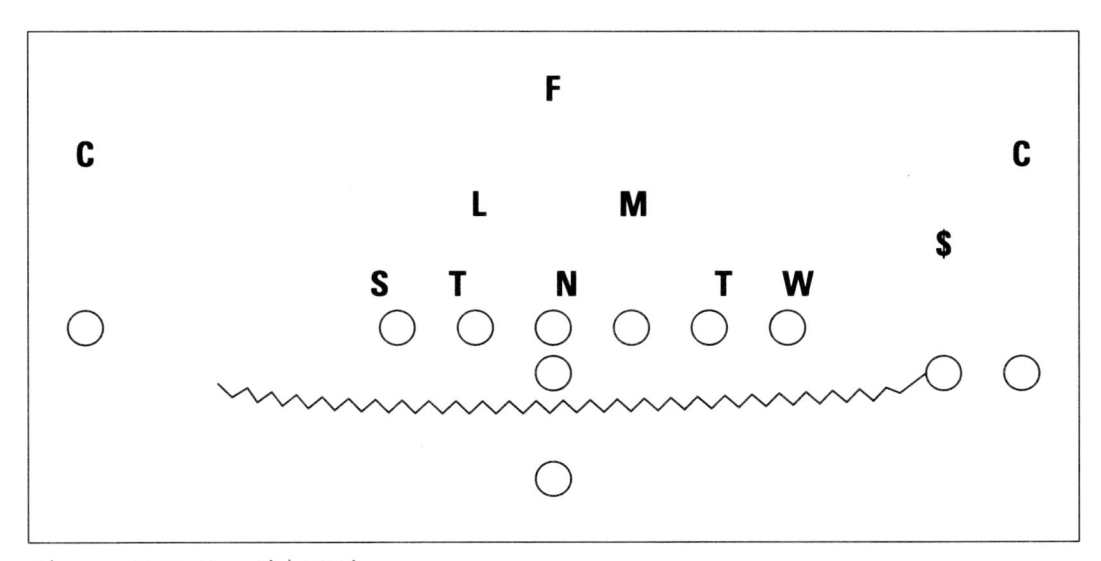

Diagram 6-46: Trey Right Z Liz

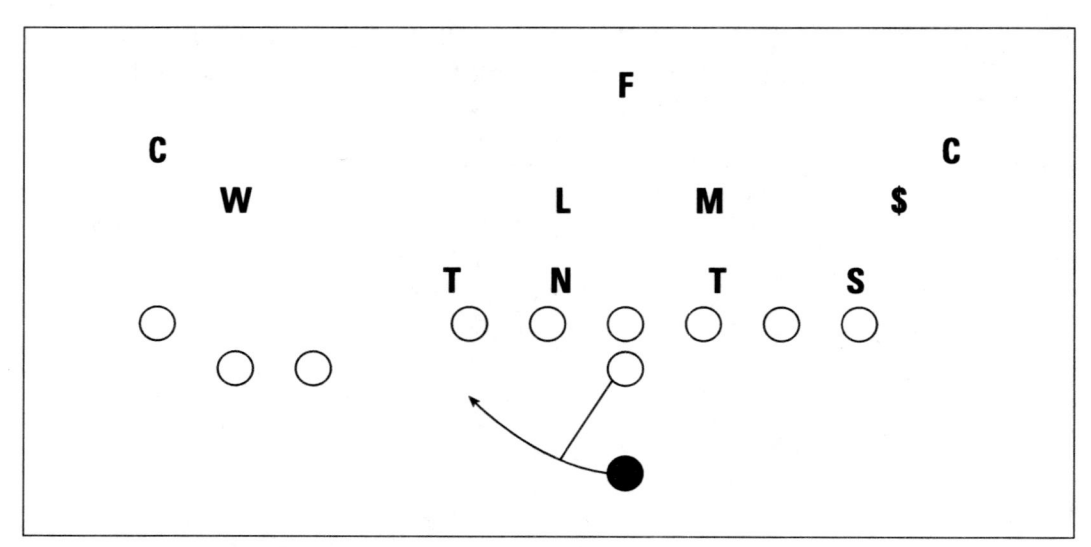

Diagram 6-47: Trips Right

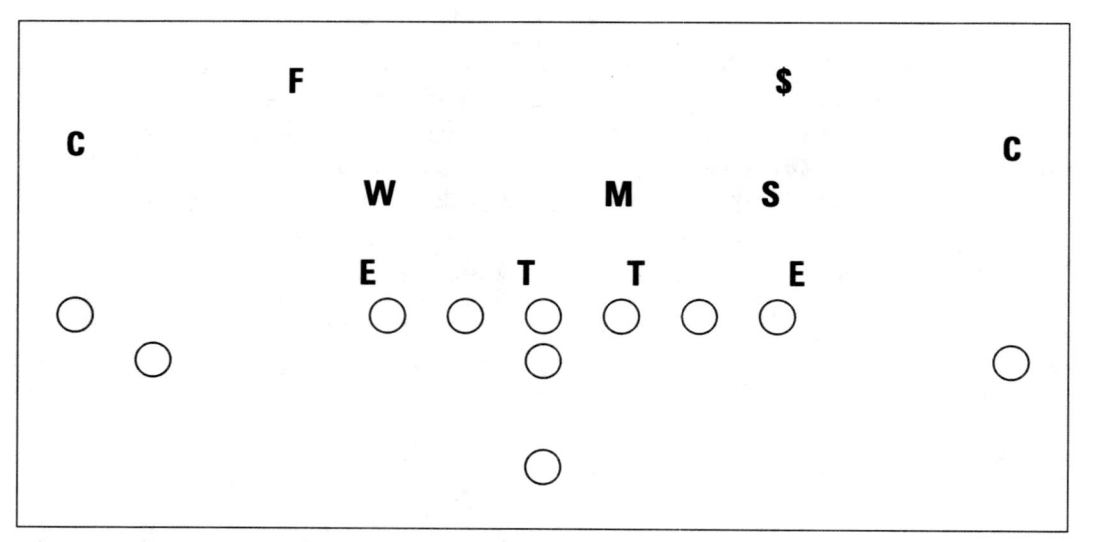

Diagram 6-48: Deuce Right

7

Zone Running Game: Trapping Game

We incorporate aspects of the trapping game into the zone attack as a change-up to keep the defense off-balance. Trapping is a way to involve the fullback and allow him to carry the ball from two-back formations. Since we went to the zone offense, we typically have run the trap less than an average of four times per game. The Inside and Outside Zone plays are the backbone of the rushing attack. The trap is still a very useful play, however, and an important part of the zone offense.

Diagram 7-1: Queen Right formation

We run 30/31 Trap from both a Queen formation (Diagram 7-1) and a King formation (Diagram 7-2). The Queen formation trap is a guard trap, while the King formation trap is a tackle trap. Both plays are designed to look like the halfback is running Stretch to the outside. The halfback will execute his normal Stretch footwork on both trap plays.

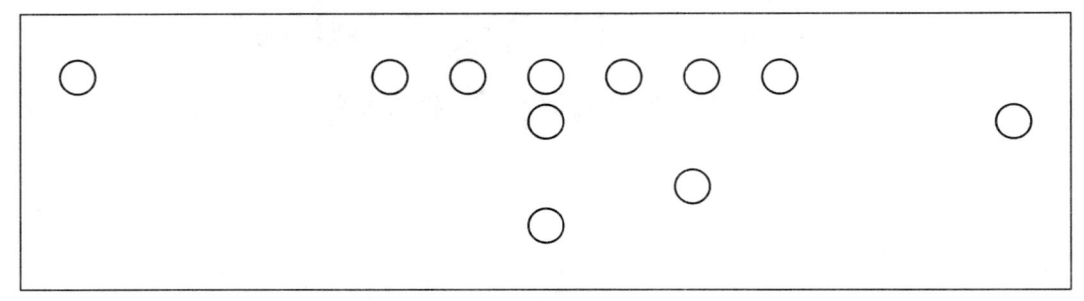

Diagram 7-2: King Right formation

Attacking an Okie Front

The play 30/31 Trap, the guard trap, is shown against an Okie front in Diagram 7-3. The trap from a Queen formation is intended to look like split-end side Stretch, with the halfback and the quarterback opening up as if they are running the split-end side Stretch play. The fullback takes a jab step with his lead foot, breaks back underneath the quarterback to receive a hand-off, and reads the guard's trap block.

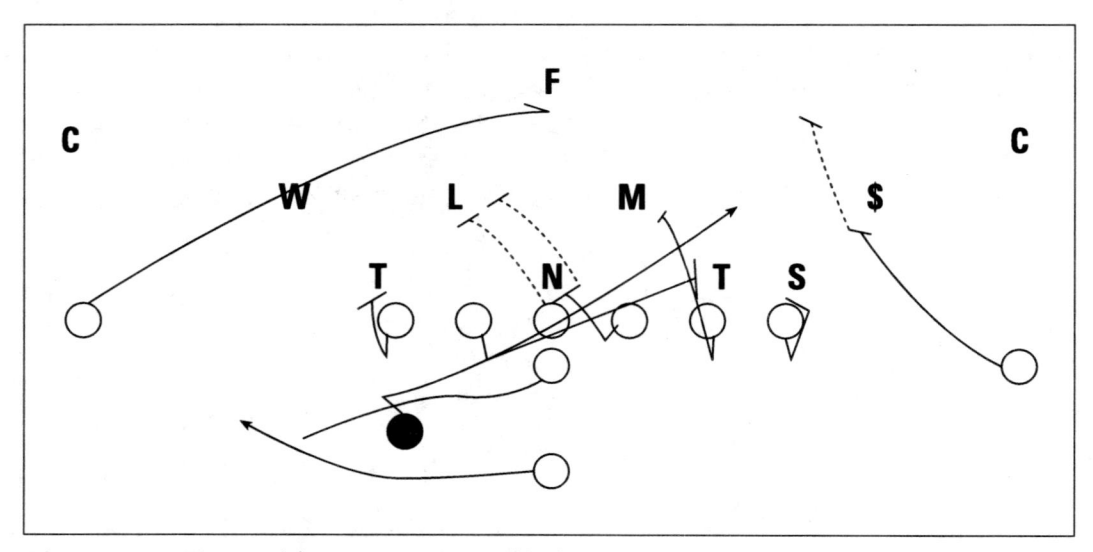

Diagram 7-3: Queen Right 30 Trap vs. an Okie front

The backside tackle blocks the 5-technique, but his primary assignment is to prevent the 5-technique from crossing his face. The backside guard is the trapper. The trapper drop steps with his lead foot, in this case his right foot, and assumes an angle of departure that allows him to slightly gain ground. Against Okie fronts, the playside 5-technique is trap blocked. The backside guard will attempt to kick out the 5-technique. The center and the playside guard will double-team/combo block the nose guard on the first level, while gaining movement and continuing on to the weak inside linebacker. This zone combination scheme is illustrated in Diagrams 7-4 and 7-5.

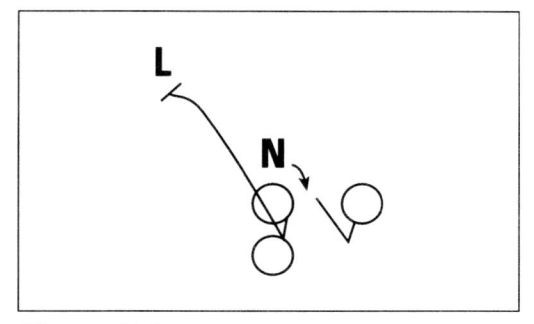

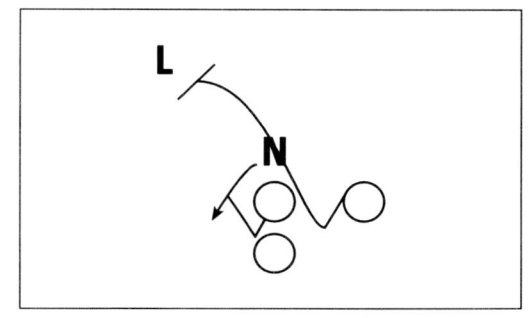

Diagram 7-4

Diagram 7-5

The playside tackle rips through the 5-technique and down blocks on the strong inside linebacker, trying to anticipate the movements of the linebacker, while always making sure that player does not cross the line of scrimmage. The tight end base blocks the 9-technique, and never allows inside penetration.

The receivers have three basic blocking assignments, depending on the coverage. If they read Cover 3, both receivers release inside to block the free safety, as shown in Diagram 7-6. They should block any wrong-colored jersey that crosses their paths. If they read Cover 2, they will block the half-field safeties aligned to their side, as shown in Diagram 7-7. If they read any form of man-to-man coverage, they will run their man off the line of scrimmage and block him, as shown in Diagram 7-8. The halfback and the quarterback carry out their split end Stretch assignments to help the trap run more effectively.

Attacking an Eagle Strong Front

The way to block an Eagle Strong front is illustrated in Diagram 7-9. Against this defensive structure, the trap scheme is changed by using a playside influence scheme. The influence trap is preferred because of the defender's ability to squeeze the trapper on his inside release.

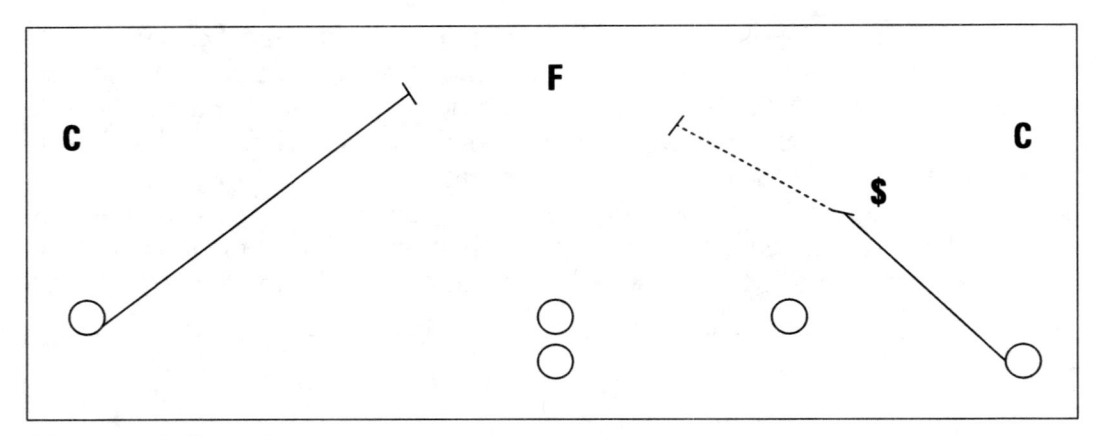

Diagram 7-6: Cover 3

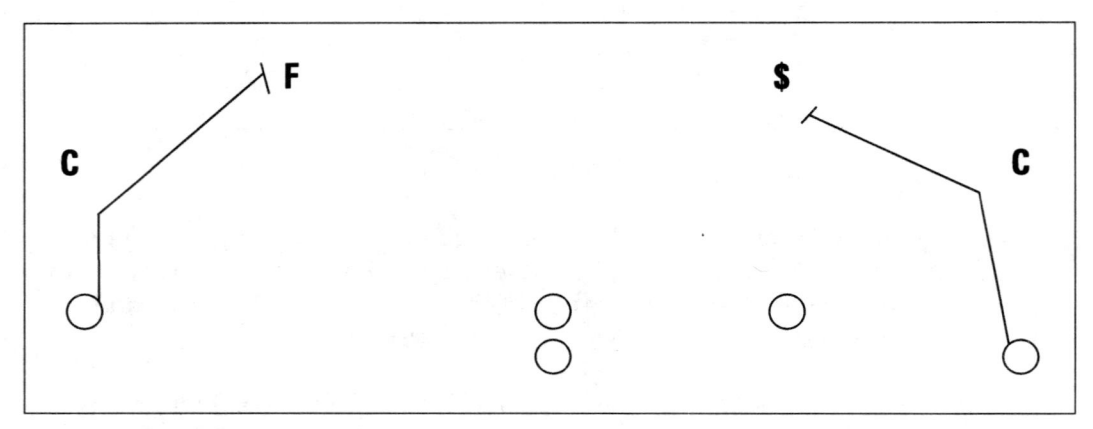

Diagram 7-7: Cover 2

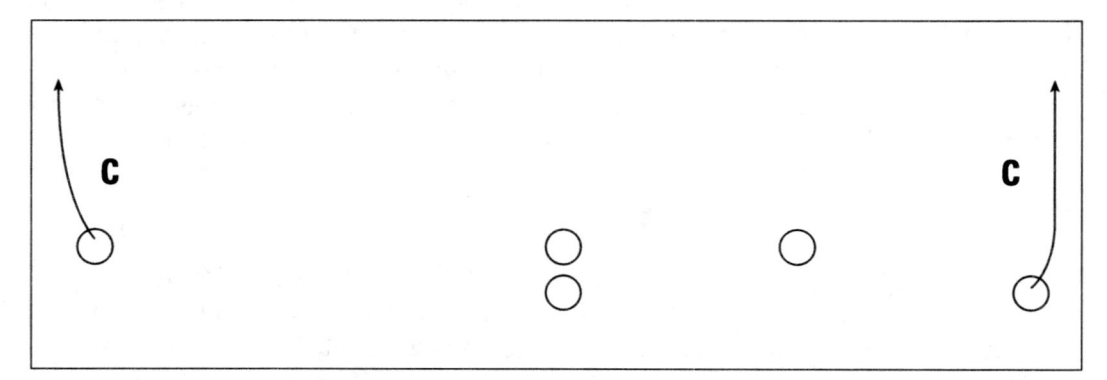

Diagram 7-8: Man-to-man coverage

The backside tackle uses a rip technique to get to the weak inside linebacker. The backside guard is the trapper and will trap block the 3-technique against an Eagle Strong front by taking a drop step with his lead foot (the left foot in this instance), executing a trap block, and kicking out the 3-technique. The center blocks back on the weak-shaded nose guard, while the playside guard uses an influence scheme to account for the 3-technique by flashing pass protection and drop stepping to invite the 3-technique upfield and outside. The guard then releases inside and blocks the 7-technique. The playside tackle blocks down on the strong inside linebacker, insuring that the linebacker does not beat him across the line of scrimmage. The tight end releases outside to widen the 7-technique and blocks the strong safety, who is the force element in this structure. The wide receivers apply their blocking rules to the secondary's coverage. The halfback and the quarterback sell Stretch, while the fullback runs his path and reads the guard's kickout block and the tackle's down block.

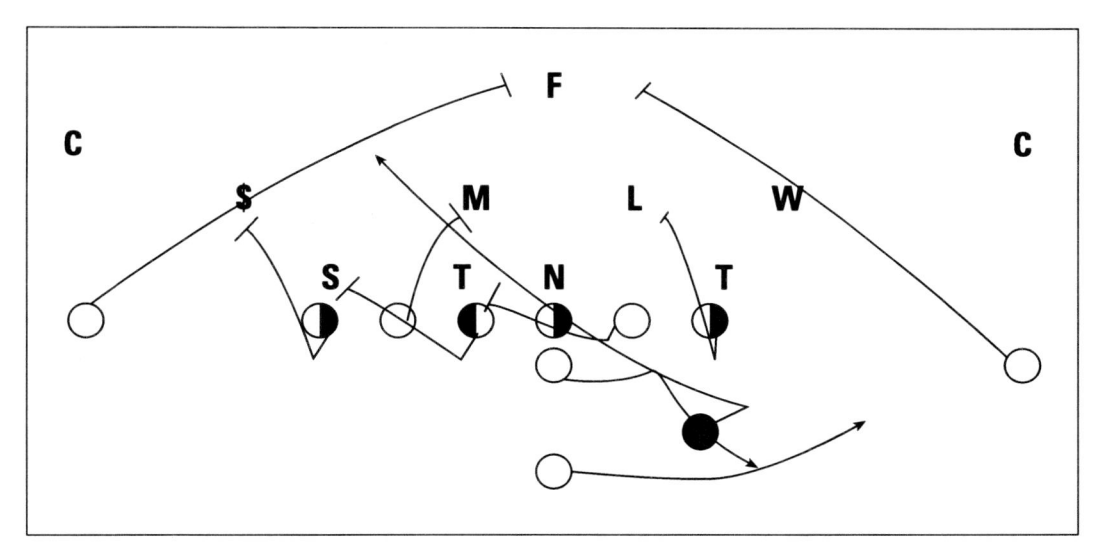

Diagram 7-9: Queen Left 31 Trap vs. an Eagle Strong front

Attacking a 4-3 Front

The way to block 4-3 is shown in Diagram 7-10. To the split-end side, the structure of a 4-3 front looks exactly like an Eagle Strong front. The backside tackle rips through the weak outside linebacker, while the backside guard trap blocks the playside 3-technique. The center blocks back on the shade, and the playside guard uses his pass influence scheme on the 3-technique, before releasing to block the 9-technique. The playside tackle down blocks on the strong inside linebacker, and the tight end releases to block the strong outside linebacker. Both wide receivers block half-field safeties, and the backfield action is exactly the same.

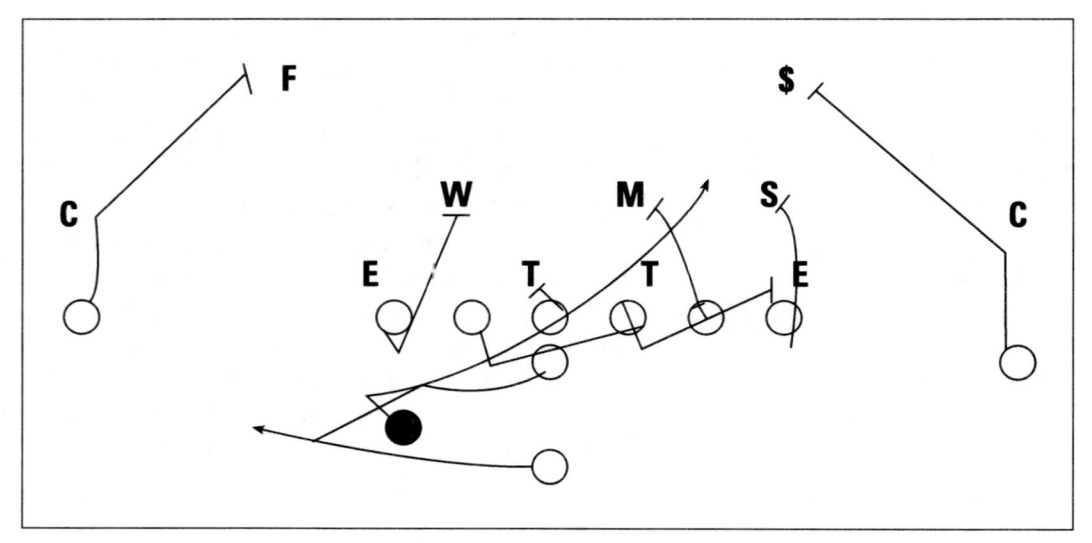

Diagram 7-10: Queen Right 30 Trap vs. a 4-3 front

Attacking a Stack Front

The way to block a Stack front is shown in Diagram 7-11. All factors considered, we would not expect to have a great deal of success with 30/31 Trap against Stack. As a result, we would prefer to audible to split-end side Stretch. If we stayed with the trap play, the backside tackle would rip and get to the weak inside linebacker, while the backside guard would drop step and trap block the first down lineman past the center, which would be the 2-technique in this structure. The center would have to block back for the trapping guard, while the playside guard would use his pass influence scheme and block the 4-technique. The playside tackle blocks down on the strong inside linebacker, and the tight end base blocks the 9-technique. Again, both wide receivers would block half-field safeties. The backfield action would remain the same, except for the fact that the fullback stays a little bit tighter because the trap block is happening one man closer to the point of attack.

Attacking a Reduced Front

The way to block a Reduced front is shown in Diagram 7-12. A Reduced structure resembles a Stack front. As a rule, we would prefer to run an Outside Zone play against this front. The backside tackle would rip through the 5-technique and continue to the weak inside linebacker. The backside guard is the trapper. He will drop step and adjust his angle to kick out the 5-technique. The center will block back for the pulling guard, and the playside guard will down block on the shaded nose guard. The playside tackle will utilize the influence pass-protection scheme on the 5-technique, flashing pass protection

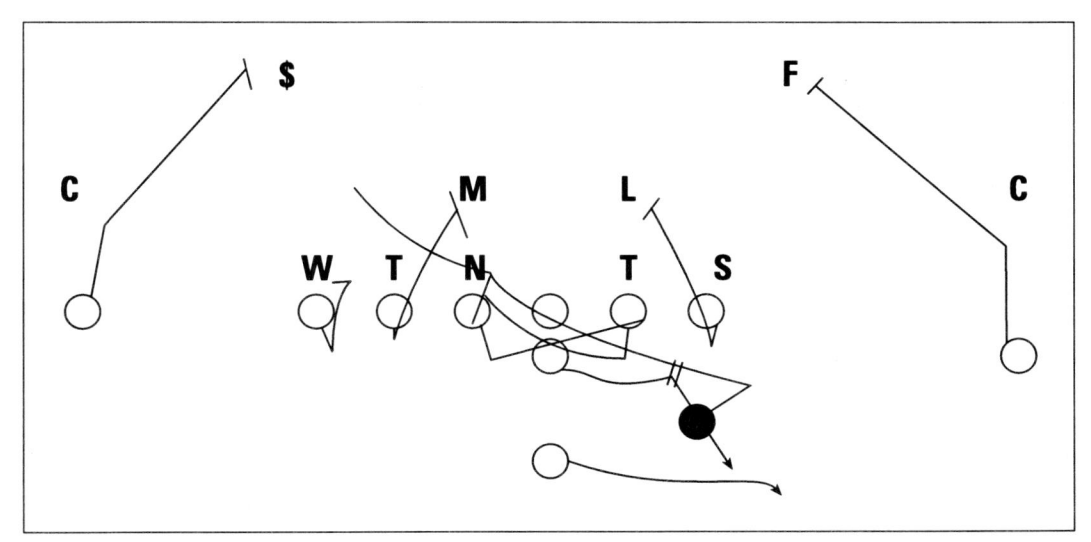

Diagram 7-11: Queen Left 31 Trap vs. a Stack front

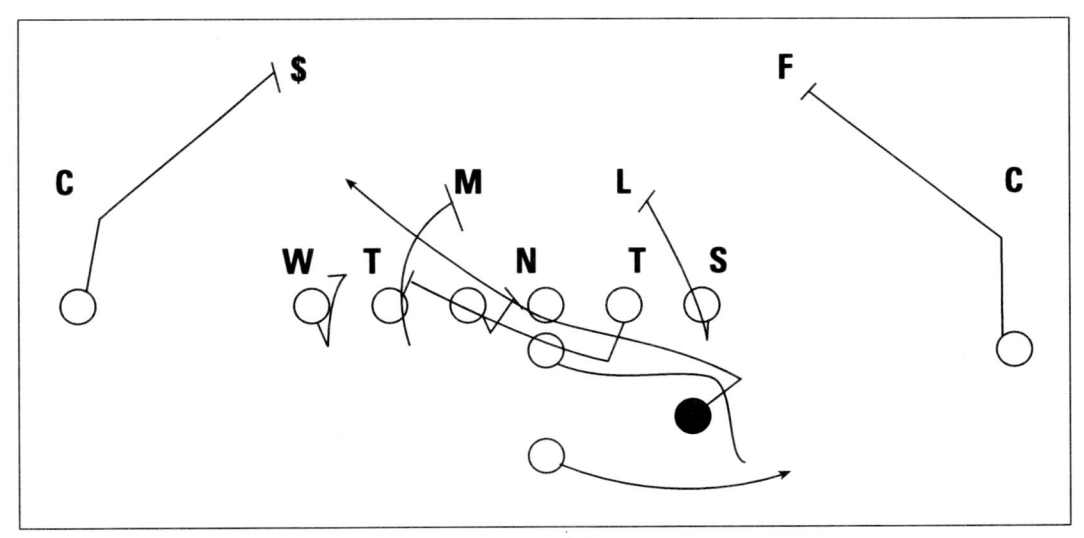

Diagram 7-12: Queen Left 31 Trap vs. a Reduced front

and blocking down on the strong inside linebacker. The tight end base blocks the 9-technique, who is actually the weak outside linebacker in a Reduced front. The backfield action remains constant, while the receivers apply their blocking rules to the coverage.

Attacking a Slide Weak Front

The way to block a Slide Weak front is shown in Diagram 7-13. The backside tackle rips through to the weak inside linebacker, and the backside guard trap blocks the 2i-technique. The center blocks back for the pulling guard, and the playside guard pass influences the 6-technique, while the playside tackle blocks down on the strong inside linebacker. The tight end releases outside to the strong safety, and the receivers release inside to block the middle third defender. The backfield action is the same as usual. The fullback runs his path, while reading the block of the pulling guard.

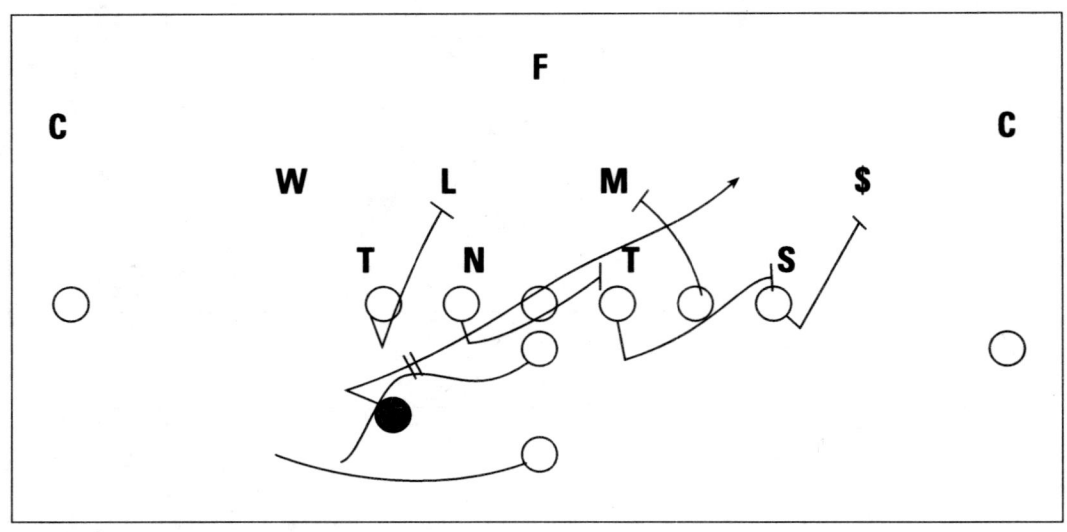

Diagram 7-13: Queen Right 30 trap vs. a Slide Weak front

Trap Game Adjustments

30/31 Trap can also be run from a Twins formation, as shown in Diagram 7-14. Another adjustment that we like to use involves the addition of flanker (Z) motion, or shifting back and forth between Pro and Twins formations, as shown in Diagrams 7-15 and 7-16. When 34/35 Trap is run out of a King formation, we change the scheme drastically and use a tackle trap rather than a guard trap. While 30/31 Trap is run with the simulation of a split-end side Stretch play, 34/35 Trap is designed to look like a tight-end side Stretch play.

Attacking an Okie Front

The play, 34/35 Trap against a standard Okie Front, is illustrated in Diagram 7-17. The playside tackle will use a pass influence scheme on the 5-technique to get him up the field and wide. The tackle knows that he cannot allow the 5-technique to get an inside rushing lane. The playside guard blocks down if he is uncovered, and uses an influence pass scheme if he is covered to widen the man that the playside tackle will block. These two possibilities are shown in Diagrams 7-18 and 7-19.

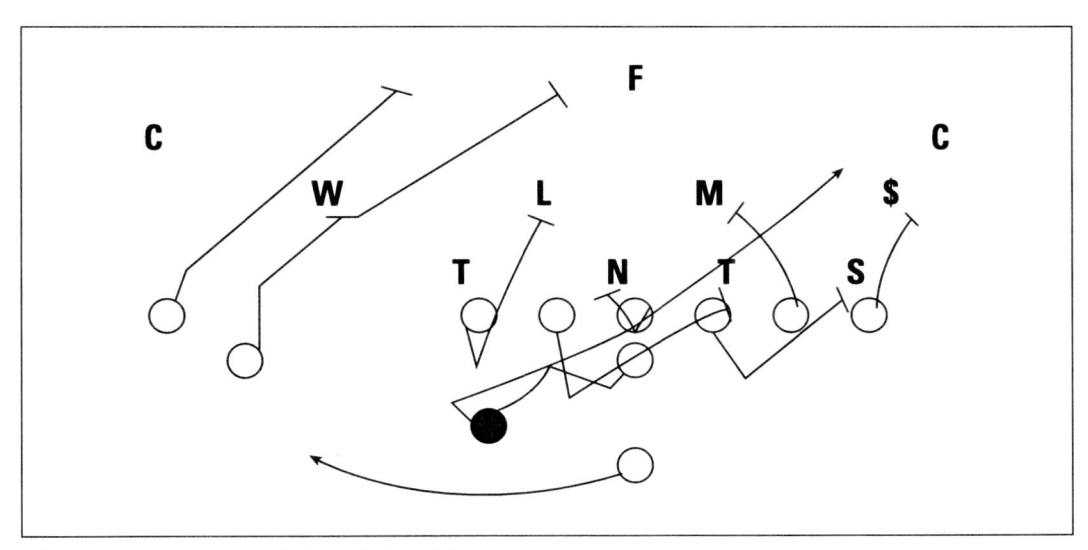

Diagram 7-14: Queen Twins Right 30 Trap

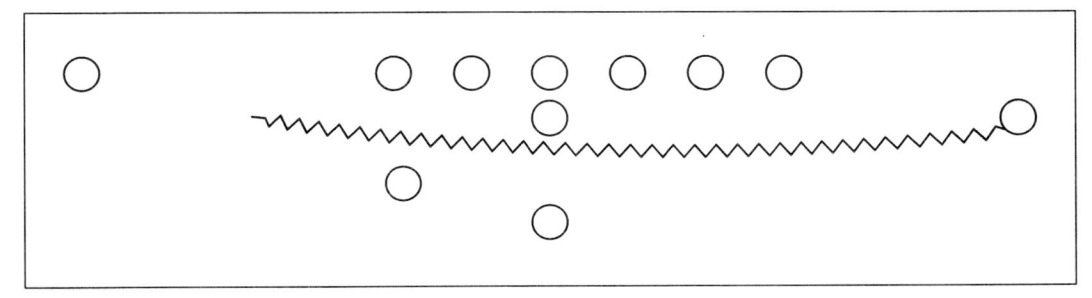

Diagram 7-15: Queen Right Z Liz

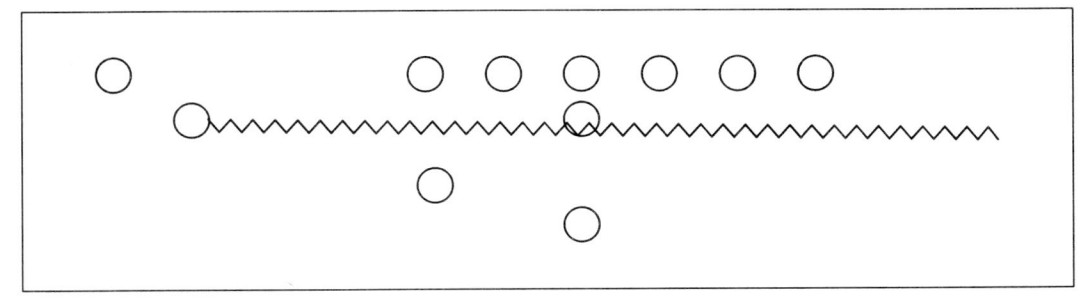

Diagram 7-16: Queen Twins Right Z Rip

Against an Okie front, the center will chip off the nose guard and get to the strong inside linebacker. In keeping with the basic zone principles, if the strong inside linebacker flowed with the Stretch fake, the center would stay on the nose guard, and the playside guard would use a combination scheme to get to the Mike linebacker. These possibilities are shown in Diagrams 7-20 and 7-21.

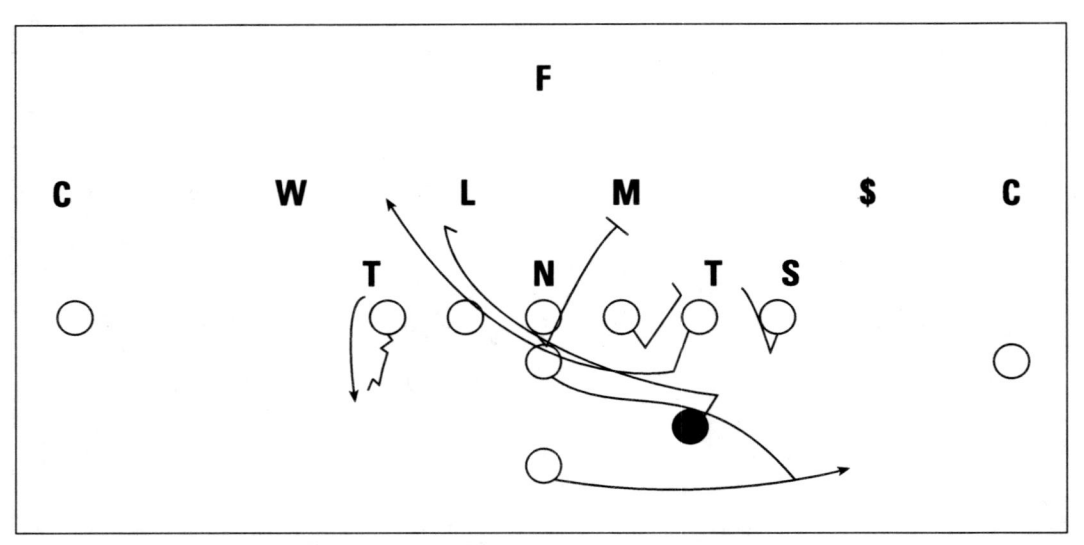

Diagram 7-17: King Right 35 Trap vs. an Okie front

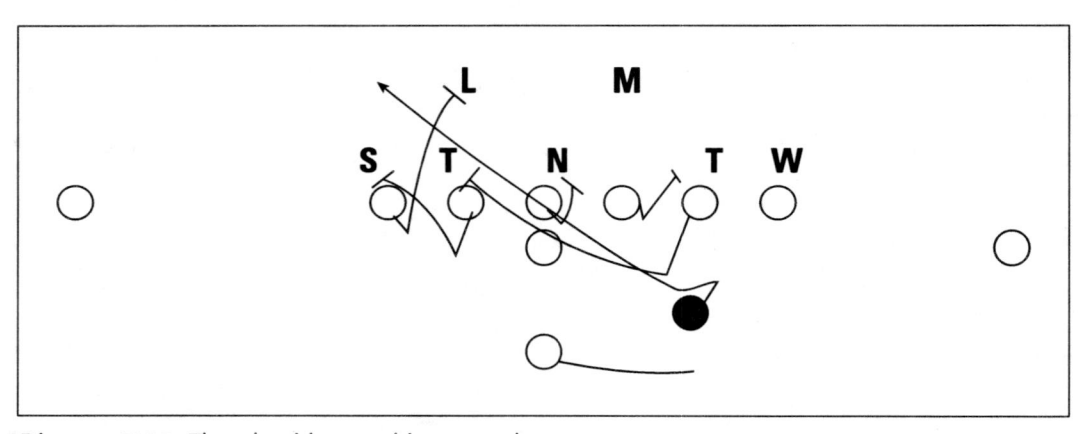

Diagram 7-18: The playside guard is covered

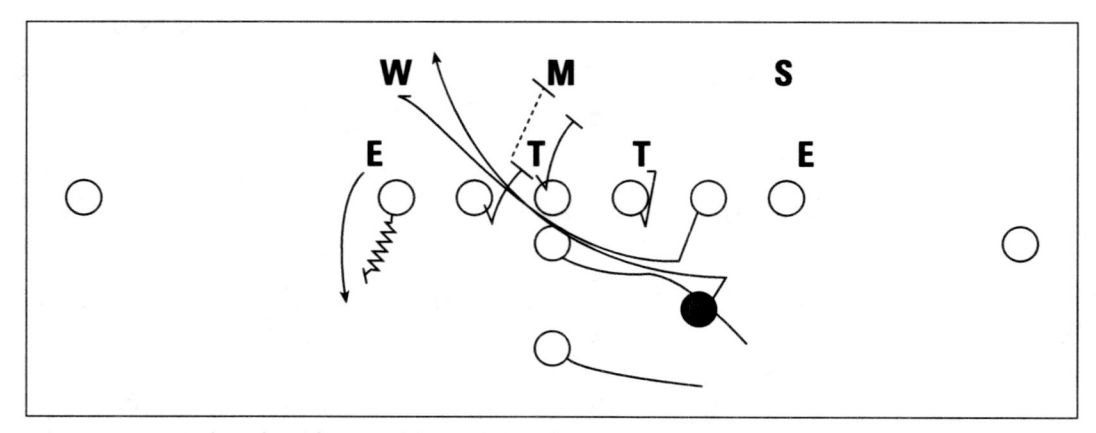

Diagram 7-19: The playside guard is uncovered

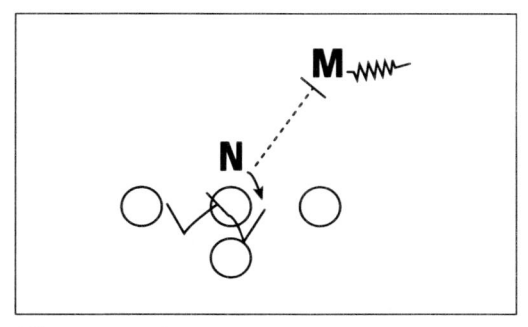

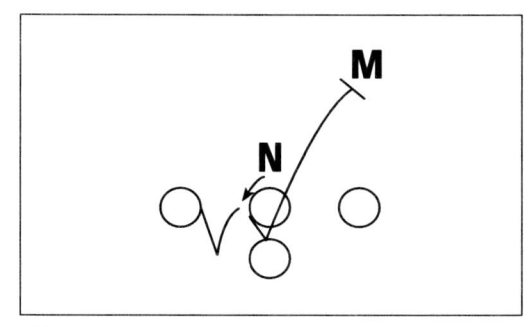

Diagram 7-20

Diagram 7-21

Against an Okie front, the backside guard fills for the pulling tackle. The backside tackle drop steps and takes a slightly upfield angle. If the playside guard has made a bubble call, then he is uncovered and must block a second-level player. The pulling tackle will kick out the defender to create a running lane for the fullback, and the tight end base blocks the 9-technique. The wide receivers have a different assignment than they do in 30/31 Trap. The split end's assignments for 34/35 Trap are shown in Diagrams 7-22, 7-23, and 7-24. The flanker always releases inside and blocks the middle-third defender. The halfback now fakes 28/29 Stretch to the tight end-side. The quarterback has to carry out his Stretch fake after handing the ball off to the fullback, who reads the block of the pulling tackle.

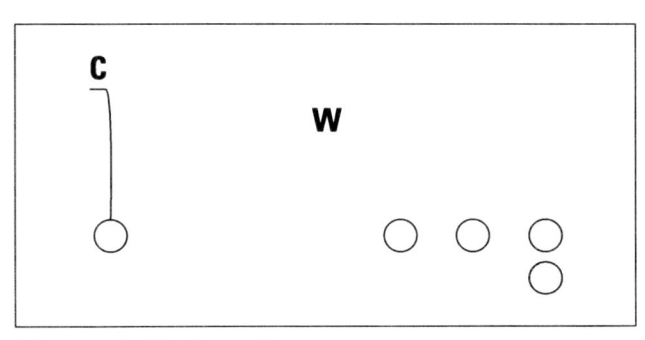

Diagram 7-22: Cover 3

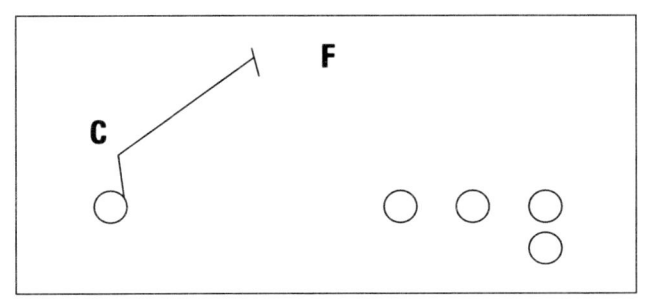

Diagram 7-23: Cover 2

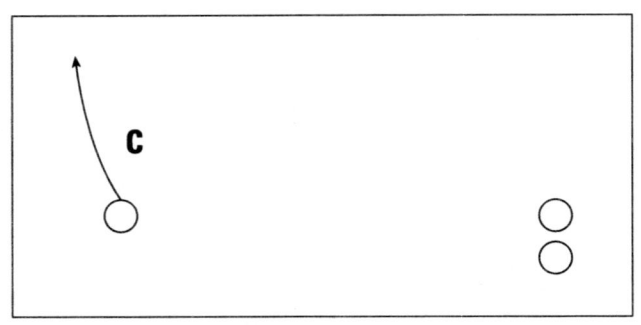

Diagram 7-24: Man-to-man coverage

Attacking an Eagle Strong Front

The way to block an Eagle Strong front is shown in Diagram 7-25. The playside tackle pass influences the 5-technique to invite him outside, while the playside guard blocks down on the shade. The center and the playside guard will use a combination scheme to work off to the strong inside linebacker. The backside guard base blocks the 3-technique, and the backside tackle pulls and trap blocks the weak inside linebacker. The tight end cuts off the 7-technique. The receivers follow their rules, while the backfield action remains the same, emphasizing the fake of the Stretch play.

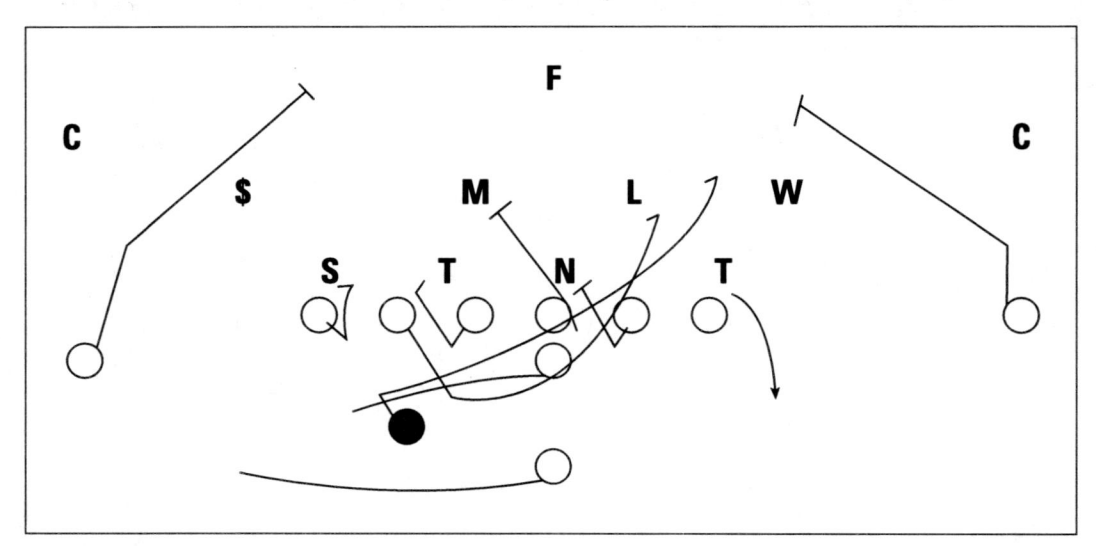

Diagram 7-25: King Left 24 Trap vs. an Eagle Strong front

Attacking a 4-3 Front

The way to block a 4-3 front is shown in Diagram 7-26. The playside tackle pass influences the 5-technique while the playside guard and the center use a zone combination scheme to block the shade and the strong inside linebacker. The backside

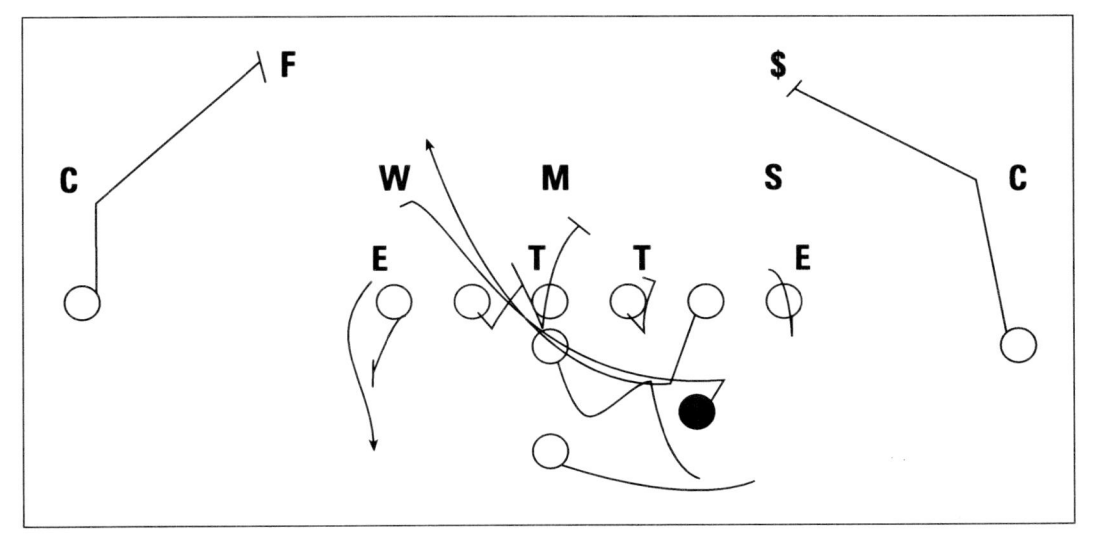

Diagram 7-26: King Right 35 trap vs. a 4-3 front

guard base blocks the 3-technique, and the backside tackle pulls and blocks a second-level linebacker. The tight end will rip through a 9-technique (not allowing that player to cross his face) and then will cut off the strong inside linebacker. The receivers block their assignments according to the coverage. The backfield action simulates Stretch, with the fullback jab stepping and running his normal course.

Attacking a Stack Front

The way to attack a Stack front is shown in Diagram 7-27. The playside tackle releases inside and blocks down on the weak inside linebacker, while the playside guard pass influences the 2i-technique and blocks out on the 5-technique. The center and the backside guard will use a zone-combination scheme to block the 2i-technique and the strong inside linebacker. The backside tackle drop steps and angles slightly upfield to trap block the 2-technique. The tight end has to snatch the 5-technique by trying to execute a backside rip and getting his face across the 5-technique, so that player cannot follow the pulling tackle. The receivers have to block their assignments according to the coverage, while the backfield action remains the same.

Attacking a Reduced Front

The trap scheme against Reduced is illustrated in Diagram 7-28. The backside tackle and the backside guard execute their normal covered assignments, while the center blocks the shaded nose guard. The backside guard waddles up to the strong inside linebacker. The backside tackle pulls and trap blocks the 3-technique, while the tight end snatches the 5-technique. The receivers block their normal assignments according to coverage. The backfield action remains the same.

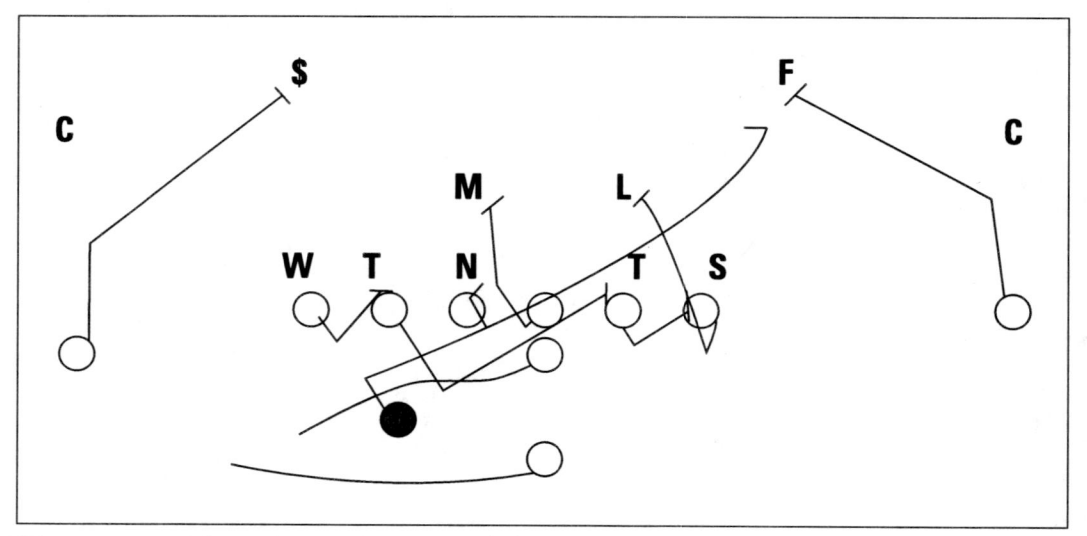

Diagram 7-27: King Left 34 Trap vs. a Stack front

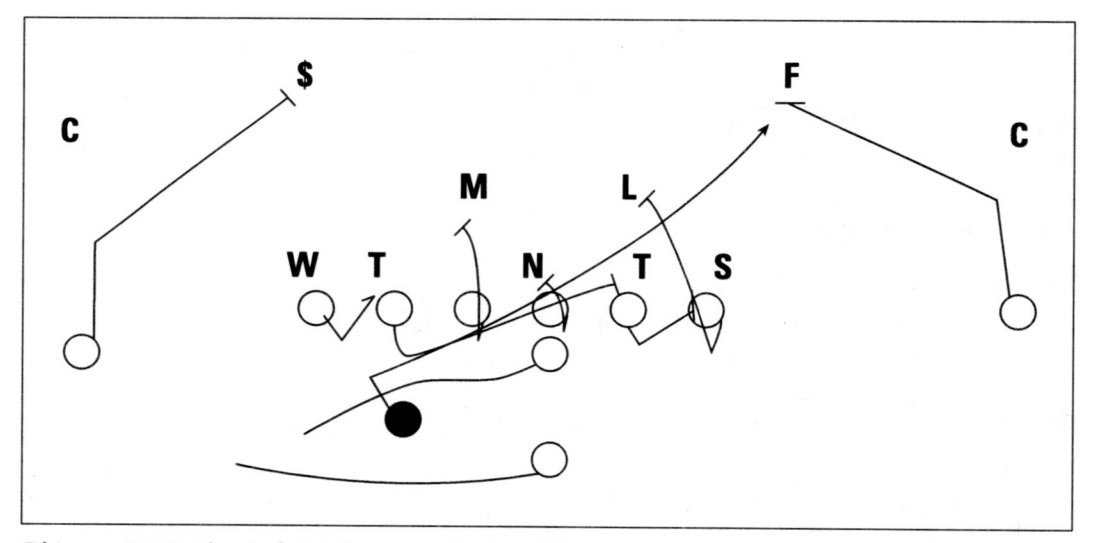

Diagram 7-28: King Left 34 Trap vs. a Reduced front

Attacking a Slide Weak Front

The way to block a Slide Weak front is illustrated in Diagram 7-29. The playside tackle and the playside guard execute their covered assignments while the center blocks the strong inside linebacker. The backside guard blocks the 3-technique and the backside tackle drop steps and traps the 2i-technique. The tight end base blocks the 6-technique, the receivers block their assignments according to coverage, and the backfield action is the same. 34/35 Trap has been a tremendous addition to our package and it gives us the ability to break formation tendencies. As always, the option of accounting for the edge by getting into a Twins formation, as shown in Diagram 7-30, exists.

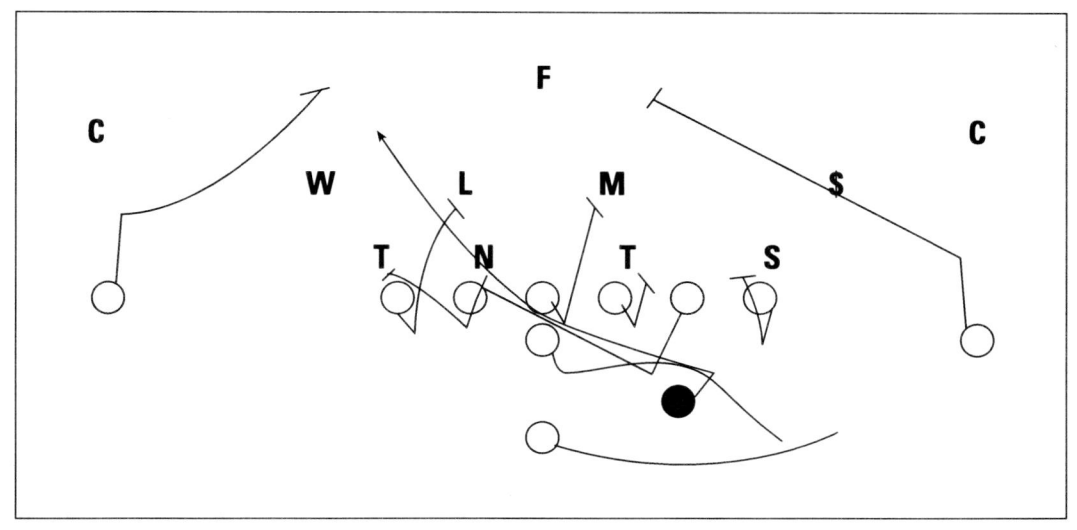

Diagram 7-29: King Right 35 trap vs. a Slide Weak front

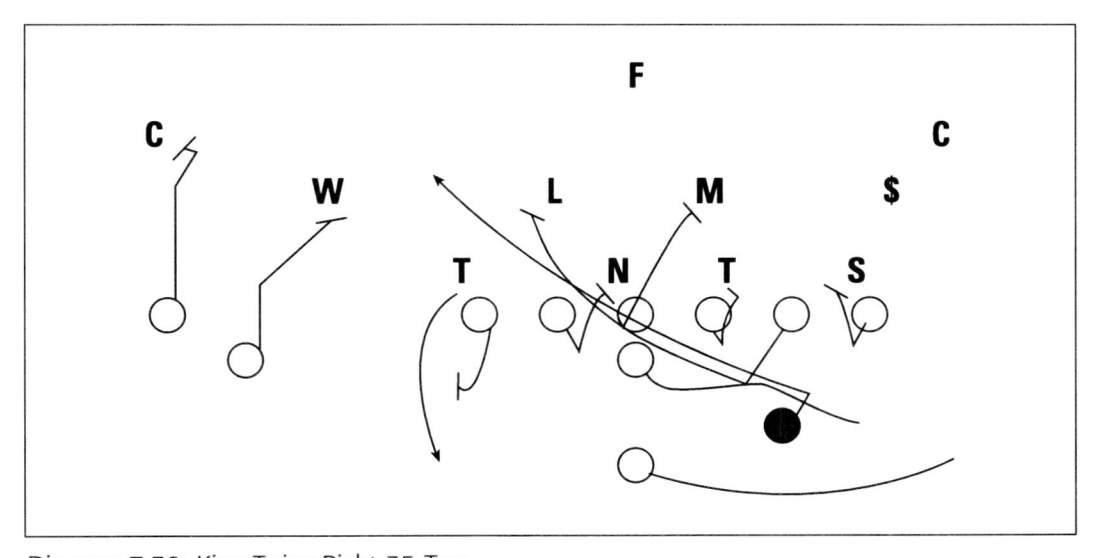

Diagram 7-30: King Twins Right 35 Trap

8

Zone Running Game: Misdirection Plays

Like every offensive system, the zone attack is at an advantage when the defense is confused, hesitant, or unsure. We attempt to create confusion in our version of the zone offense through the execution of a long counter play, which we refer to as 26/27 GF, and by running a number of reverses involving both the split end and the flanker. GF stands for guard and fullback—the two lead blockers on this misdirection play.

The long counter play initially resembles the basic Inside Zone play, just as the trap initially resembles the basic Stretch play. The long counter misdirection play is run in conjunction with a fake of the basic 24/25 Inside Zone. We run two different long counter plays. Diagram 8-1 shows 26 GF run from a Queen formation.

From the start, 26 GF resembles 25 BOB, the standard Inside Zone play to the split-end side. It becomes a long counter misdirection play to the tight-end side of the formation. Diagram 8-2 illustrates 27 GF run from a King formation. In King formation, the long counter initially appears to be 24 Back, a tight-end side Inside Zone run. In diagramming the long counter, we will first consider some 26/27 GF schemes from a Queen formation, and then execute the same plays from a King formation.

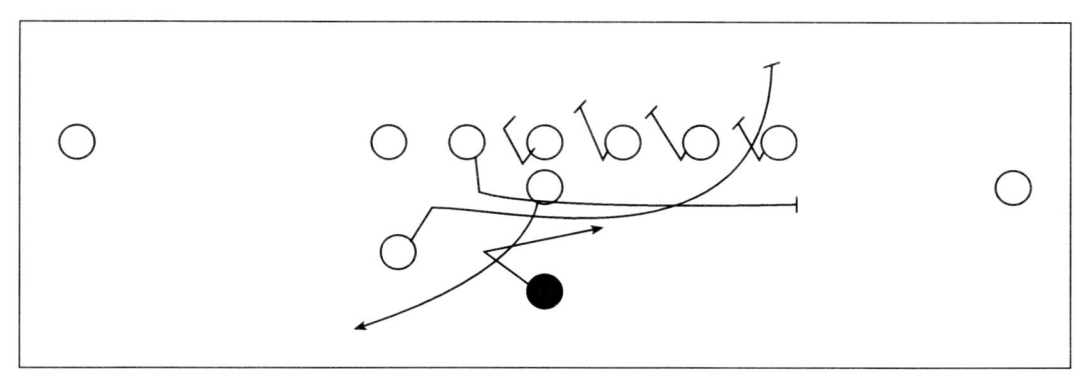

Diagram 8-1: Queen Right 26 GF

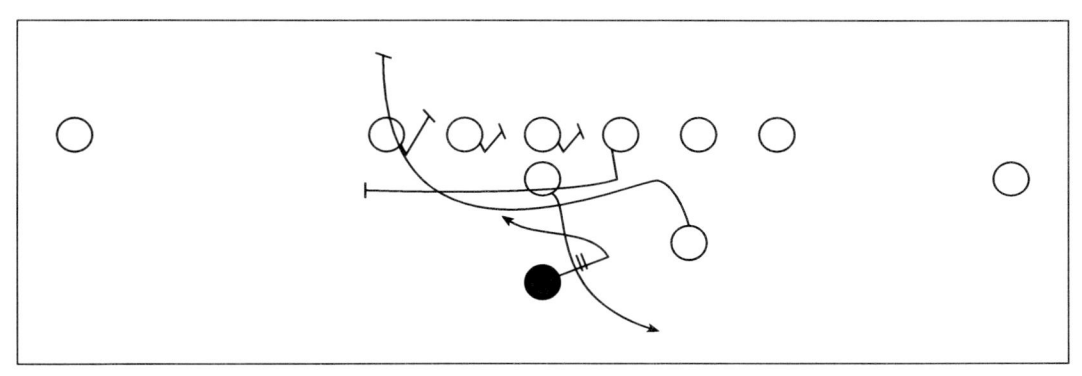

Diagram 8-2: King Right 27 GF

Attacking an Okie Front

Diagram 8-3 illustrates 26 GF from a Queen formation. The backside tackle sets up for an influence pass-protection block. In other words, he sets up hard to the inside and invites the 5-technique to take a wide outside pass-rush lane in order to effectively block him. The backside guard drop steps with his right foot and then takes a path slightly upfield to kick out the first wrong-colored jersey outside of the tight end's down block. Two different types of blocks are taught to the pulling guard, who always assumes that he will kick out the defender, as illustrated in Diagram 8-4.

Sometimes the defender will close on the down block and wrong shoulder the kickout block, in which case the pulling guard is instructed to log block the defender. The guard should maintain outside leverage and turn the defender inside, as shown in Diagram 8-5.

Against an Okie front, the center and the playside guard will stay on the double-team block of the nose guard and come off on a late combo to the weak inside linebacker. The two members of the double-team are told that they should have four

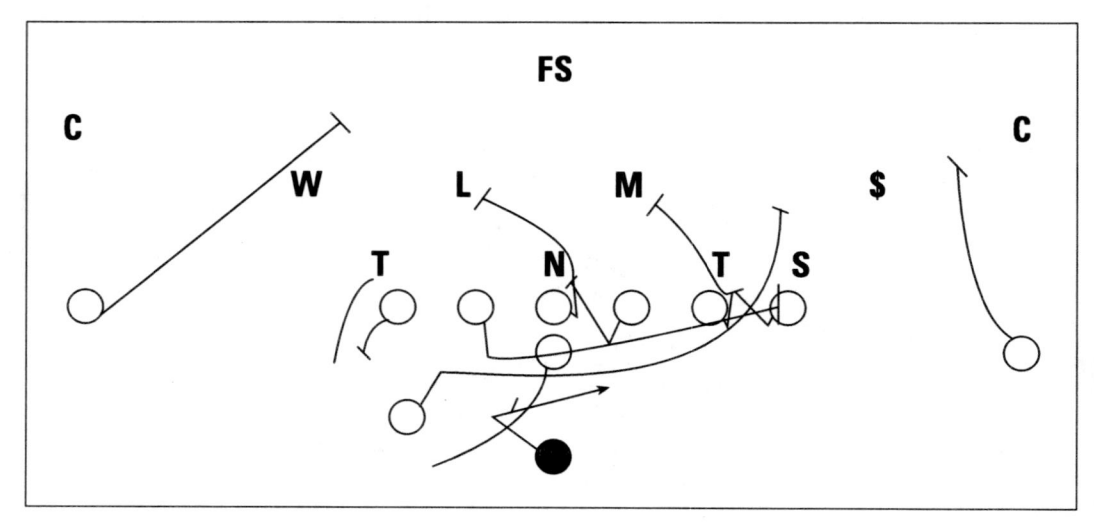

Diagram 8-3: Queen Right 26 GF vs. an Okie front

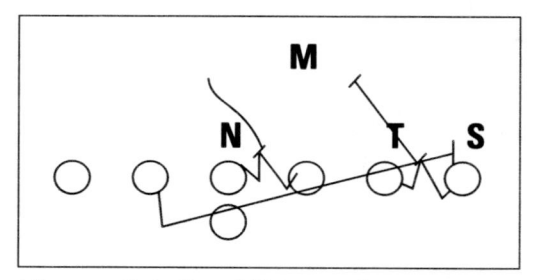

Diagram 8-4: Guard kickout scheme

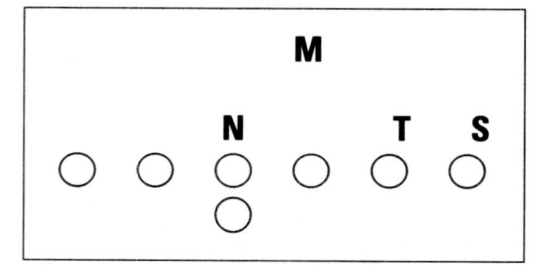

Diagram 8-5: Guard log scheme

hands on the nose guard and four eyes on the weak inside linebacker. The playside tackle and the tight end execute a double-team block on the 5-technique, which is vital to the play. The playside tackle and the tight end have to get vertical movement in order to let the guard and the fullback react on the run and secure their blocks. After movement, they also have a late combo to the strong inside linebacker. The tackle will come off if the strong inside (middle) linebacker shoots, as shown in Diagram 8-6.

The fullback in 26/27 GF fakes 24 or 25 BOB and then assumes his path parallel to the line of scrimmage. While on his path, he keeps an eye on the strong inside (middle) linebacker and attempts to go outside the double-team block of the tackle and the tight end, but inside of the pulling guard's kickout block. The fullback is instructed never to pass up a wrong-colored jersey. The fullback has to be able to read the kickout scheme, as shown in Diagram 8-7. As such, the fullback has to be able to distinguish the kickout scheme from the log scheme, because he has to step around the log block, as shown in Diagram 8-8.

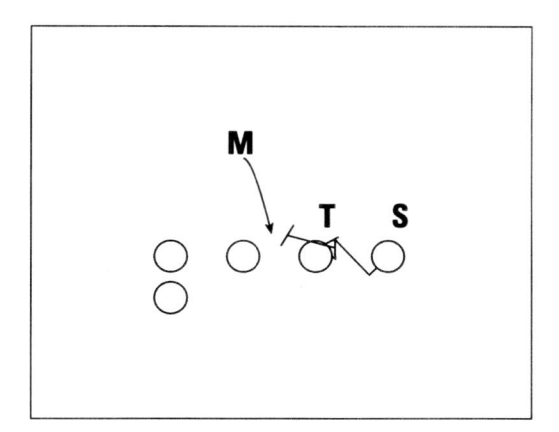

Diagram 8-6: Strong inside (middle) linebacker blitz scheme

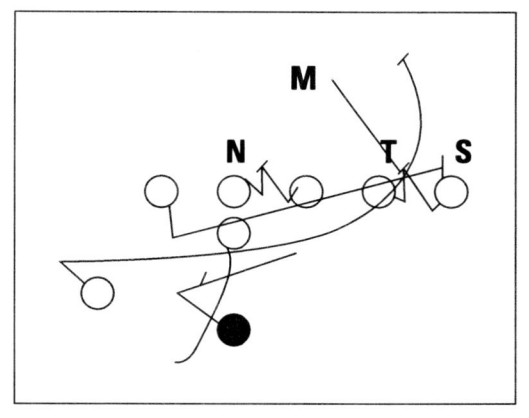

Diagram 8-7: Fullback path on the guard kickout scheme

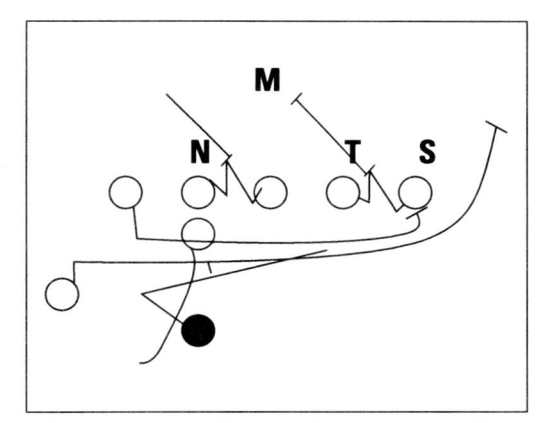

Diagram 8-8: Fullback path on the guard log scheme

This play is actually a hybrid form of the guard-tackle counter that the Washington Redskins made famous with John Riggins and the Hogs, a play that was called counter trey. The reason we made the fullback the second blocker in this scheme is because he is a better athlete. We also like the separation that is created between the path of the guard and the path of the fullback. This separation, in depth and width, gives the fullback a little more time to identify the blocking scheme and to react accordingly.

The blocking scheme for receivers adheres to the following rules:

- Cover 3—block the cornerback (Diagram 8-9).
- Cover 2—block the near half-field safety (Diagram 8-10).
- Man coverage—block the man responsible for them (Diagram 8-11).

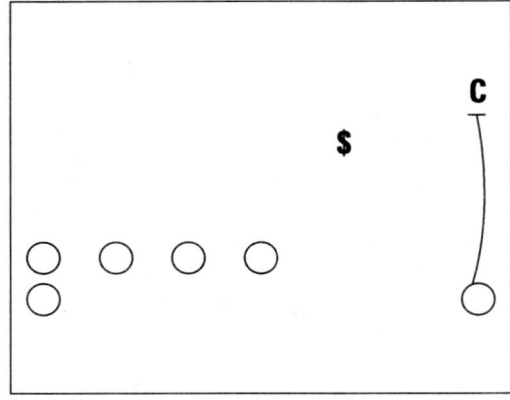

Diagram 8-9: Flanker assignment vs. Cover 3

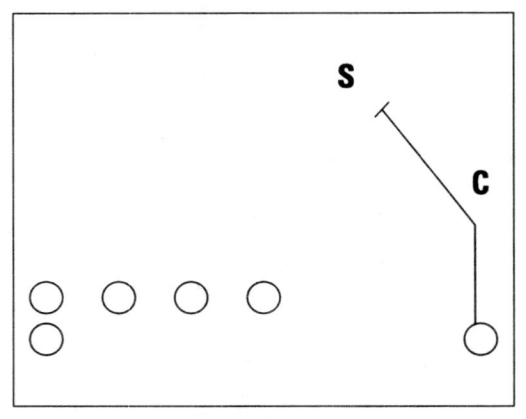

Diagram 8-10: Flanker assignment vs. Cover 2

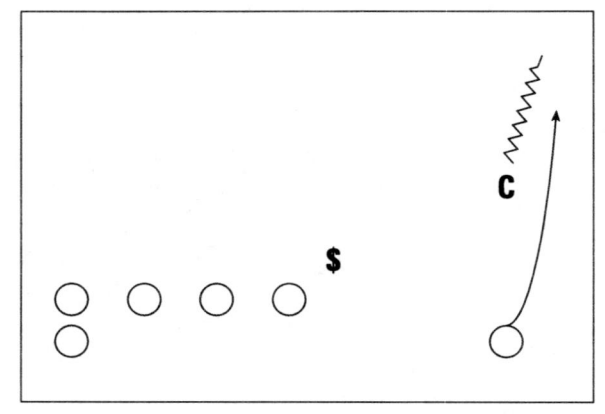

Diagram 8-11: Flanker assignment vs. man coverage

The backside split end has one rule that he must follow when GF is run to the tight-end side, regardless of coverage—he has to release to block any defender in the middle third of the field. The halfback takes a lead step (with his left foot on 26 GF and his right foot on 27 GF), and then follows it with two more steps on the same path he normally takes when running 24/25 BOB. His footwork sequence is shown in Diagram 8-12. On the halfback's third step, he plants and turns over on his inside foot and receives a back hand-off from the quarterback. He brings his eyes directly to the block of the pulling guard, who will kickout or log block, and reacts accordingly. The halfback should take any running lane that appears. He has to hit the first open lane, as shown in Diagram 8-13.

The quarterback opens for 26 GF exactly like he does when he runs 25 BOB. On the quarterback's third step, he hands back to the halfback, and then continues on his naked/bootleg path to hold the backside edge, as shown in Diagram 8-14.

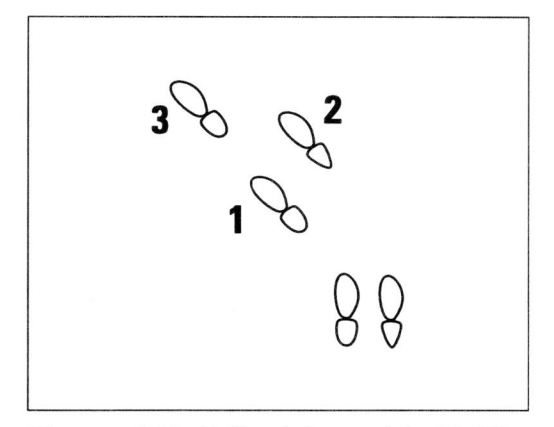

Diagram 8-12: Halfback footwork in 26 GF

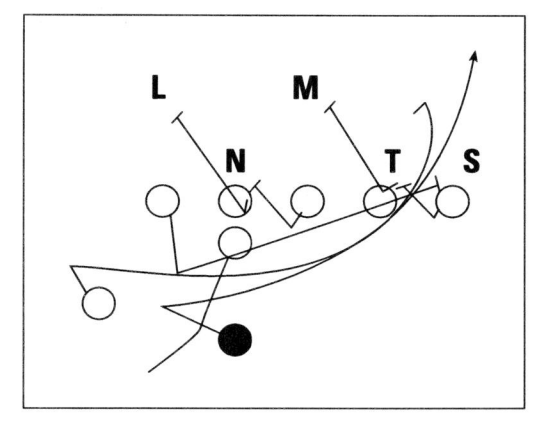

Diagram 8-13: Halfback's path

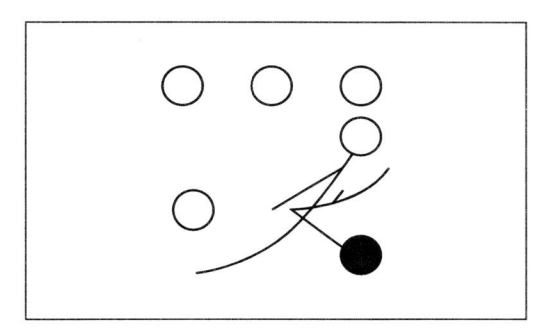

Diagram 8-14: Quarterback's path

Attacking an Eagle Strong Front

GF has been an excellent misdirection play for us and provides tremendous down-blocking angles for our offensive linemen. It also provides some play-action passing options to further confuse the second-level defensive players. GF is shown against an Eagle Strong front in Diagram 8-15.

Similar to his actions against an Okie front, the backside tackle sets up to pass protect and invites an outside rush by the 5-technique. The backside guard pulls and runs his kickout path toward the 7-technique. The center blocks the weakside shade by himself. The playside guard and the playside tackle now apply the double-team/combo scheme against the 3-technique, with four hands on the 3-technique and four eyes on the weak inside linebacker. The tight end releases outside and tries to get the 7-technique to widen along with his release, thus helping the guard execute his kickout block. The tight end is responsible for the strong safety, while the receivers apply their rules based on the coverage read they make based on alignment. The backfield action remains exactly the same.

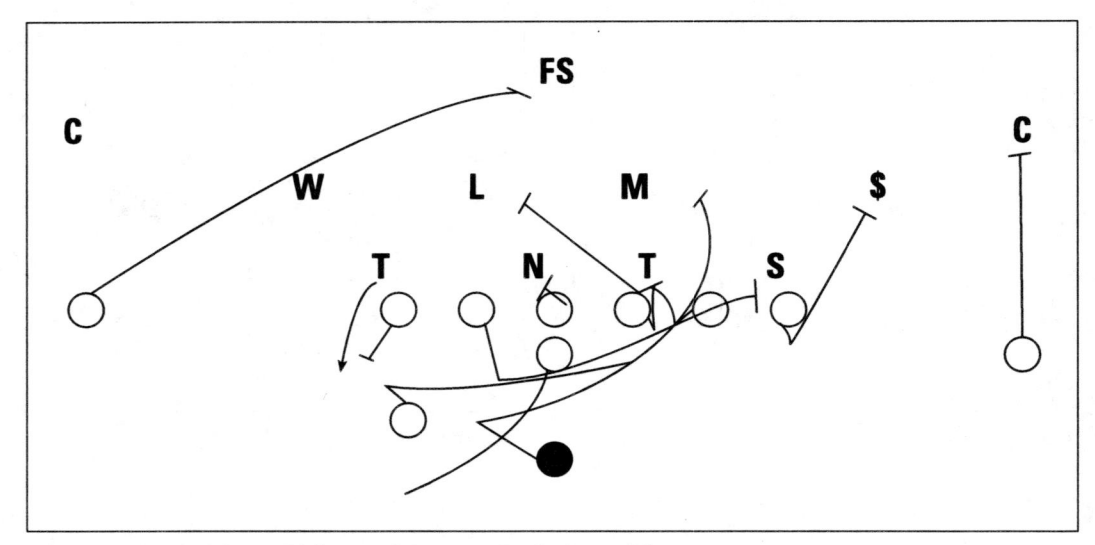

Diagram 8-15: Queen Right 26 GF vs. an Eagle Strong front

Attacking a 4-3 Front

Diagram 8-16 illustrates 26 GF against a 4-3 front. The backside tackle again uses influence pass protection on the 5-technique, while the backside guard drop steps and pulls to kick out the playside 9-technique. The center blocks back on the weakside shade, while the playside guard and the playside tackle execute a double-team/combo scheme on the 3-technique and the weak outside linebacker. It is important to note that while the guard and the tackle execute their scheme against the 3-technique, they

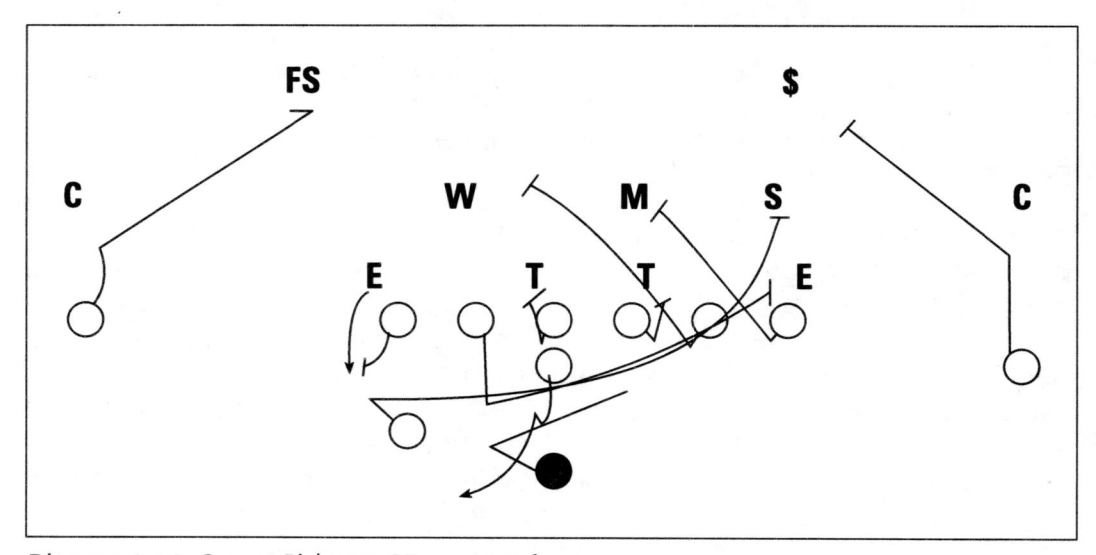

Diagram 8-16: Queen Right 26 GF vs. a 4-3 front

have to also keep an eye on the strong inside (middle) linebacker, looking for a blitz run-through of some kind. If there is a run-through by the strong inside linebacker, then someone has to come off the double-team/combo block immediately. If the strong inside (middle) linebacker flows, then the double-team/combo block will go all the way to the weak outside linebacker.

The tight end inside releases and blocks the strong inside linebacker, unless the strong inside linebacker disappears into the double-team/combo on some kind of a stunt or blitz. The tight end then continues flat across the formation and looks for the first wrong-colored jersey, which will probably belong to the weak outside linebacker. The fullback jab steps, as he does on 25 BOB, and then assumes his path, while keeping an eye on the strong outside linebacker and reading the block of the pulling guard.

An adjustment is made for the playside flanker against a Cover 8 coverage that is frequently played behind a 4-3 front that involves four deep zones (or deep quarters). In this zone coverage, the safety provides primary run support. In their words, the flanker drives off the line of scrimmage and keeps an eye on the near quarter-field safety. Diagram 8-17 illustrates this blocking adjustment.

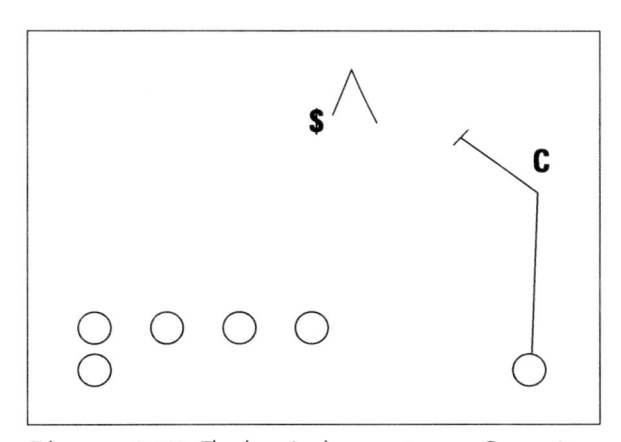

Diagram 8-17: Flanker Assignment vs. a Cover 8

After the flanker pushes the cornerback off the line of scrimmage with his vertical release, he keeps an eye on the two quarter-field safeties and prepares to push inside to cut off the far safety and take away his ability to provide force. The split end follows his blocking rules and releases inside to the near quarter-field safety. The halfback takes three steps along his normal BOB path, takes a back hand-off, and reads the block of the pulling guard. After the hand-off, the quarterback runs his naked path like he does on a play-action pass.

Attacking a Stack Front

The Stack front is actually a 50 front that leaves the center uncovered. The scheme used to block a stack front is shown in Diagram 8-18. The backside tackle and the backside guard have the same assignment. The center blocks back for the pulling guard, who will execute a kickout/log technique. The playside guard blocks the 2i-technique by himself, while the playside tackle and the tight end have to be able to block all of the possible defensive looks. Diagrams 8-19, 8-20, and 8-21 illustrate three of the possible alignments. Against a team playing a Stack front, the playside tackle and the tight end have to block the technique they face. The fullback reads the block of the guard and keeps his eyes on his assignment—the strong inside linebacker. The flanker blocks the half-field safety on his side, while the quarterback and the halfback execute their normal GF techniques.

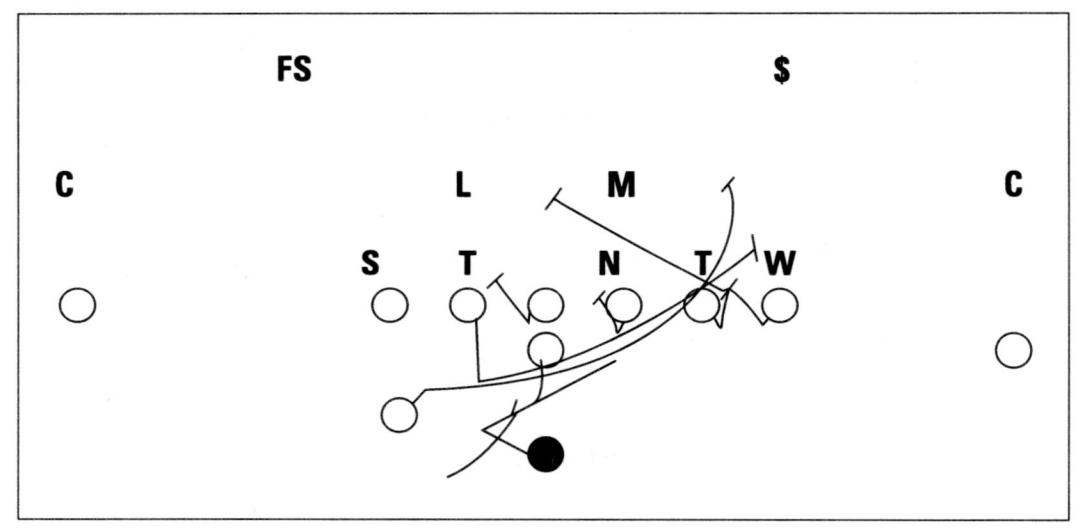

Diagram 8-18: Queen Right 26 GF vs. a Stack front

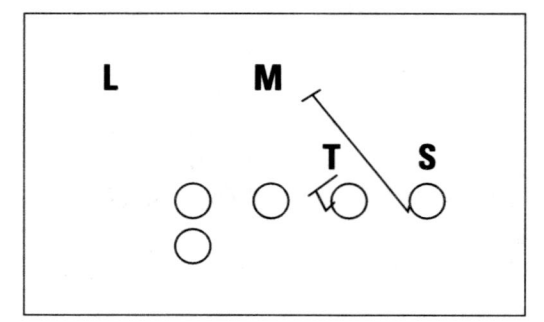

Diagram 8-19: The tight end and the playside tackle vs. a 4i-technique

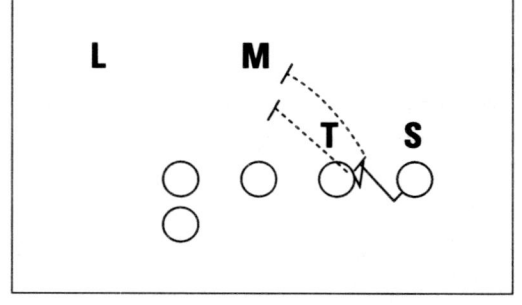

Diagram 8-20: The tight end and the playside tackle vs. a 4-technique

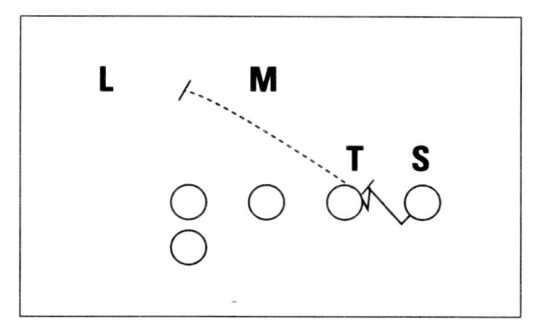

Diagram 8-21: The tight end and the playside tackle vs. a 5-technique

Attacking a Reduced Front

Diagram 8-22 illustrates a way to block a reduced front. The backside tackle pass influences the 5-technique, while the backside guard pulls and tries to kick out the 9-technique. The center executes a chip block, meaning that he flattens out and blocks the 3-technique for the pulling guard. The playside guard blocks down on the strongside shade, while the playside tackle and the tight end double-team/combo block the 5-technique back to the weak inside linebacker. The fullback runs his normal path and blocks the strong inside linebacker. The receivers block their respective half-field safeties, and the quarterback and the halfback execute their normal techniques.

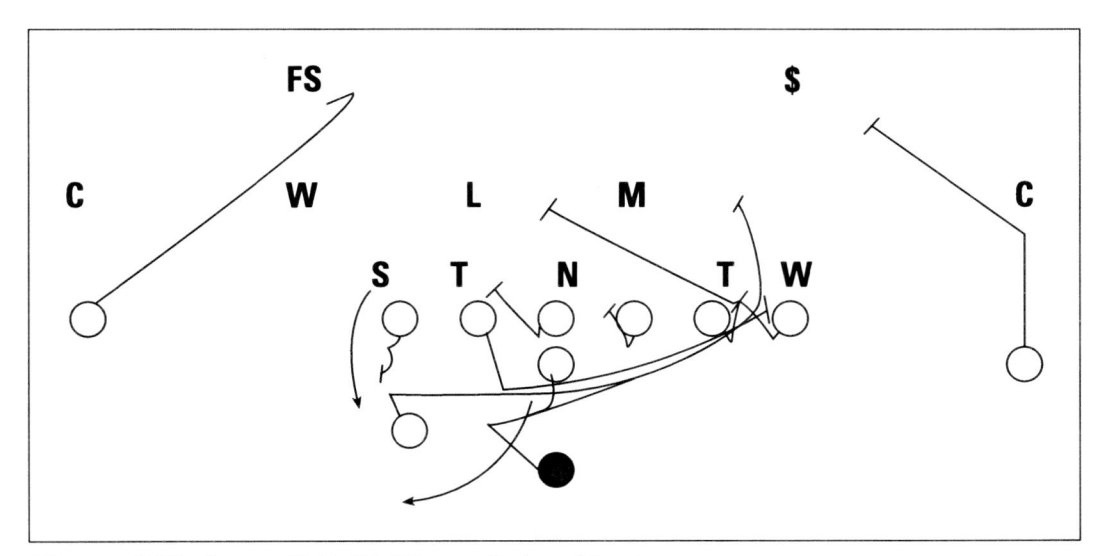

Diagram 8-22: Queen Right 26 GF vs. a Reduced front

Attacking a Slide Weak Front

Diagram 8-23 illustrates a way to attack a Slide Weak front—a true eight-men front. The backside tackle executes his pass protection influence scheme, and the backside guard runs his kickout path against the 6-technique. The center blocks back for the pulling guard, while the playside guard and the playside tackle double-team/combo block the 3-technique back to the weak inside linebacker. As he does against Eagle Strong fronts, the tight end releases outside and attempts to widen the 6-technique, while actually blocking the force of the defense, which is the strong safety.

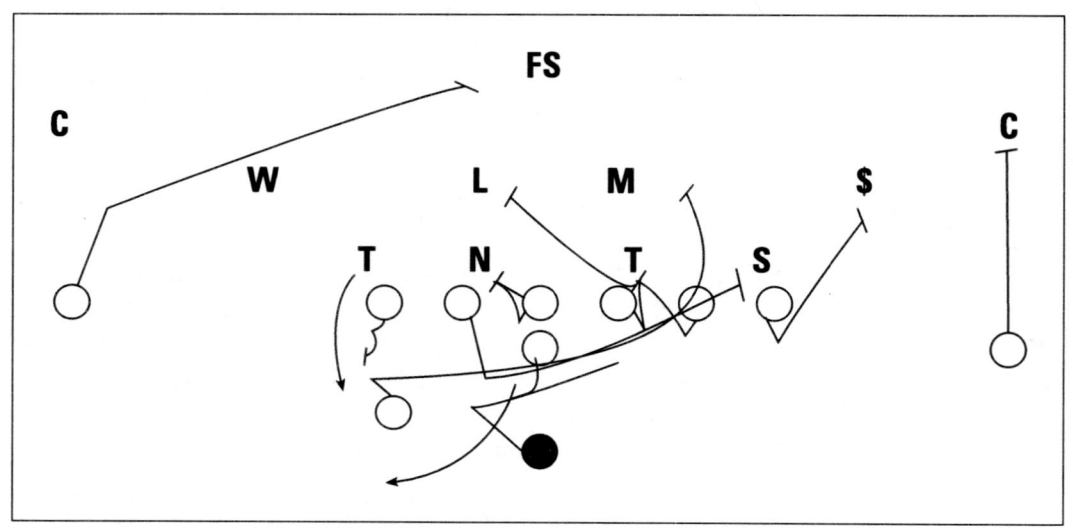

Diagram 8-23: Queen Right 26 GF vs. a Slide Weak front

The receivers apply their normal rules. The flanker blocks the cornerback, and the split end releases inside to block the free safety. The fullback keeps his eyes on the strong inside linebacker, and the halfback reads the block of the pulling guard. The quarterback, following the hand-off to the halfback, has to carry out his bootleg play action pass path to hold the edge player.

26/27 GF can be run many ways from a variety of formations. One such adjustment is shown in Diagram 8-24, which illustrates the same play run from a Twins formation.

Attacking a Reduced Front

Against a Reduced front, we can get a soft cornerback by utilizing a Twins formation. We can also use flanker motion to create a coverage adjustment, as shown in Diagram 8-25.

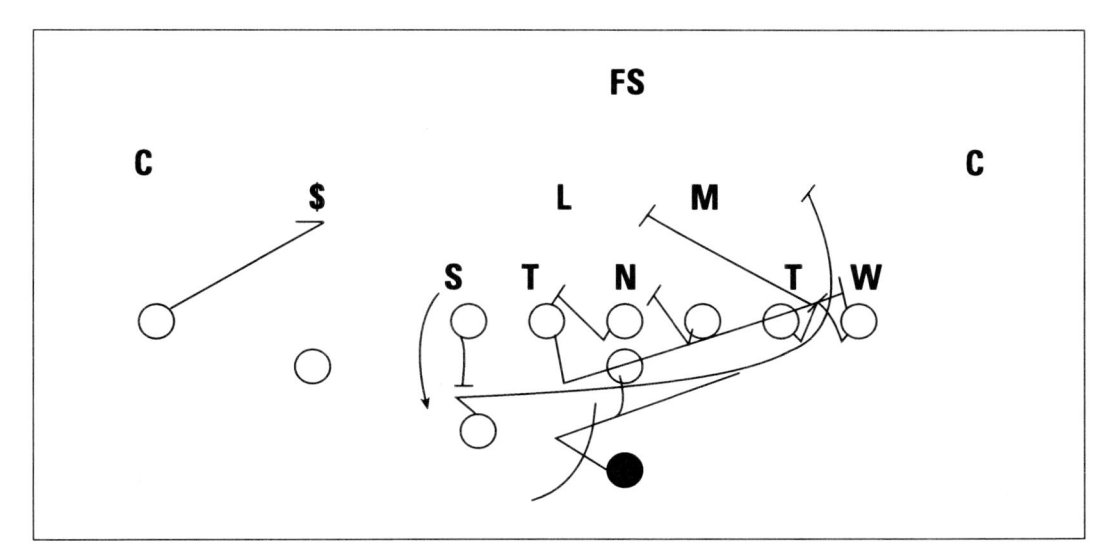

Diagram 8-24: Queen Twins Right 26 GF

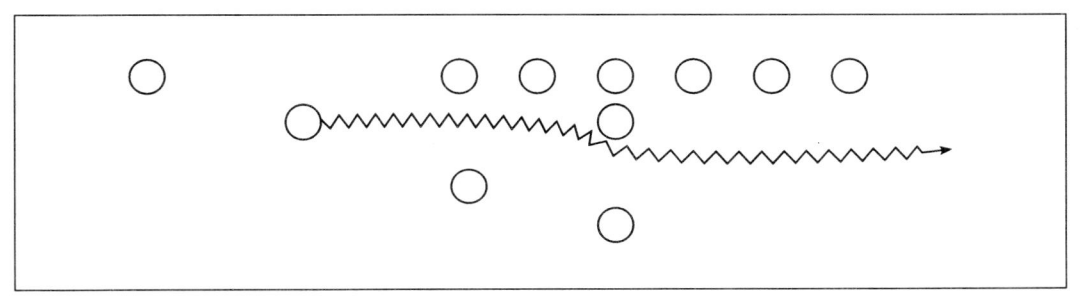

Diagram 8-25: Flanker motion

Another way to dictate coverage and front adjustments to the defense is by trading a tight end. The formation would start as a King formation and then, by trading the tight end, it becomes a Queen formation. This adjustment is shown in Diagrams 8-26 and 8-27.

Attacking an Okie Front

We also run 26/27 GF from a King formation, running to the split-end side of the formation. The first defensive structure that is attacked is the Okie front. 27 GF is illustrated in Diagram 8-28.

The backside tight end drop steps with his left foot and cuts off the 9-technique. The backside tackle cuts off the 5-technique, while the backside guard drop steps with his left foot and takes a slightly upfield course to kick out the 5-technique. The center

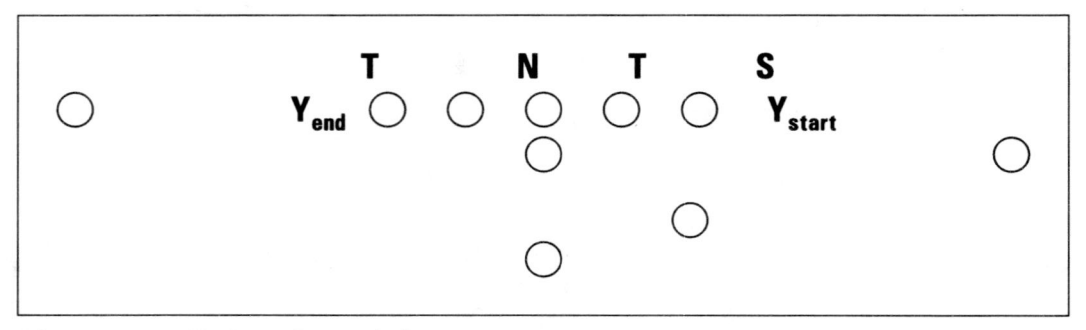

Diagram 8-26: Trade to Queen Left

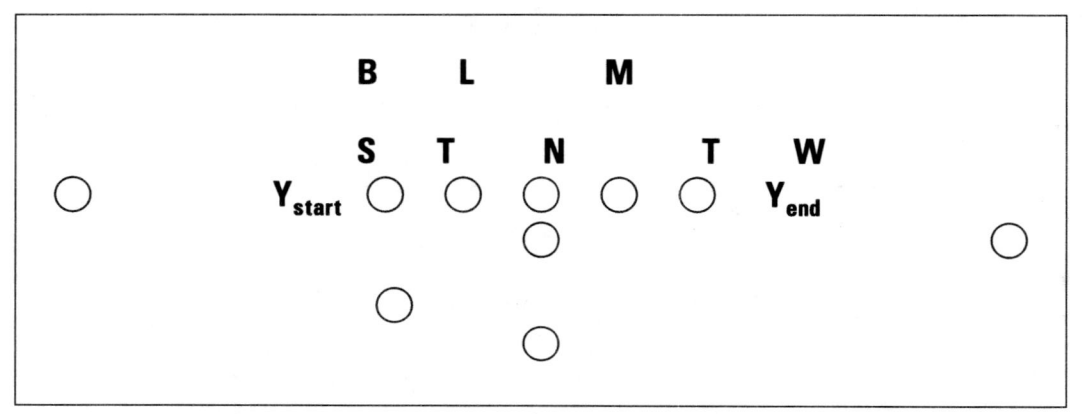

Diagram 8-27: Trade to Queen Right

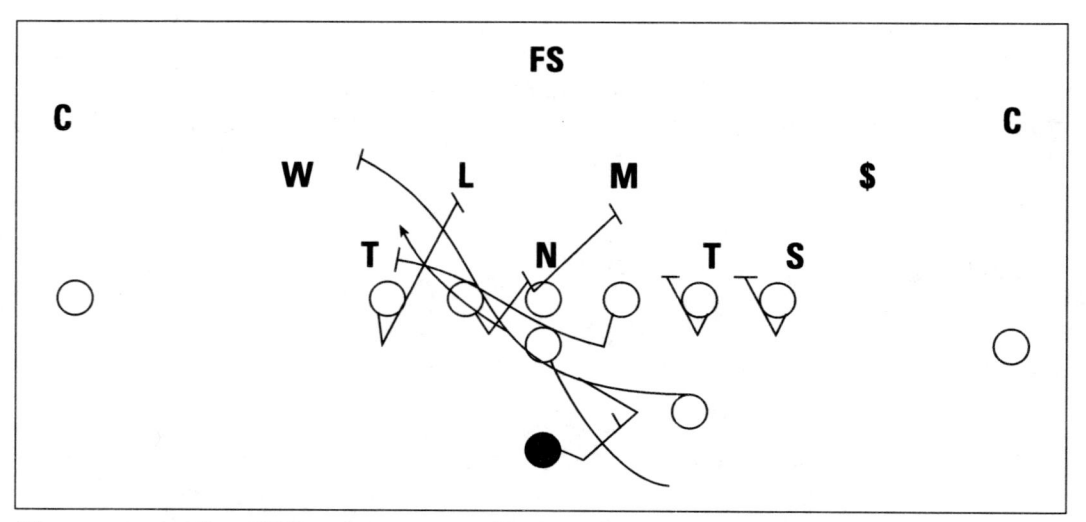

Diagram 8-28: King Right 27 GGF vs. an Okie front

and the playside guard double-team/combo the nose guard back to the strong inside linebacker. The playside tackle tries to help the kickout block by flashing pass protection, before releasing inside to block the weak inside linebacker. The fullback jab steps backside, then takes his course, and reads the block of the pulling guard. The fullback has the weak outside linebacker; as a result, after he runs inside the kickout block, he looks to the outside. The halfback takes a right-foot lead step, a second step, and then a third step where he plants and takes a back hand-off from the quarterback and reads the guard's kickout block. The quarterback hands the ball back to the halfback after opening like it is tight-end side Inside Zone (with a back call to the fullback). The quarterback then continues on his naked play-action pass course, while trying to hold the perimeter defensive player. The receivers switch their assignments from tight-end side 26/27 GF, because the split end will now be on the playside. The split end applies the rules that are illustrated in Diagrams 8-29, 8-30, and 8-31.

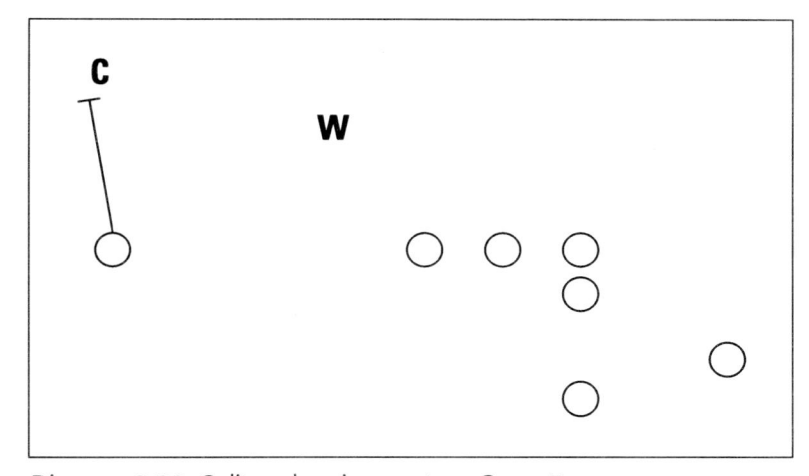

Diagram 8-29: Split-end assignment vs. Cover 3

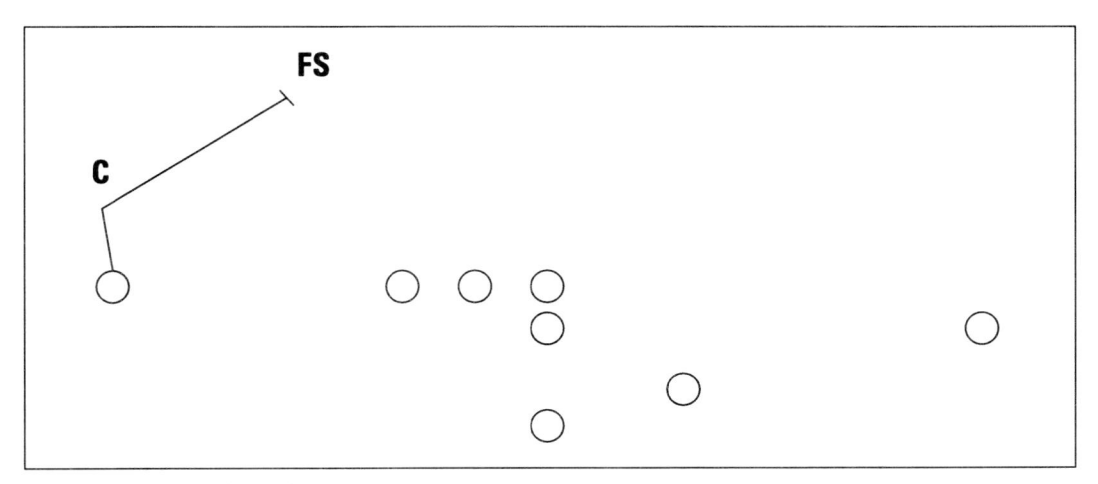

Diagram 8-30: Split-end assignment vs. Cover 2

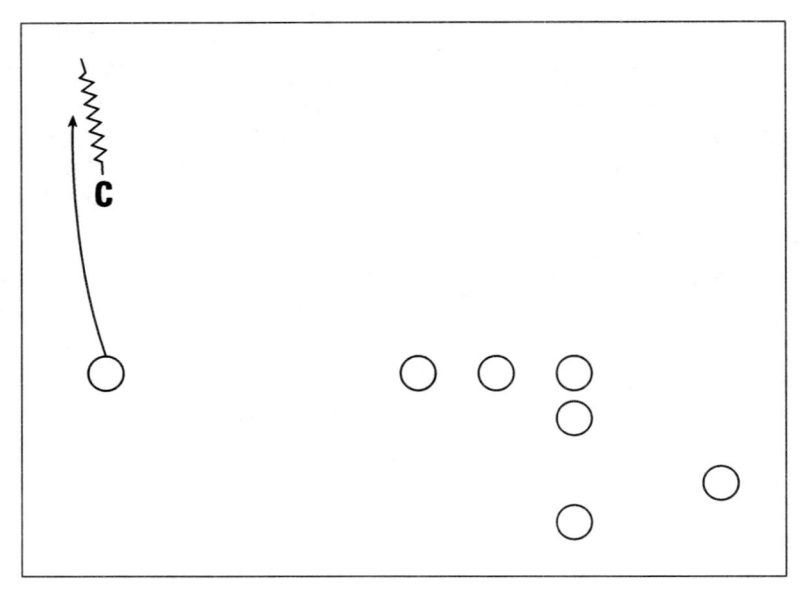

Diagram 8-31: Split-end assignment vs. man coverage

Against man coverage, the scheme for the split end simply involves a vertical release and blocking the man responsible for coverage. Our playside adjustment to Cover 8 by the split end is shown in Diagram 8-32. The flanker or the backside receiver on 26/27 GF releases inside and blocks the nearest defender—the player responsible for covering the deep middle third of the field.

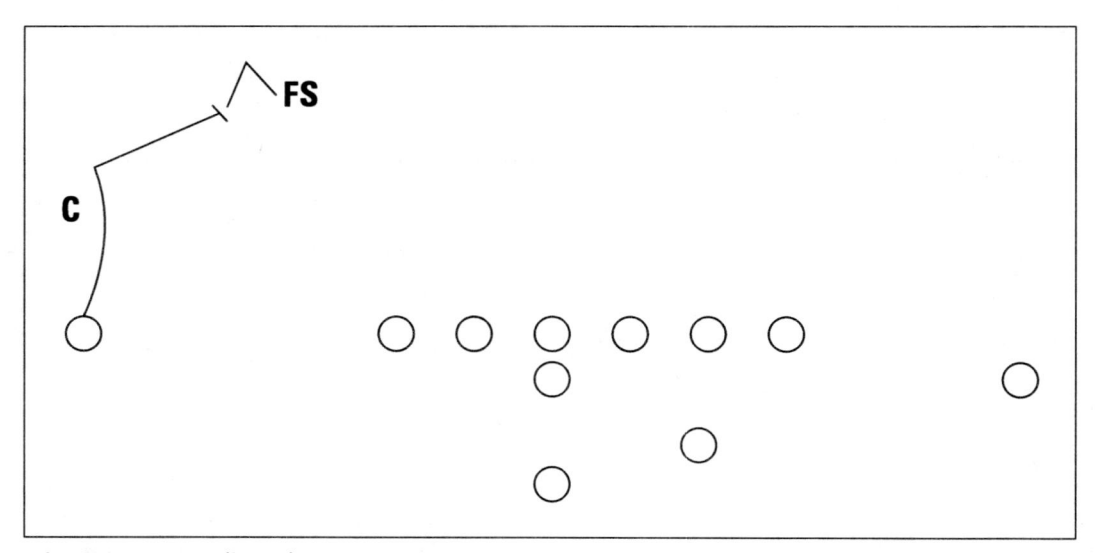

Diagram 8-32: Split-end assignment vs. Cover 8

Attacking an Eagle Strong Front

Diagram 8-33 illustrates the scheme used against an Eagle Strong front. The tight end cuts off the 7-technique, using a backside rip technique to accomplish his assignment. The backside tackle is uncovered, and the adjacent guard has a 3-technique. The backside tackle uses a snatch technique to block the 3-technique, while the backside guard pulls and runs his kickout path. The center and the playside guard double-team/combo block the weak shade back to the strong inside linebacker. The playside tackle flashes pass protection and then releases to the weak inside linebacker. The fullback runs inside the kickout block and looks outside for the weak outside linebacker. The quarterback and the halfback simulate 24 Back. The quarterback runs his naked fake, while the halfback follows the blocking scheme. Both the split end and the flanker apply their usual rules based on coverage.

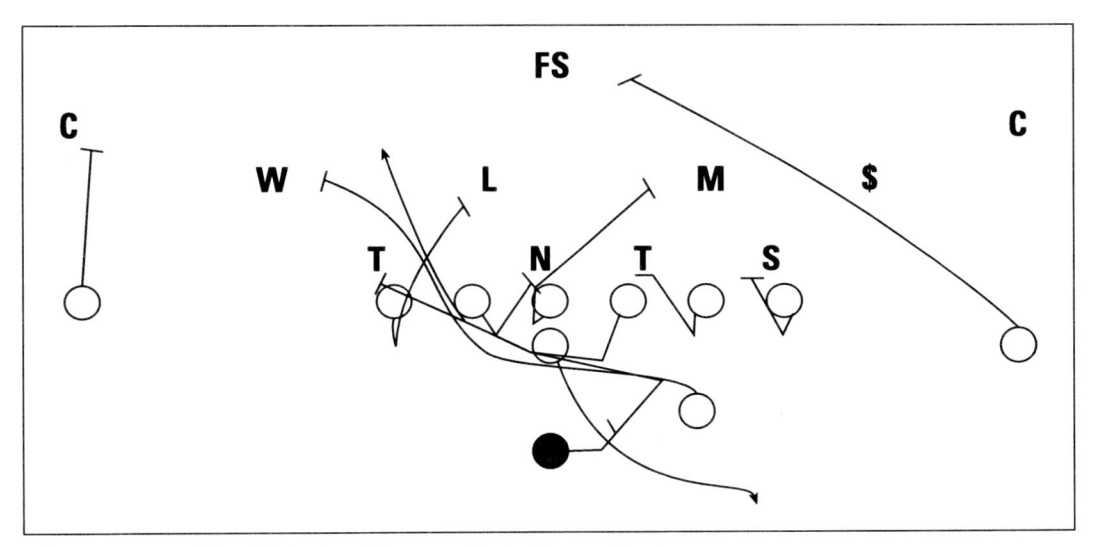

Diagram 8-33: King Right 27 GF vs. an Eagle Strong front

Attacking a 4-3 Front

The way to attack the 4-3 front is illustrated in Diagram 8-34. The backside tight end cuts off the 9-technique, and the backside tackle snatches the 3-technique. The backside guard pulls and runs his path to kick out the 5-technique. The center and the playside guard double-team/combo all the way back to the strong outside linebacker, while the playside tackle flashes pass protection and works to the strong inside linebacker. The fullback makes a slight adjustment, because the weak outside linebacker is now inside of the 5-technique, instead of being to that player's outside. The quarterback and the halfback execute their normal assignments. The split end blocks according to his quarter-coverage rule, running off the cornerback and blocking inside against the near safety. The flanker releases inside and blocks the safety aligned closest to him.

4-3 defenses would like the football to bounce or be run parallel to the line of scrimmage in order top prevent the running back from turning upfield. When we face this type of front, we practice the possibility of the kickout block becoming a log block, and this play becoming a Counter Sweep. Diagram 8-35 illustrates this play.

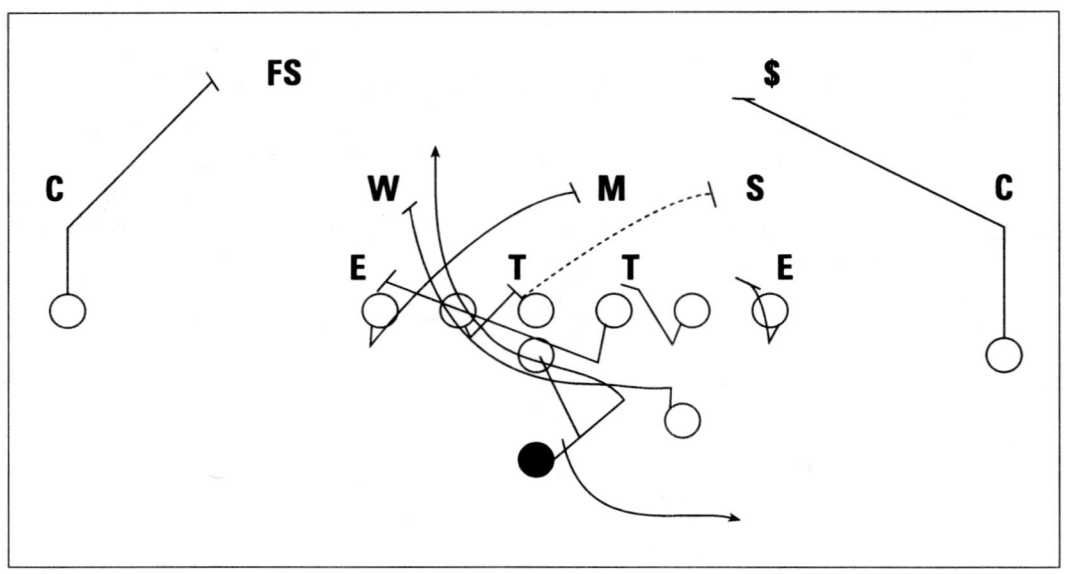

Diagram 8-34: King Right 27 GF vs. a 4-3 front

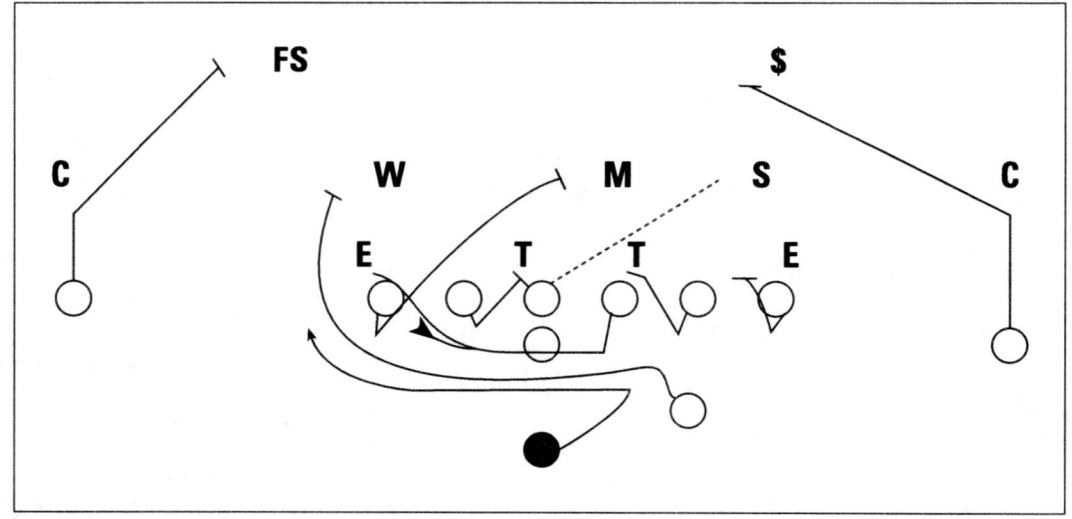

Diagram 8-35: King Right 27 GF as a counter sweep vs. a 4-3 front

Attacking a Stack Front

The way to attack a Stack front is illustrated in Diagram 8-36. The backside tackle and the tight end cut off the 5-technique and the 9-technique, respectively. The backside guard pulls and executes his kickout/log scheme against the 5-technique. The center blocks back on the 2i-technique for the pulling guard, while the playside guard and the playside tackle double-team/combo the 2-technique back to the strong inside linebacker. The fullback blocks the weak inside linebacker, while following the path of the pulling guard. The receivers apply their Cover 2 rules and block the near safeties, while the quarterback and the halfback execute 27 GF.

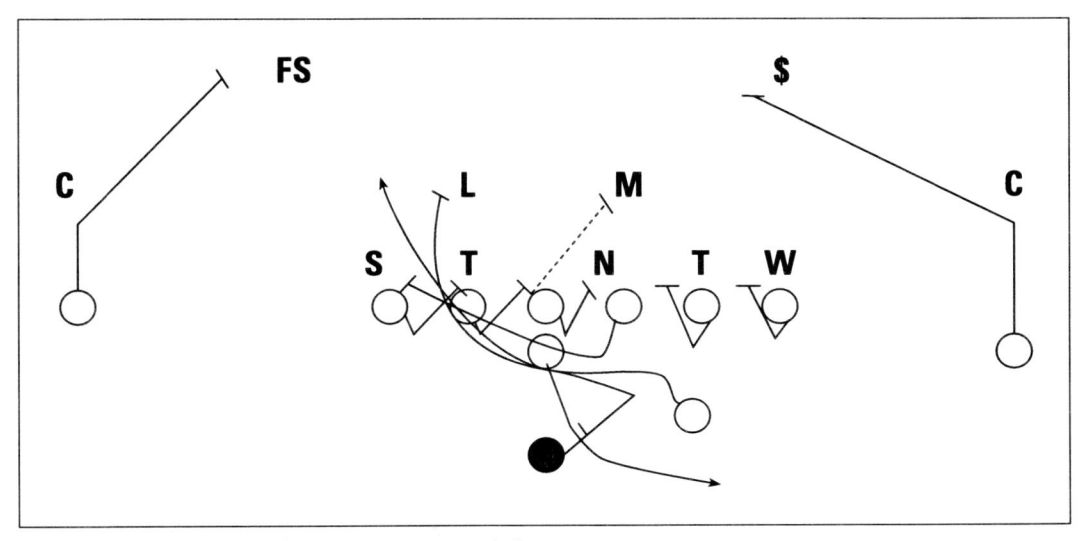

Diagram 8-36: King Right 27 GF vs. a Stack front

Attacking a Reduced Front

The way to attack a Reduced front is shown in Diagram 8-37. A Reduced front is blocked exactly the same as a Stack front with one exception—the fullback keeps his eyes on the weak inside linebacker, because the weak inside linebacker is a gap player and might jump up into the weak A gap when reading the play.

Attacking a Slide Weak Front

This play can be run against a Slide Weak front, as shown in Diagram 8-38. As can be seen, the tight end cuts off the 6-technique. The uncovered backside tackle snatches the 3-technique, communicating with the center to account for the strong inside linebacker. Diagrams 8-39 and 8-40 illustrate the problems that a Slide Weak front can present to the center and the backside tackle.

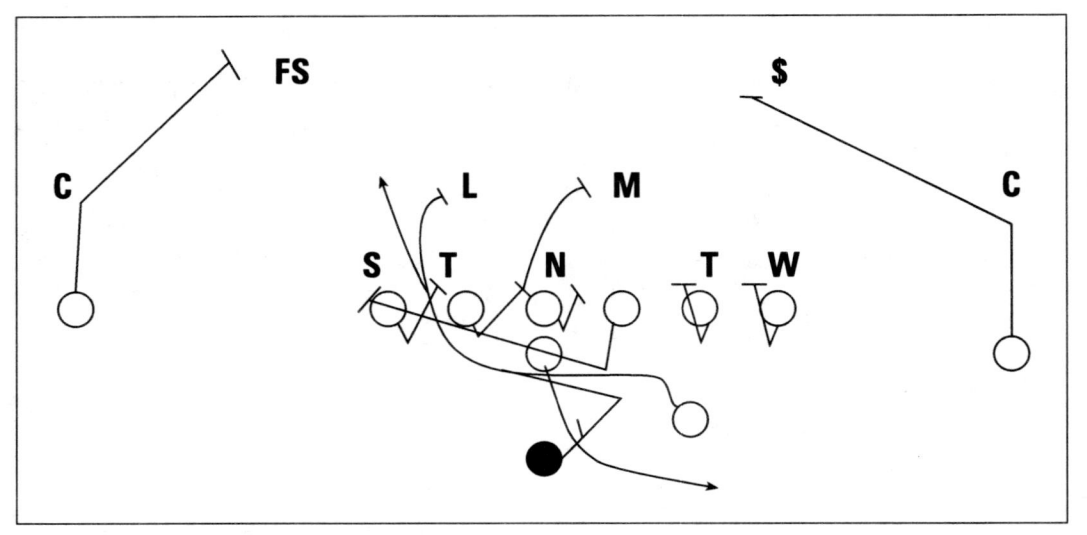

Diagram 8-37: King Right 27 GF vs. a Reduced front

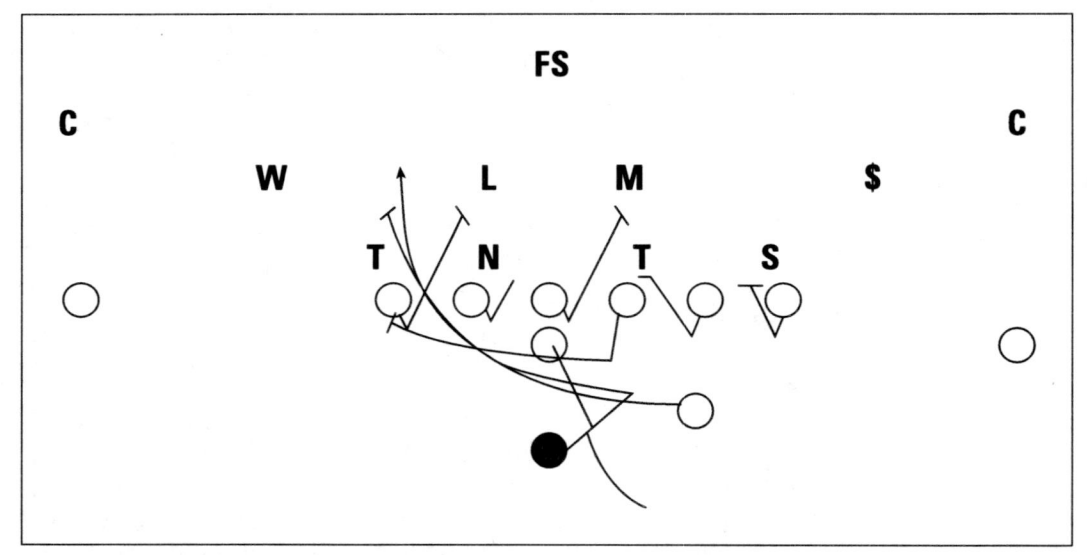

Diagram 8-38: King Right 27 GF vs. a Slide Weak front

The center and the backside tackle account for the strong inside linebacker and the defensive lineman over the backside guard. This assignment has to be practiced and given many repetitions. The playside guard blocks down on the 2i-technique, and the playside tackle flashes pass protection and releases inside to block the weak inside linebacker. The fullback adjusts his path to the outside and looks for the weak outside linebacker as he runs up inside the kickout block of the pulling guard. All other players keep the same assignments. Some of the variations that we use against a Slide Weak front include the use of a Twins formation, the use of motion to shift from Twins to Pro or from Pro to Twins, and the trading of the tight end.

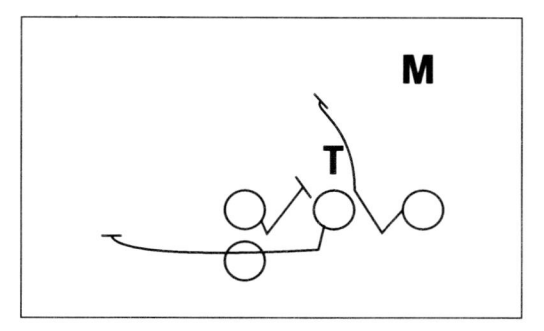

Diagram 8-39: The center and backside tackle vs. a Slide Weak front (2-technique)

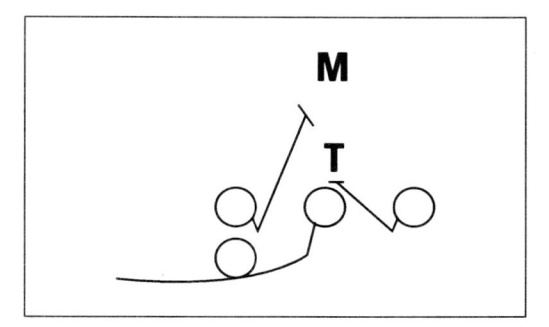

Diagram 8-40: The center and the backside tackle vs. a Slide Weak front (3-technique)

9

The Play-Action Pass: The Naked and Bootleg Series

A logical extension of the zone running concept is utilizing a play-action passing attack that simulates the Inside and/or Outside Zone play. While play action is not a new concept for offenses committed to running the football, it remains fundamentally important to be able to execute the play action series effectively. At the University of Wisconsin-Whitewater, the play-action pass has become the backbone of our throwing attack over the past several seasons.

The term "naked" refers to play action in which the quarterback fakes an Inside or an Outside Zone running play to one side of the offensive formation. The quarterback then redirects himself away from the fake to the opposite side of the formation, maintaining a run/pass option without an offensive lineman blocking for him or leading him to that side. The basic naked scheme is shown in Diagram 9-1.

The term "bootleg" (or simply boot) refers to a play-action pass in which the quarterback fakes an Inside or an Outside Zone running play, and then redirects himself in exactly the same manner as naked, only this time maintaining his run/pass option with the aid of an offensive lineman. The guard that lines up on the playside, where the play is being simulated, pulls across the center and protects the quarterback as he runs his option path. The basic bootleg scheme is shown in Diagram 9-2.

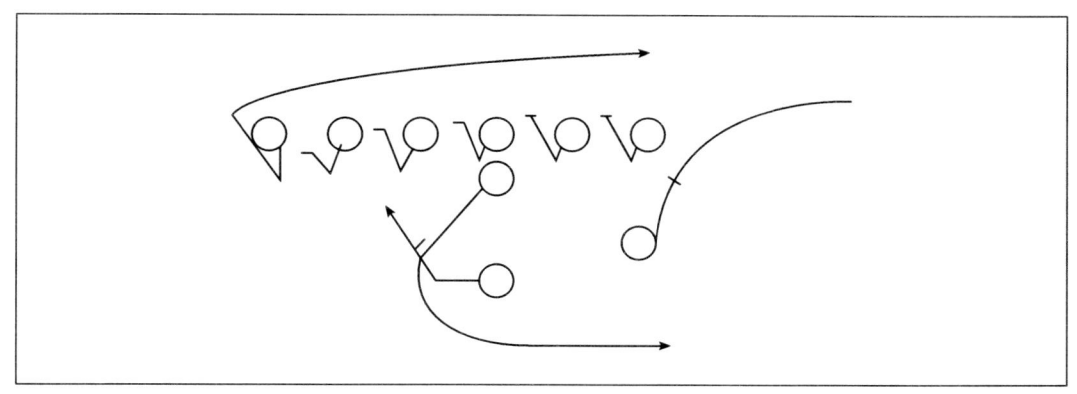

Diagram 9-1: Naked action

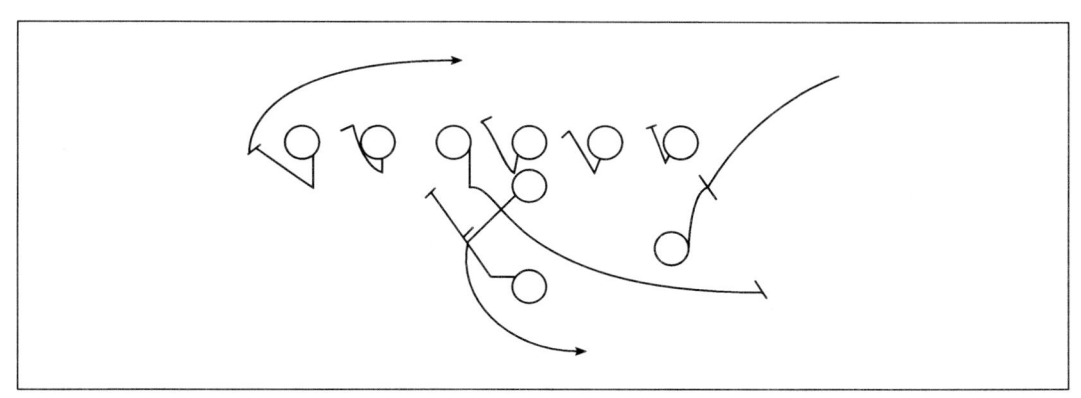

Diagram 9-2: Bootleg action

We use both naked and bootleg action when calling a play-action pass. It is more a matter of personal preference to lead with a pulling guard than it is a necessity or a requirement. In theory, the obvious benefit of the bootleg action is the added protection given to the quarterback by the guard—a situation that allows more time for the quarterback to make a good decision about what to do with the football. The chief drawback of the bootleg scheme is that pulling a guard deviates from the normal zone-blocking scheme and can tip off the defense earlier on in the play than the offense would prefer. The naked action more closely resembles an actual zone running play and gives the play a more deceptive beginning. Unfortunately, the quarterback is put in a more vulnerable position than he is when running boot action, because a greater potential exists for him to face immediate pressure.

We usually call the boot series when we are operating from a one-back formation, or when the quarterback's action after the fake takes him away from the fullback in a two-back set. When the play action goes toward the fullback, that player is able to blunt or neutralize the charge of a defensive end or an edge blitzer before releasing out into a pattern—an action that hopefully will buy a little more time for the quarterback.

We have used the boot series in all play-action situations (i.e., two-back formations, one-back formations, play action toward the fullback, and play action away from the fullback) to help the quarterback when the defense adjusts or defends effectively against the naked series. On the other hand, there have been games where we rarely use the boot series, preferring instead to better disguise our play intent and relying solely on the quarterback's natural ability to make a positive play.

Regardless of whether the play-action pass utilizes naked or boot action, it can be an effective weapon in any zone offensive arsenal because:

- It so closely resembles the zone running scheme and leads to extremely high pass completion percentages.
- It takes pressure off the zone running game by not allowing defenses to gang up on the run without fear of or respect for the pass.
- It's potential to fool defenders with assigned pass-coverage responsibilities gives it big-play potential. In one recent season, for example, our play-action passing attack averaged over 15 yards per completion, with 24 pass receptions of more than 25 yards, and 14 touchdown passes in a 10-game schedule.
- It makes the quarterback a constant threat to the contain element of the defense, thereby forcing pass defenders to decide whether to stay in coverage with a receiver or to attack the quarterback when he breaks contain.
- It can be thrown out of multiple formations, with each formation possessing the ability to threaten the defensive coverage underneath, intermediately, deep, or backside. Given the nature of the play-action pass and where the receiver routes could potentially be run from, it is impossible for a defense to be able to cover all of the potential receivers.
- It is a relatively low-risk pass play that is fairly easy to execute. Aside from a few basic principles and reads, the quarterback is not required to sit back and dissect coverages, or make a myriad of decisions about where to throw the ball. His receivers only need to be aware of their position relative to the offensive formation in order to know what their route should be. Very few incorrect routes will be run, no matter what the initial formation alignment is. In one recent season, for example, we called 115 play-action passes and threw only 1 interception.

Among the rules that can help a zone play-action passing attack produce positive results on a consistent basis are the following:

- The offense should run and pass from similar formations. It is decidedly easier for the opposition to defend either play successfully when the offense primarily runs or passes from certain formations.
- The play-action pass should be called in all situations where an Inside or Outside Zone running play could also be run. Unpredictability is one of the biggest assets of

the play-action pass. Creating uncertainty and keeping the defense off-balance and having to guess about exactly what is coming from a certain type of action are critical factors to the success of both the zone running and play-action passing attacks.

- The initial action of the offensive linemen, except for the guard on a boot call, should look like the complementary running play. If the demeanor of the offensive line is passive, soft, or otherwise drastically different from the run action, all members of the defense who key or focus through the line will notice the difference and react more readily to the pass.
- The quarterback and the halfback should make the defense believe that an Inside or Outside Zone play is being run. Their mesh and body language should resemble the running play as much as possible. The quarterback should carry out his play-action pass course to its completion every time he actually hands off the ball on a zone running play. If the demeanor of either the quarterback or the halfback changes according to the run or the pass, the defense will be tipped off, and the effectiveness of both plays will be reduced.
- Once the play is underway, the quarterback should be able to identify and take advantage of whatever weaknesses the defense is displaying. He cannot predetermine where the ball is going to go (short pass, long pass, quarterback run, etc.), or he will inevitably lead the offense to failure, regardless of what actually unfolds during the course of the play.
- The quarterback should have an awareness of what might happen once the play is initiated based on what the defense is showing him prior to the snap. He should also be able to lock on to a single aspect of the defense with the precision of a laser guidance system; no matter what occurs once the ball is snapped. These two tasks must be grasped by both the trigger man of the offense and his coach in order for the play to have a chance.

Developing a Play-Action Passing Attack

In order to design a play-action passing attack, it is necessary to consider the basic assignments, reads, and coaching points for the quarterback, the receivers, and the running backs. In a relatively simple format, this section addresses four of the routes that we use in our attack. It is essential to know how the routes are called, to be aware of what similar routes can be run out of different formations and/or using motion, and to realize which defensive coverages against which certain routes tend to be especially successful.

One of the most fundamental plays in our play-action passing attack is the basic play-action pass route, a play that is run from a two-back formation off an Inside Zone fake to the tight-end side of the formation. This play is diagrammed using the naked series in Diagram 9-3.

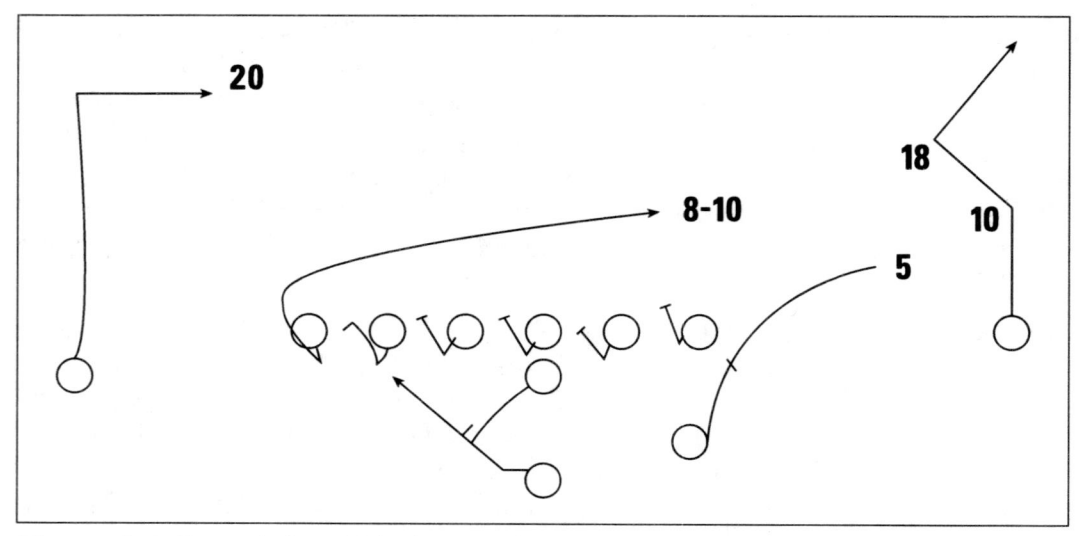

Diagram 9-3: Queen Left 25 Naked

Option #1—Split End (X): Post Corner Route. The goal of this play-action pass route is to stretch the defensive coverage vertically, while attempting to get behind all the defenders. This basic route is shown in Diagram 9-4.

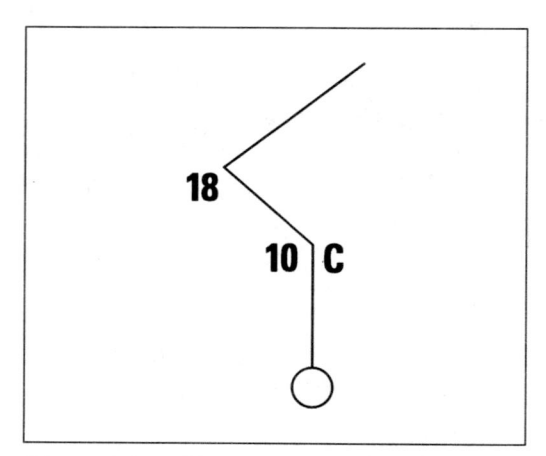

Diagram 9-4: Post corner

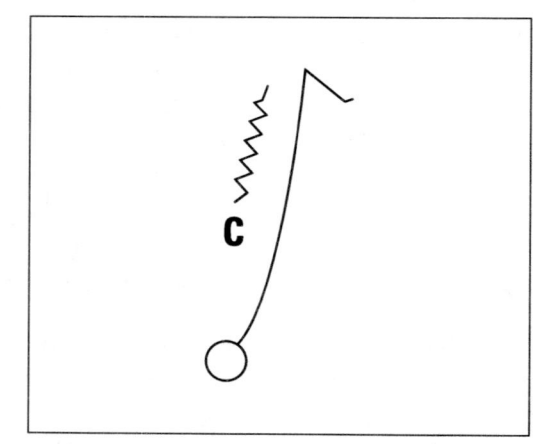

Diagram 9-5: Adjustment vs. deep corner

If the coverage is extremely soft, and no chance exists of getting behind the defense, the receiver will flatten his route out underneath the defender toward the sideline. This adjusted pattern is shown in Diagram 9-5.

The route will vary somewhat according to the type of coverage and how the defense reacts. The standard rule is for the receiver to make the first break toward the corner at approximately 12 yards, while aiming toward the sideline to a point approximately 25 yards from the line of scrimmage. The route is shown against a standard two-deep coverage in Diagram 9-6. In this situation, the split end should drive at the safety to hold that player inside.

Option #2—Fullback (F): Flat Route. When the fullback runs the flat route, he takes a path that aims at the outside shoulder of the defensive end, who will be unblocked by the offensive tackle. The fullback will blunt the charge of the defensive end by knocking that player off his path to the inside of the fullback's own pass release, before the fullback heads out into the route. This route is shown in Diagram 9-7. If the receiver running this route is not the fullback (i.e., it could be a wide receiver or a tight end depending on the formation), he will attempt the same technique from an alignment much closer to the defensive end. If the defensive end widens, loops out, or otherwise makes it impossible to be blunted inside, the receiver will slip underneath him and be ready to accept the ball from the quarterback quickly while on the move to the outside. This situation is shown in Diagram 9-8.

The actual flat route entails blunting the edge, staying on the move to the outside, and aiming toward a point on the sideline five yards from the line of scrimmage. If a

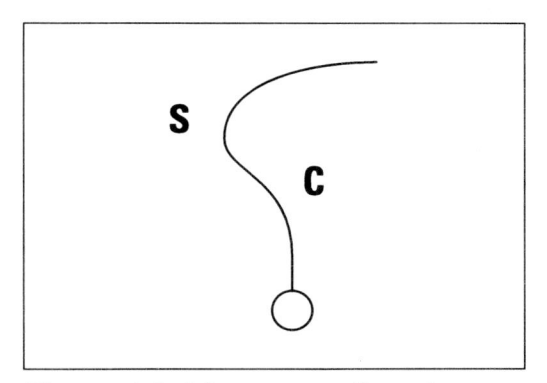

Diagram 9-6: Adjustment vs. Cover 2

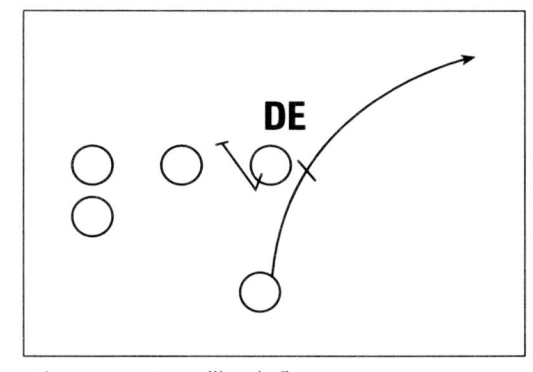

Diagram 9-7: Fullback flat route

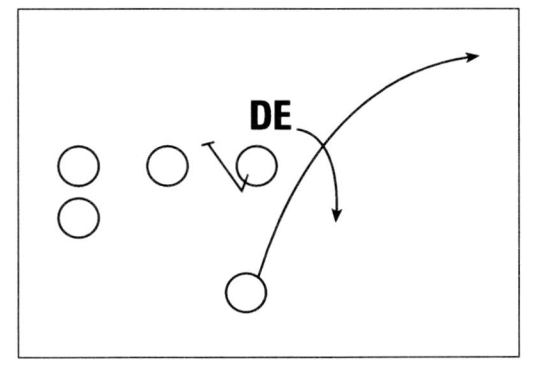

Diagram 9-8: An out stunt by defensive end

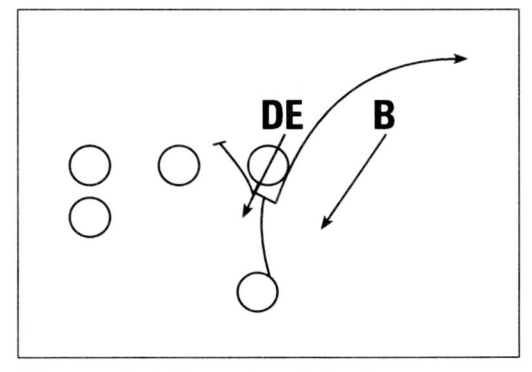

Diagram 9-9: Two edge defenders

defensive end and another defensive player are lined up on the edge with the potential to blitz, the receiver running the flat route should block the inside man first. The inside man is considered the most dangerous to the quarterback, because his alignment gives him a shorter route to the passer. This situation is shown in Diagram 9-9. If the receiver reads blitz, he should be ready to receive the ball from the quarterback much more quickly than in a non-blitz situation.

Option #3—Tight End (Y): Shallow Crossing Route. When the tight end runs this route, he zone steps in the direction of the play action, and then finds the best possible release to run the shallow crossing route. If a wide receiver is running this route, he will release into the route immediately. This route entails gaining depth as the receiver crosses the formation, and is run behind the linebackers. The basic route is shown in Diagram 9-10.

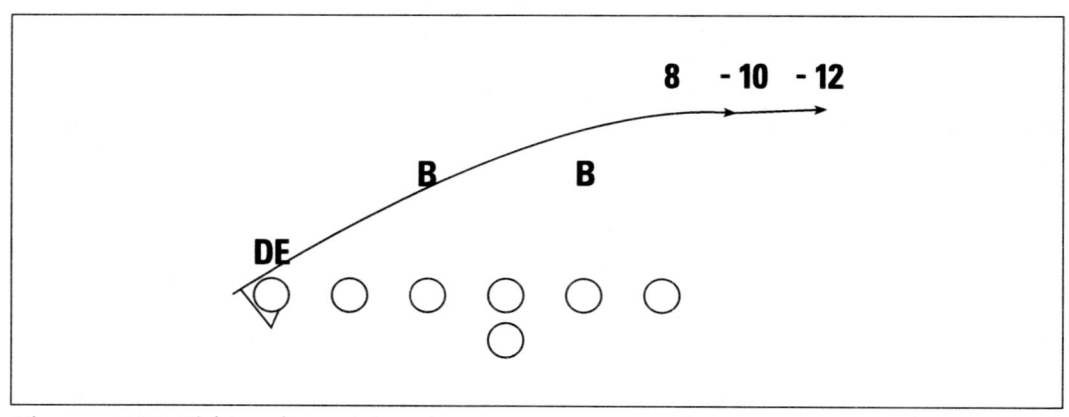

Diagram 9-10: Tight end crossing route

Generally, we expect the route to be run between 8-12 yards from the line of scrimmage as the receiver crosses the formation. The depth of the route, however, could vary depending on the underneath coverage. The receiver should attempt to find a clear passing lane between himself and the quarterback. Diagram 9-11 shows the shallow crossing route adjusted for a linebacker who has ignored the run fake and has taken a deep pass drop. As he widens, the receiver will stay on the move with the quarterback. Against zone coverage, the receiver will attempt to settle into an opening once he crosses the hashmark heading into the sideline, as shown in Diagram 9-12. If the receiver reads man-to-man coverage, he will stay on the move, "climbing the stairs" for two steps and continuing across the field, as shown in Diagram 9-13.

Option #4—Flanker (Z): Come Open Late Route. The backside route is the last option to be considered by the quarterback before he opts to run the ball himself. The flanker runs vertically upfield for 15 yards, being sure to stay away from the receiver running the shallow crossing route. The flanker then flattens out across the field,

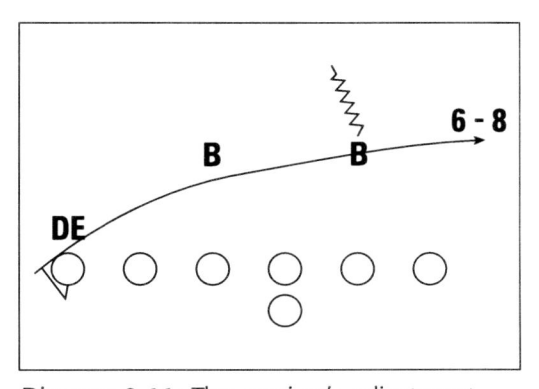

Diagram 9-11: The receiver's adjustment underneath a linebacker

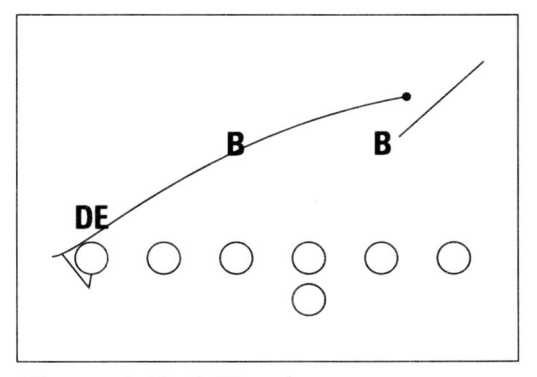

Diagram 9-12: Settling down

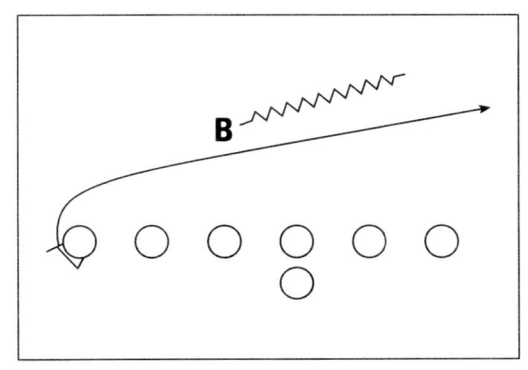

Diagram 9-13: The receiver's adjustment vs. man coverage

working to find an open window between himself and the quarterback. As shown in Diagram 9-14, the flanker has to stay behind all other receivers in the pattern in order to maintain proper spacing.

Occasionally, if a deep-middle defender is too aggressive in covering the shallow crossing route, the receiver running the come open late route is allowed to convert his pattern to a climb post route over the top of the deep-middle defender, as shown in Diagram 9-15. When running the climb post route, the receiver gains depth toward the deep middle and keeps working away from the backside defender.

Halfback (H): Zone Fake

On the halfback's zone fake, the halfback runs his normal zone path and simulates the Inside or Outside Zone play. He sells the run fake by positioning his arms as if he is receiving the football, and leans forward at the mesh point to execute a rollover fake

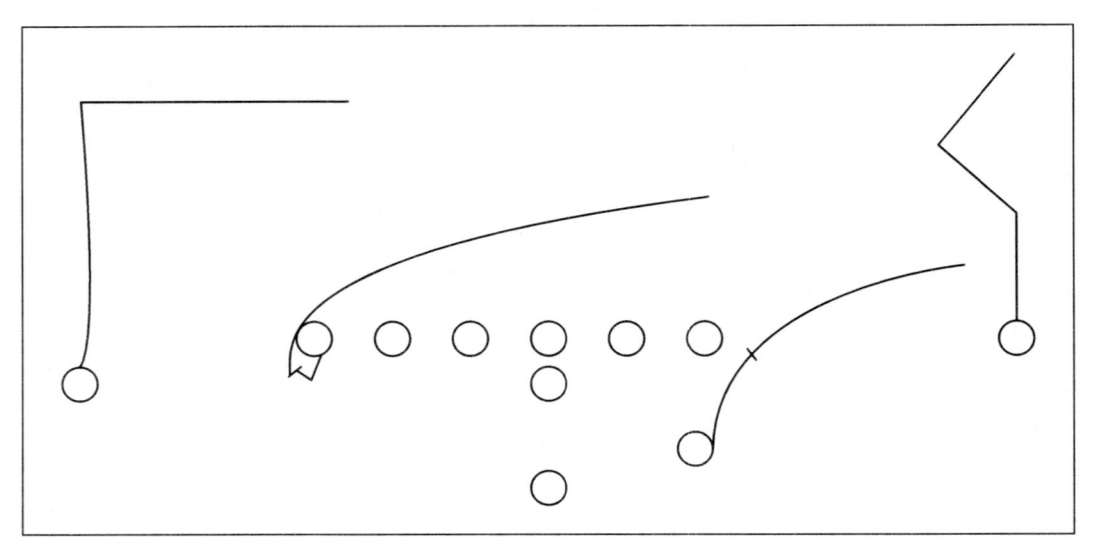

Diagram 9-14: Come open late route

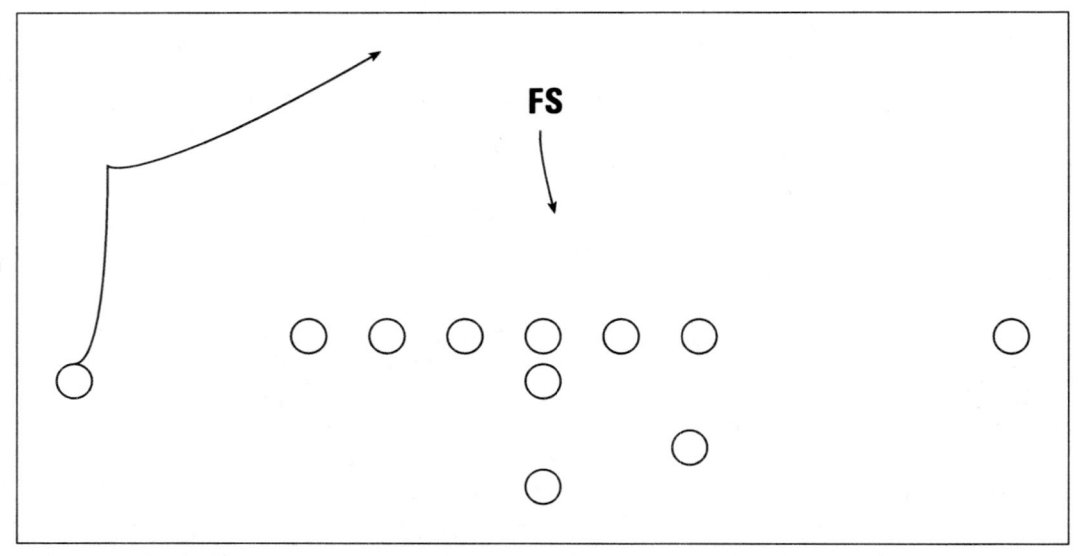

Diagram 9-15: Climb post route

with the quarterback. Ideally, as he continues on his path following the fake, the halfback will be tackled by a host of defenders. On occasion after this sequence unfolds, he trickles out into the route and becomes a safety-valve option for the quarterback, if the play otherwise breaks down. This situation is illustrated in Diagrams 9-16 and 9-17. It is important to remember that becoming a safety-valve option is not actively taught. The halfback's primary job is to sell the running play completely.

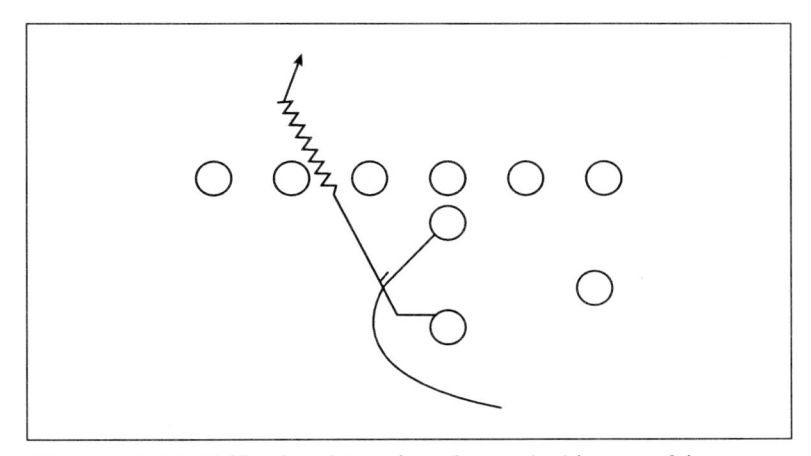

Diagram 9-16: Halfback safety valve after an inside zone fake

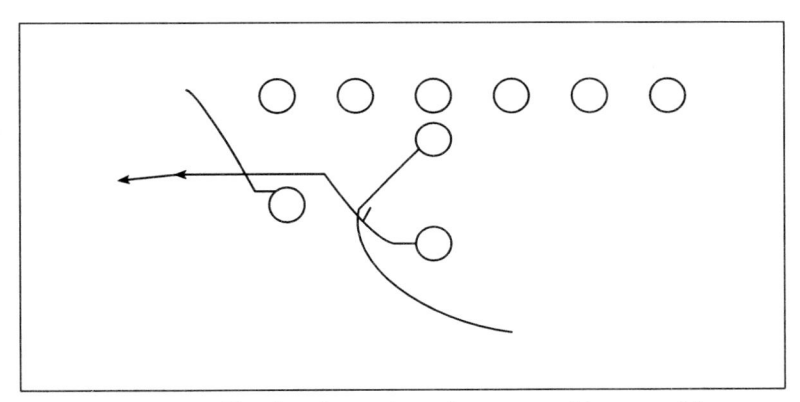

Diagram 9-17: Halfback safety valve after an outside zone fake

Quarterback (Q): Zone Fake and Bootleg

The success of the zone play-action pass play usually depends on the quarterback's ability to react on the move and make a play once the ball has been snapped. Having the most difficult task, he has to correctly ascertain how the defense reacts to the routes being run by the receivers. Prior to the ball being snapped, the quarterback should determine:

- The offensive formation and the pass routes being run by each receiver

- The defensive pass coverage—two-deep zone, three-deep zone, four-deep zone, man-to-man with a free safety, man-to-man with a blitz, etc.

- The defensive alignment and scheme to the side of his run/pass option, and whether he is seeing a base front, an unusual alignment, or a blitz look

- The width of the defensive end
- How many defenders are on the edge, and what positions they play

Correctly perceiving these factors will at least give the quarterback an idea of how quickly he will have to make a decision, or where he may initially be thinking of going with the football immediately following the play fake. After the center exchange, the quarterback should execute the following options:

- *Run fake.* The quarterback has many adequate techniques at his disposal to effectively sell the run fake. We prefer to use what we call the "show ball" method. The quarterback presents the ball openly with an extended arm, and pulls it back in just prior to contact with the ball-carrier. As he pulls the ball in, the quarterback turns his back to the line of scrimmage, bobs his head and shoulders as he fakes, and pauses momentarily—all actions designed to sell the fake.

- *Run/pass option.* The run fake will normally take place four to five yards from the line of scrimmage. Following the fake, the quarterback will belly back to a depth of seven to nine yards from the line of scrimmage as he moves to the outside, away from the play fake. The quarterback will generally gain ground toward the line of scrimmage as he breaks contain, while always attempting to throw the ball with his momentum carrying him toward the line of scrimmage. This path can be abruptly altered based on how the defense plays the quarterback while he is running his path. He should be aware of what is happening on the defensive edge and be ready to execute a variety of escape maneuvers. He should also be able to see through the defense in order to locate an open receiver and deliver the ball when necessary. The quarterback will almost always throw on the move, stopping to set his feet only if he has an open receiver and ample time to throw the ball to that player.

- *Defensive pass-coverage read.* The coverage read will be based on a pre-snap read and an awareness of what happens when the ball is snapped. Against two-deep zone coverage, the quarterback reads deep to shallow (post corner > shallow cross > flat > come open late). This read is illustrated in Diagram 9-18. Against three and four-deep zone coverage, the quarterback reads shallow to deep, as shown in Diagram 9-19 (flat > shallow cross > post corner > come open late).

Against man-to-man coverage with a free safety, the quarterback looks for his best receiver match-up, reading from deep to shallow, as he does against two-deep zone coverage. Against man-to-man coverage with a blitz look, the quarterback reads from shallow to deep, as he does against three-deep zone coverage.

- *Decision.* If the quarterback sees an open receiver, he should then deliver the ball to that player. If all receivers appear covered, the quarterback can face extreme pressure. If the quarterback is unsure, then he should run with the football or attempt to buy time in order to deliver it to a receiver. If both the run and the pass

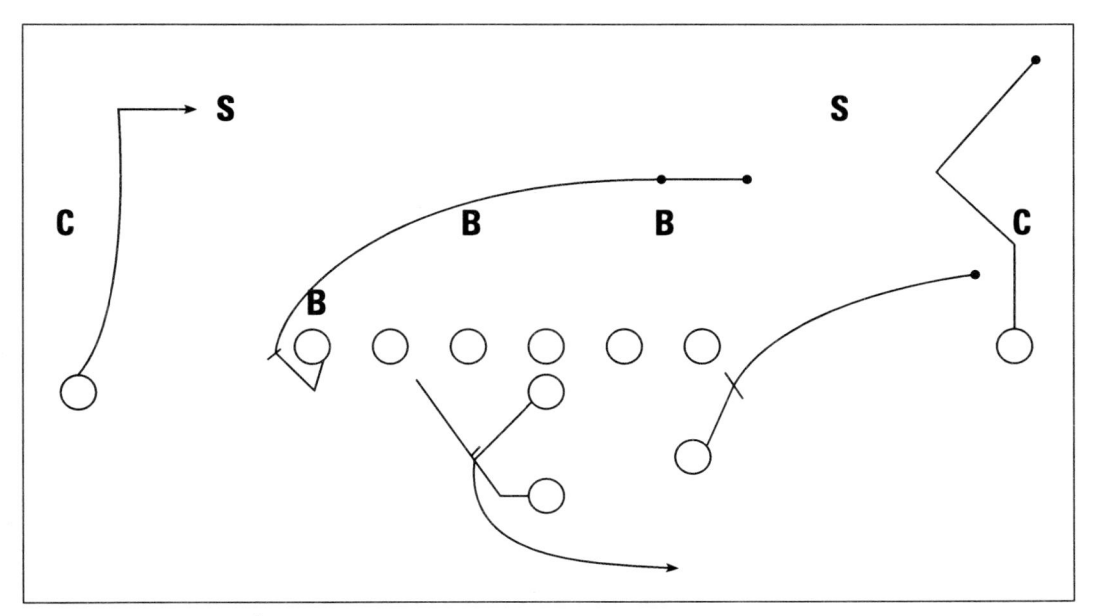

Diagram 9-18: Two-deep zone coverage

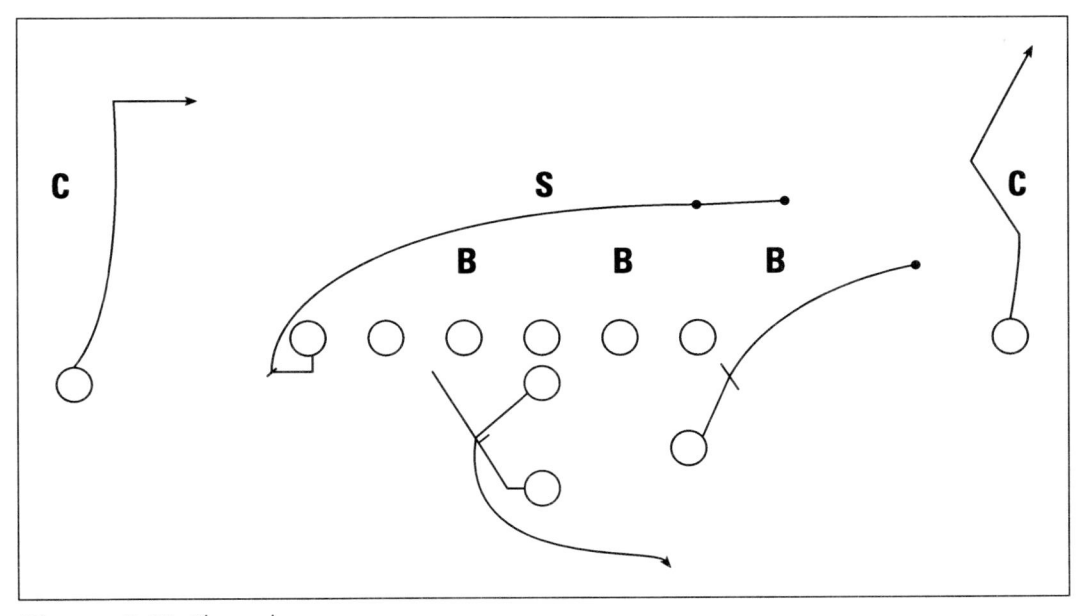

Diagram 9-19: Three-deep zone coverage

are available to the quarterback, and he can get as many yards running as he can throwing, then he should run with the ball. In short-yardage, goal-line, and fourth-down situations, the quarterback should run instead of pass if he can run for the required yardage.

Coaches should keep in mind that every quarterback makes poor decisions from time to time that are apparent on the bench, in the press box, and in the stands. The quarterback should, however, be given the freedom to do what he believes is correct on each play on a case-by-case basis. It is important to remember that certain scenarios hardly ever present themselves the same way twice. Even when the quarterback makes a poor decision on one play, it is quite possible he should make exactly the same decision the next time the same play is called.

Basic Play Action Routes

Diagrams 9-20 to 9-32 illustrate several of our play-action routes. Where further clarification for a particular play is necessary, additional comments and explanations are included as appropriate. The standard 24/25 Inside Zone fake bootleg and/or naked pass has generally proven to be successful in any circumstance against any pass coverage (Diagram 9-20).

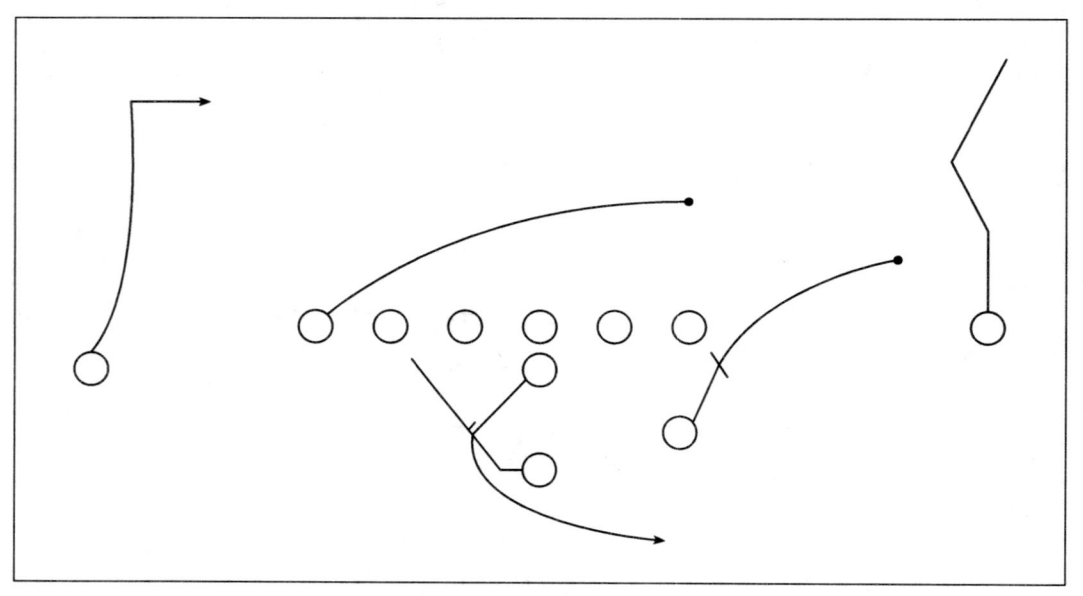

Diagram 9-20: Basic play action from a Queen Left formation

The tight end's standard rule is as follows: if the quarterback's run/pass option course is coming toward the tight end's side of the formation, the tight end runs the flat route (Diagram 9-21). If the quarterback's run/pass option course is going away from the tight end, the tight end runs the shallow crossing route.

A slot receiver can be used to perform the fullback's blunt-and-release responsibility in a one-back formation (Diagram 9-22). The slot receiver is aligned in a variety of positions. Motion is used to get him into the right position when the ball is snapped.

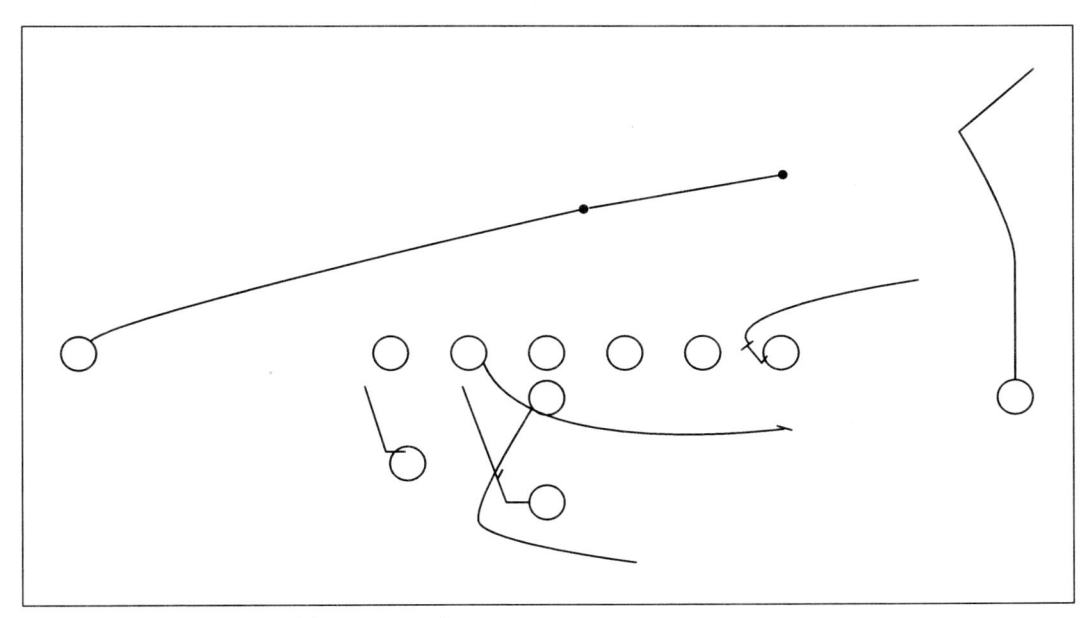

Diagram 9-21: Queen Right 25 BOB boot pass

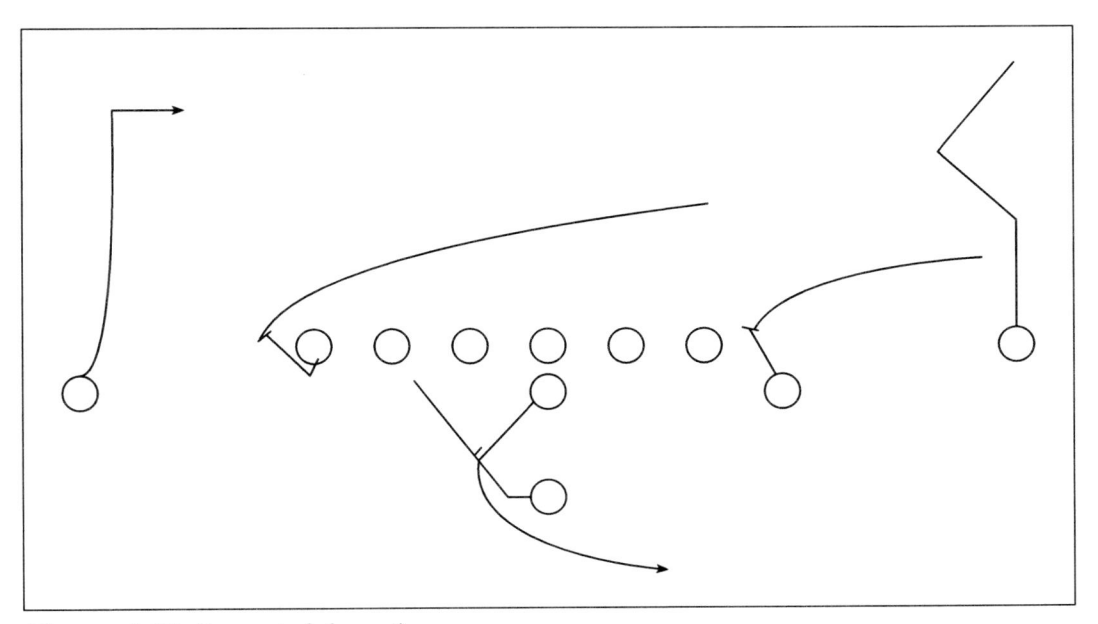

Diagram 9-22: Deuce Left formation

The sail pass is most likely to be effective when the defensive safety on the tight-end side of the formation tends to support the run aggressively, or when the deep-third Cover 3 cornerback consistently bites on an out cut run by the number one receiver. Sail simply tells the tight end to run a corner route (Diagram 9-23).

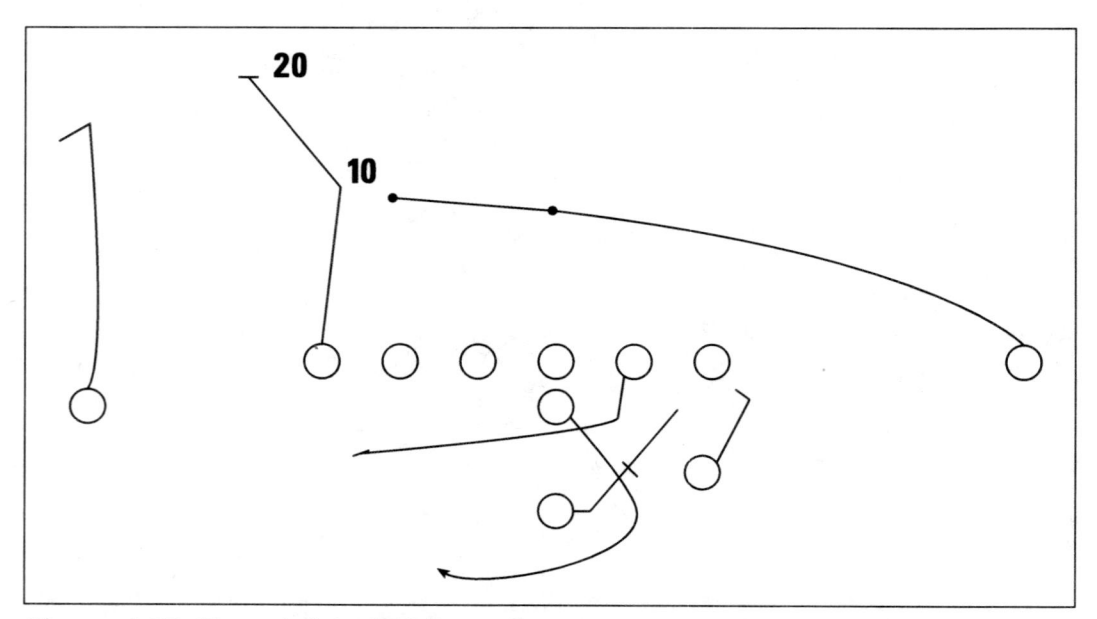

Diagram 9-23: Queen Left 24 BOB Boot sail pass

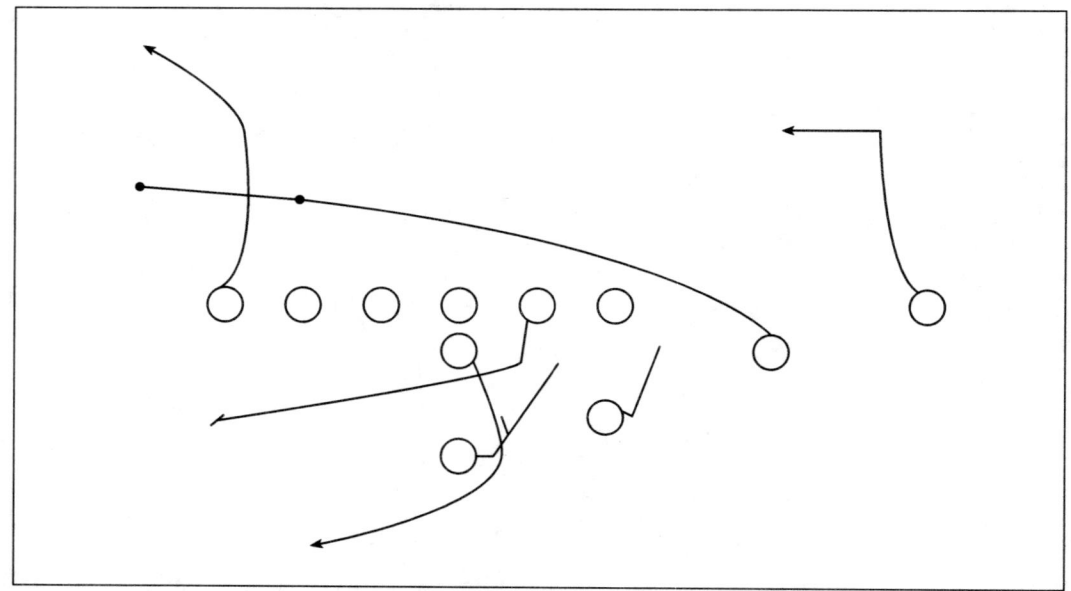

Diagram 9-24: Queen Twins Left 24 BOB boot pass

The boot pass is effective when there is a cornerback with a deep-zone responsibility on the tight-end side. If two receivers are on the backside of the route, the inside receiver runs the shallow crossing route and the outside receiver runs the come open late or the climb post (Diagram 9-24).

The naked sail pass is an effective call in the same circumstances as BOB boot out of a Twins formation (Diagram 9-25). Anytime two or more receivers are on the same side of the formation as the quarterback's run/pass option, the #2 receiver should be given a route designation. The #2 receiver runs the called route, and the #1 receiver runs the complementary route. Throwing nakeds and/or bootlegs toward the Twins receivers can be an extremely successful play against any coverage, especially zone.

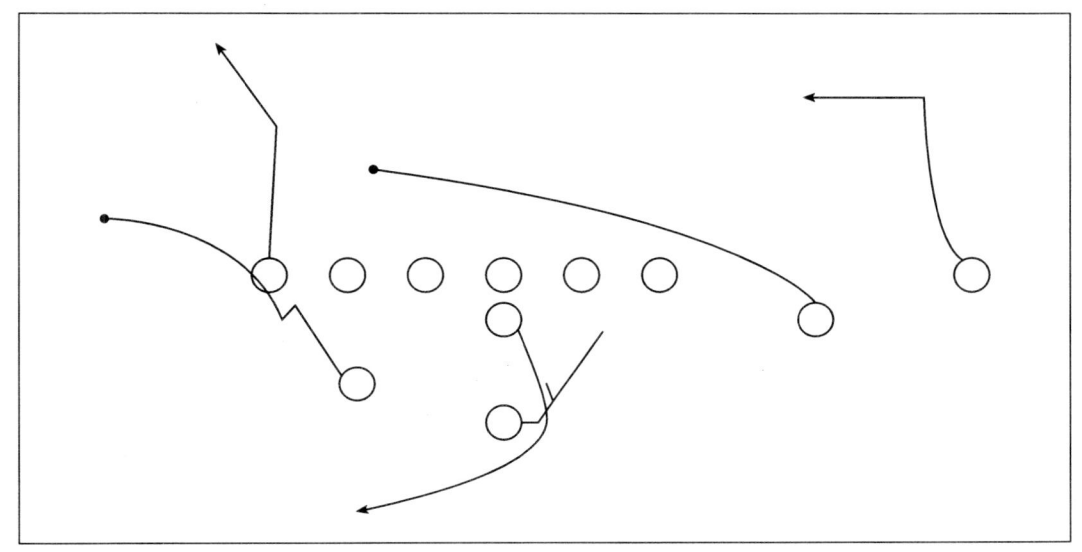

Diagram 9-25: King Twins Left 24 naked sail pass

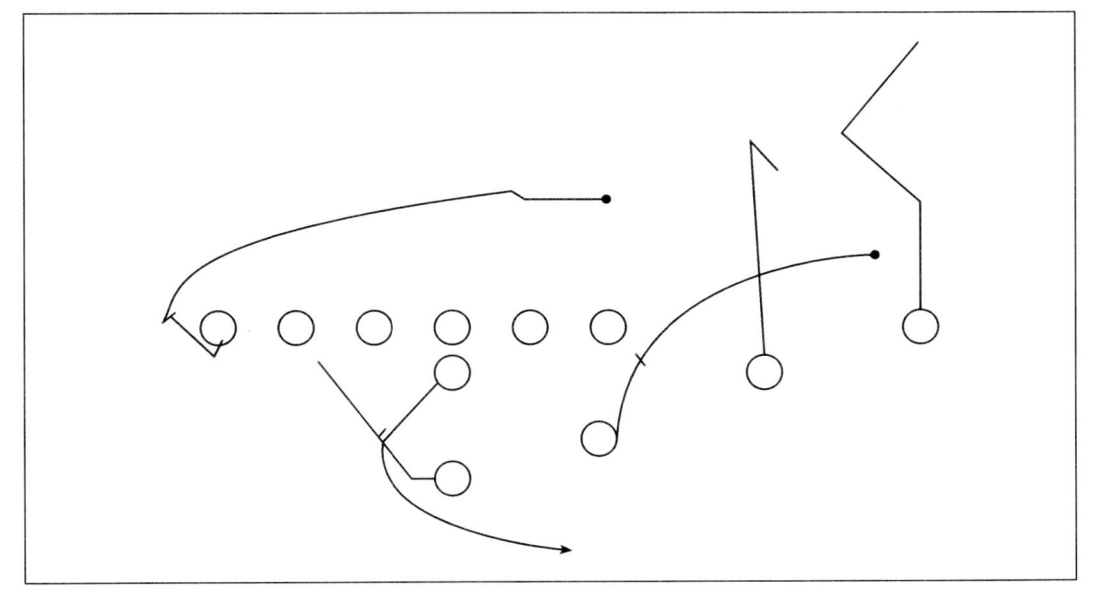

Diagram 9-26: Queen Twins Left 25 naked out pass

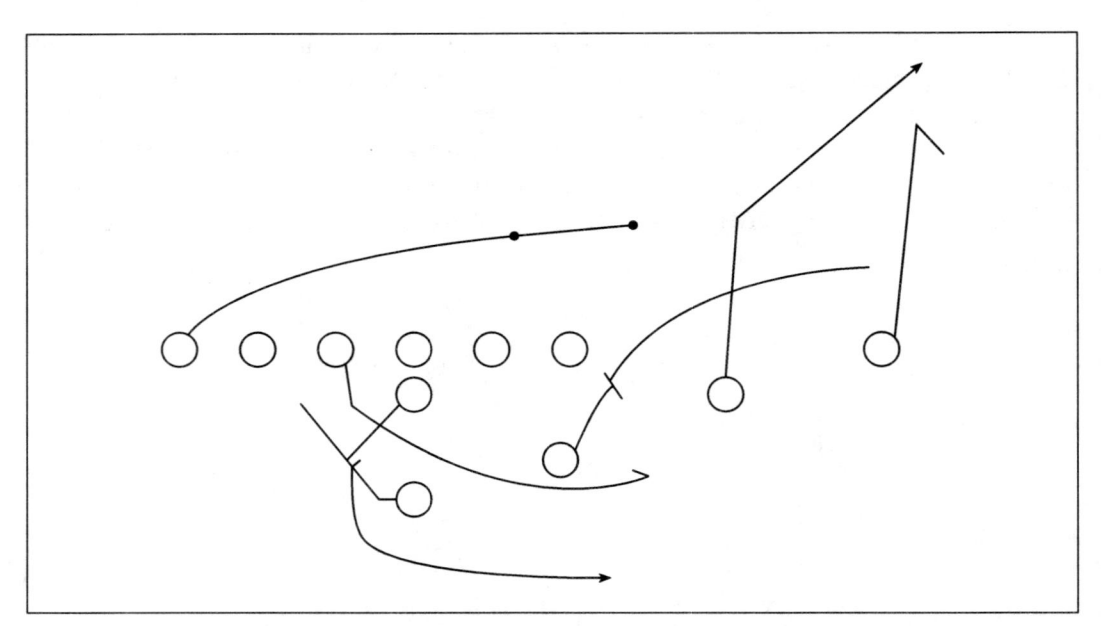

Diagram 9-27: Queen Twins Left 25 boot corner pass

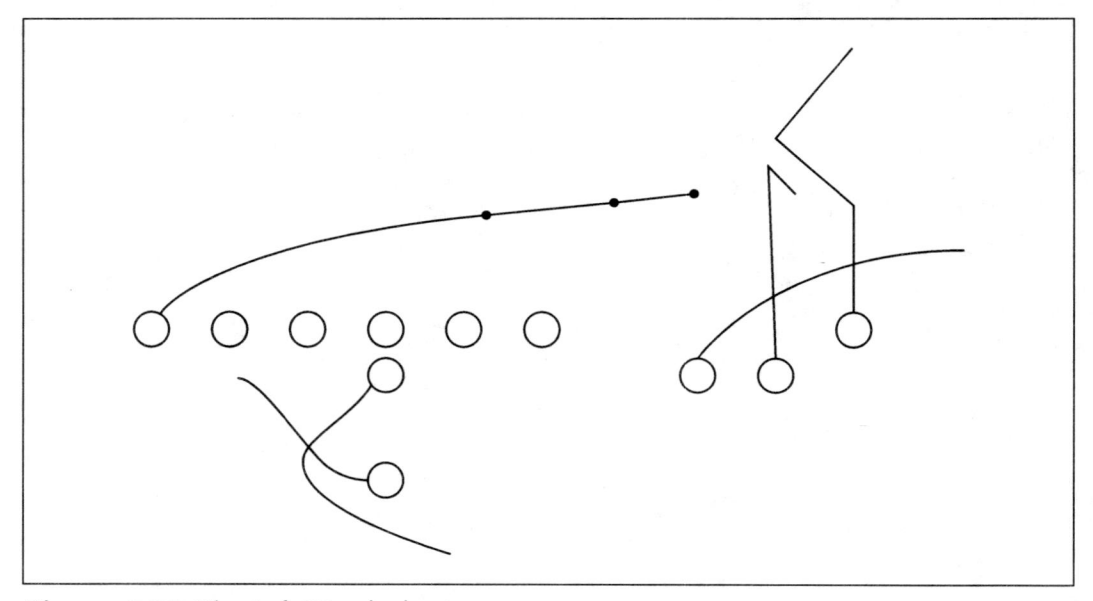

Diagram 9-28: Trips Left 25 naked out pass

On a naked out pass, the #3 receiver does the fullback's job of blunting and releasing. A variety of motions and shifts are used to get into this formation. Naked stay tells either the slot receiver or the fullback to stay in and block the defensive end. We use this protection when the defensive end proves to be too difficult for the quarterback to get away from, or when we want to insure that the quarterback will break contain.

Diagram 9-30 illustrates a tight-end side Trips formation that we often use. In this situation, we have to give the #2 receiver a route designation.

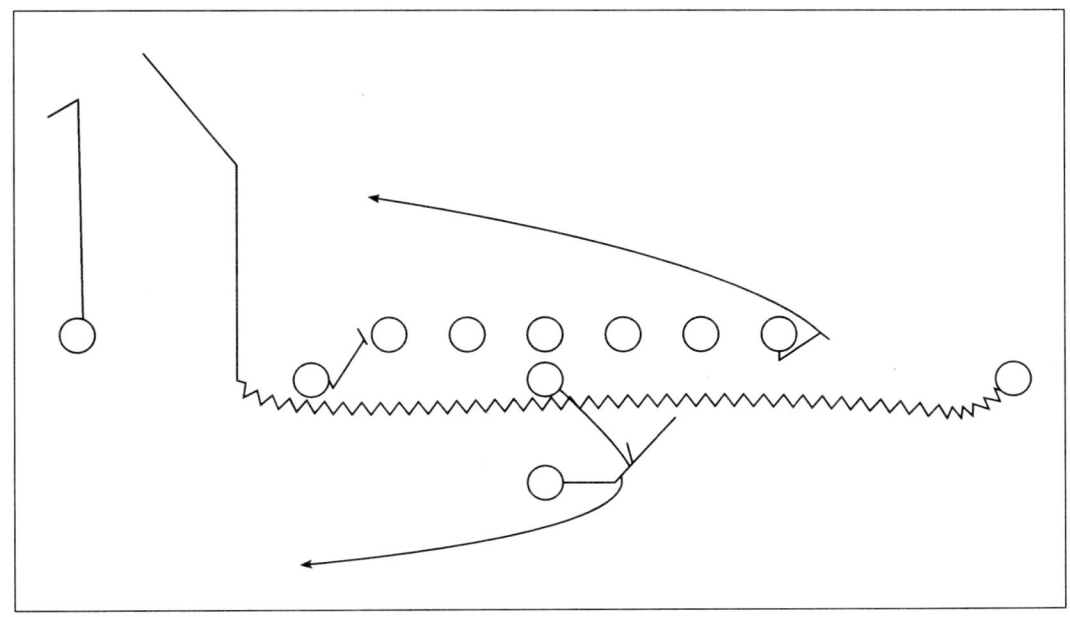

Diagram 9-29: Deuce Right Z Liz 24 naked stay corner pass

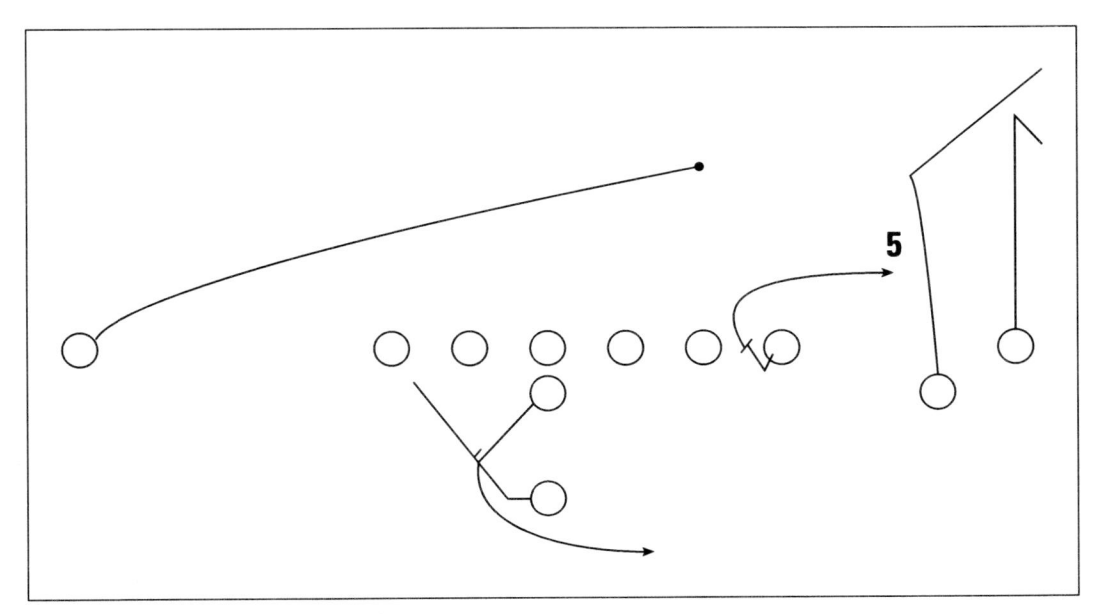

Diagram 9-30: Trey Right naked corner pass

Diagram 9-31 illustrates a no-tight end, four-receiver formation. The play shown in Diagram 9-32 is also run from a no-tight end, four-receiver formation, but to the side of the Trips receivers.

Diagram 9-31: Four-wide receiver formation

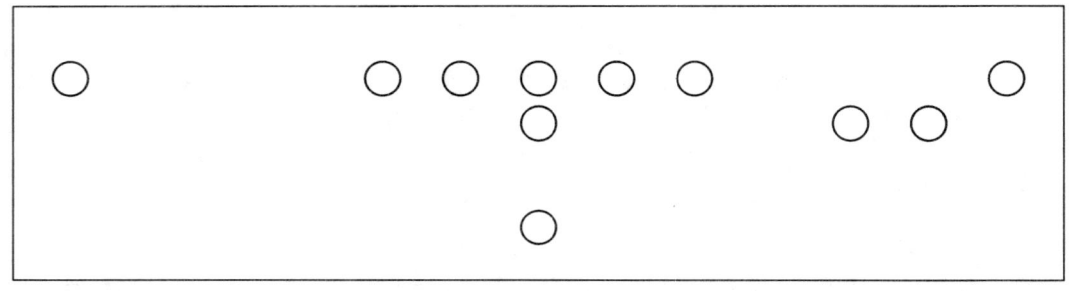

Diagram 9-32: Four-wide receiver formation to the side of the Trips receivers

10

The Play-Action Pass: The Dropback Series

The play-action pass is a sound football play that can help any offense disrupt a defensive game plan. Obviously, it is extremely important to integrate the running game and the passing game in order to develop an efficient offensive attack. A well-executed play-action pass looks like a running play to the defense, and it puts a great deal of pressure on the linebackers and the defensive backs. When receivers use effective route techniques, and running backs execute convincing fakes, the defense will never know for sure when the offense is intending to run or throw.

The play-action pass is the single best tool offenses have in an attempt to take advantage of disciplined defenses. It gives offenses a way to slow down aggressive, blitzing, charging, intense, and pressure-oriented defensive structures.

Teams have to commit themselves to practicing the play-action pass as a normal part of daily offensive practice sessions. It is highly unlikely that the play-action pass will ever be effective after only a minimal amount of repetitions. Proper execution only results from running the play over and over at practice in order to achieve the perfection necessary from every position. The play should look like a running play. Proper ball handling, play faking, carrying out blocking assignments, and following a proper running path all help sell the run. These skills have to be practiced, and every offensive player should take pride in the perfect execution of his individual assignment.

When we run play action, we are simply hoping to freeze a cornerback, safety, or linebacker by forcing them to react to a running play. We do not have to trick defenses into penetrating the line of scrimmage and tackling the ballcarrier, because good defenses will already perform those tasks. It does not matter exactly how a linebacker is fooled. Once he hesitates or is not quite sure what a play is, the damage is done, and the intended goal is accomplished.

The receivers simply want to drive defensive backs off the ball, and work down the field and behind the pass-coverage drops of the linebackers. If receivers can get behind the linebackers, then the pass should be thrown between or behind the linebackers, depending on their reaction to the run fake.

When developing a game plan and analyzing videotapes of opponents, we attempt to identify specific individuals we want to attack. For example, if we see an outside linebacker who is slow moving into the flat area, or an inside linebacker who aggressively attacks the line of scrimmage every time the offense runs play action, we will gear our game plan toward taking advantage of these weaknesses. When evaluating video we essentially look for four things:

- Can we attack a specific cornerback?
- Is there an overly aggressive free safety who likes to bite on the run fake?
- How quickly do the outside linebackers react?
- How aggressive are the inside linebackers, and how quickly do they react?

Each week, we look to alter our game plan to attack one or more areas of the defense, based upon the answers to the aforementioned questions. All factors considered, we will do everything we can to attack a vulnerable area or a vulnerable man with the play-action pass.

The play-action pass is another category of play, just like Inside Zone, Outside Zone, trap, draw, dropback pass, reverse, and screen. Each week we analyze the potential effectiveness of each type of play against the structure we expect to see. Play-action passes are generally best run on first and second downs, or in short-yardage situations when teams would normally expect to run the ball.

The Benefits of the Play-Action Pass

We have come to rely on the play-action pass as a valuable weapon in our offensive attack because of several factors, including:

- It is one of the best tools we have available to effectively break down a defense and take advantage of a mistake or a weakness.

- The defense cannot prepare to defend a well-executed play-action pass without becoming much less aggressive on run support. When defenders lose their aggressiveness, we can rely on the zone running game to dominate the defense up front and completely destroy the defense's continuity.
- Proper execution will slow down an opponent's pass rush, thereby making the three-step passing game more effective.
- We can ensure that the inside linebackers will be forced out of proper pass coverage position by our success on the ground.
- Defensive backs can be frozen for a split second, thereby giving our receivers an opportunity to gain an advantage when they are running their routes.
- We can isolate specific defenders by forcing them to react to fakes and to ignore their coverage responsibilities.
- Defenses have a difficult time preparing to face the play-action pass because they cannot predict when we are going to run it. The advantage to the zone attack is that virtually all run and pass plays start exactly the same way.

Factors Increasing the Effectiveness of the Play-Action Pass

As a rule, we focus on the following factors to help make the play-action pass more effective and help it look like a running play:

- The offensive line should look like it is run blocking.
- The running backs should run the exact same path that they do in the actual run play, and should deliberately hold the fake through the line of scrimmage.
- The quarterback's mechanics should look exactly like those he executes on the running play. His actions on both the run and the pass should be uniform on every play.
- We want to find a successful running play that is repeatedly directed at a specific defender.
- On a regular basis, we focus segments of practice time on ball handling and faking.
- We incorporate play-action passes into our offensive scripts during the inside run and team segments of practice.
- On short-yardage and goal-line situations, we want to aggressively block underneath the pad level of the defensive linemen in order to sell the run play.
- We make the quarterback and the running back aware of which defender we are trying to freeze, and to direct their fakes to fool that defender.

When we get into short-yardage (i.e., third down and two or less yards to go) or goal-line situations, and defenses adjust their defensive structure by changing personnel, the play-action pass techniques also change. The offensive linemen should use a lower-body position and a more aggressive zone technique. The run fake by the back is more intense. He should drive low into the line of scrimmage, and simulate that he has the ball in order to attract the safeties who will be supporting the run.

Basic Play-Action Pass Routes

We call our play-action passes by using the numbers assigned to the desired running play (24 or 25, for example) and then adding a call of 01 to 09, to indicate the pass route the receivers will run. Our patterns are numbered 1 through 9, and the 0 preceding the route number tells our offensive linemen to utilize play-action pass protection, and to simulate the blocking scheme for the play specified by the first two digits. The last digit tells our receivers what route to run.

Diagrams 10-1 to 10-6 illustrate several basic play-action pass routes and the blocking schemes we use against various defensive fronts. Diagram 10-1 illustrates a play-action route run in conjunction with our basic 24/25 Inside Zone play.

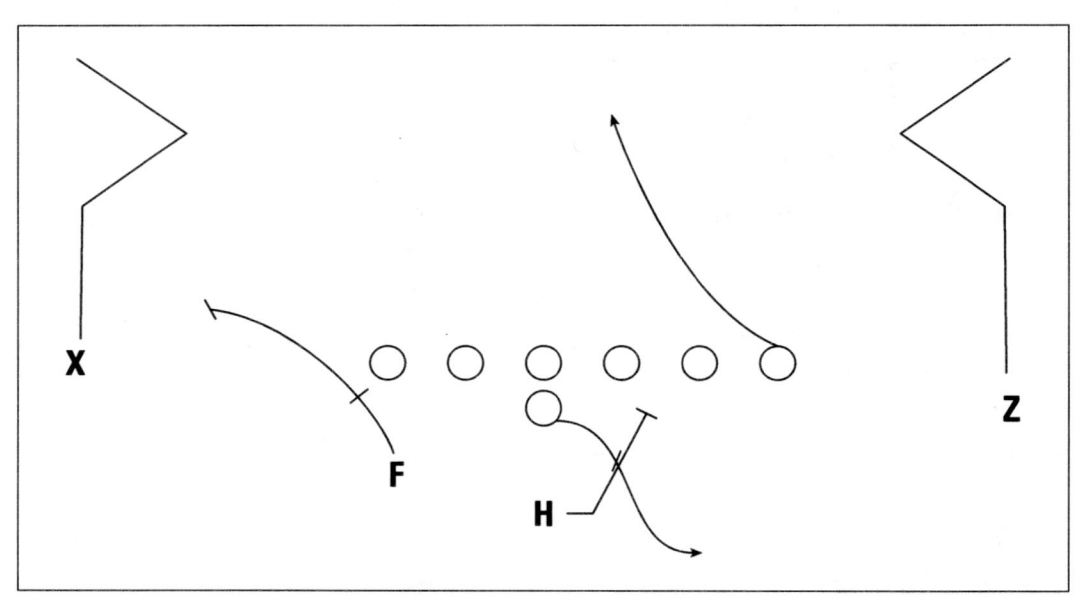

Diagram 10-1: Queen Right 2405

The split end (X) and the flanker (Z) run post corner routes, while the tight end (Y) releases inside and runs a seam route. These routes allow us to stretch the defense vertically as we run our fullback (F) on a flat route. The quarterback reads flanker (Z) to tight end (Y), depending on the coverage, and has the fullback in the flat as a third option. Diagrams 10-2, 10-3, and 10-4 show this route against three different defensive schemes.

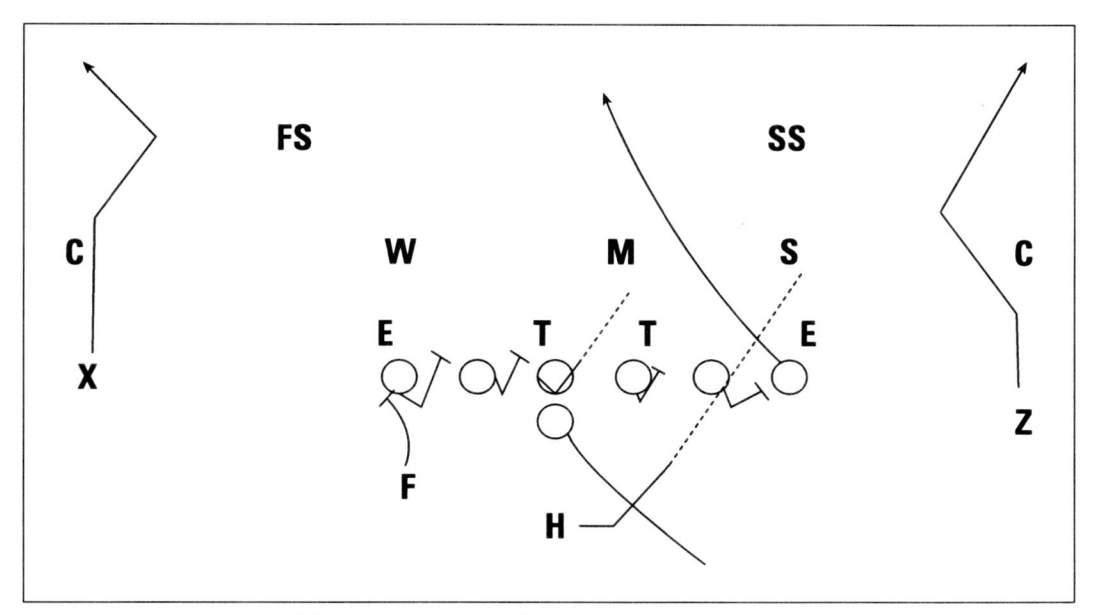

Diagram 10-2: Queen Right 2405 vs. a 4-3 front

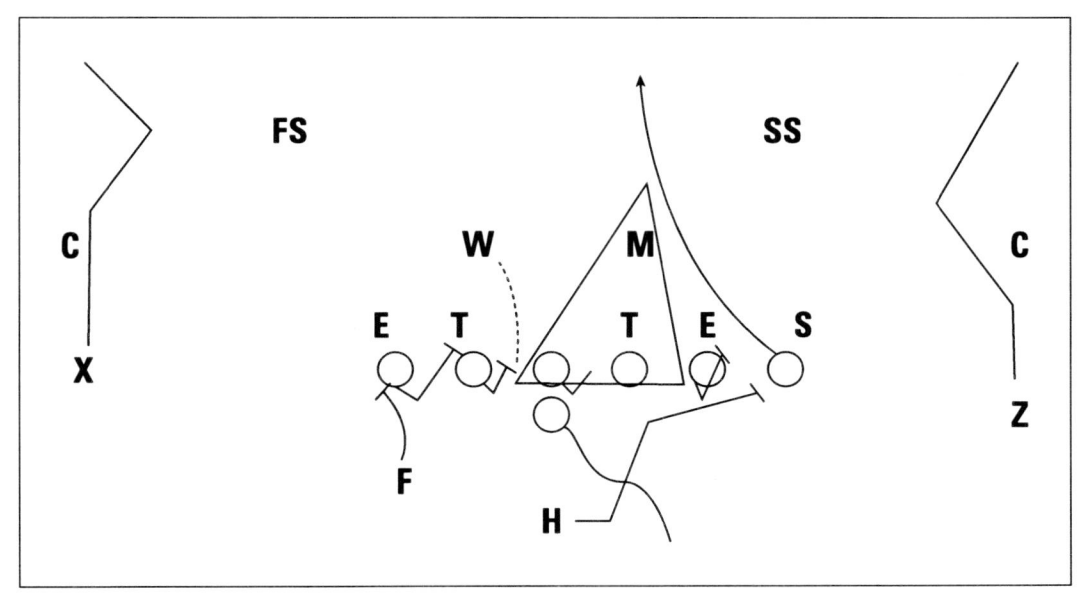

Diagram 10-3: Queen Right 2405 vs. a Stack front

Another one of our base play action routes is shown in Diagram 10-5. The only limits to the possible routes are a coach's imagination, and the way in which the coach has designed the normal dropback-passing attack. This illustrated play shows all three receivers running curl routes at various depths. The split end (X) and the flanker (Z)

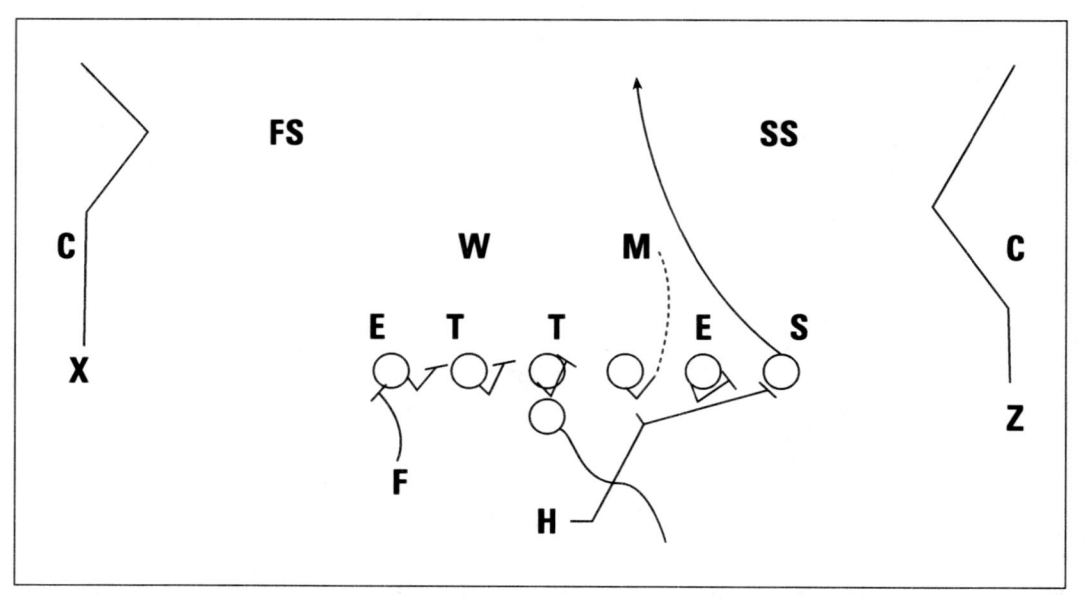

Diagram 10-4: Queen Right 2405 vs. a Reduced front

run 12- to 14-yard routes, and the tight end (Y) runs a 10- to 12-yard route. The fullback (F) looks for a linebacker blitz and then runs a five-yard flat route. The halfback (H) runs a normal 24 Inside Zone path, scans for a linebacker blitz, and runs a five-yard flat route.

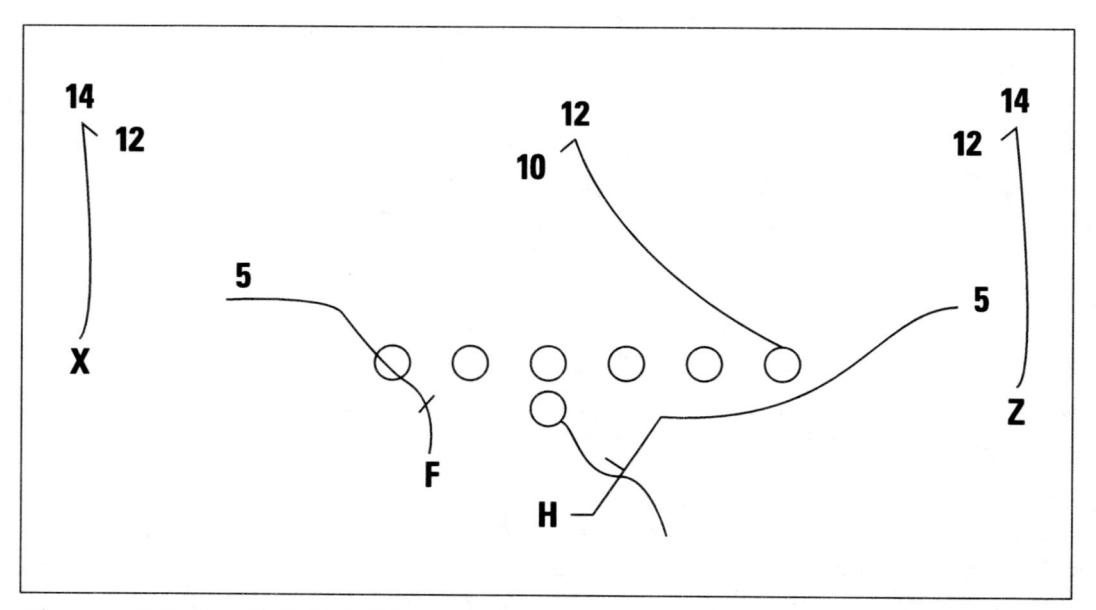

Diagram 10-5: Queen Right 2404

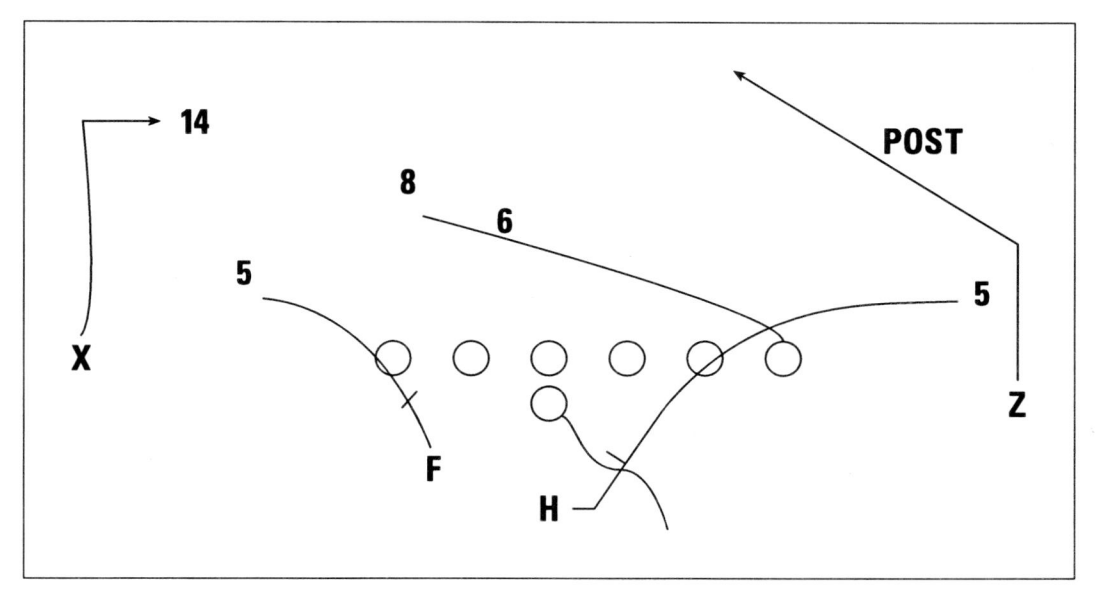

Diagram 10-6: Queen Right 2406

Diagram 10-6 shows yet another example of a play-action route we run. We are again faking our base 24 Inside Zone running play. The quarterback reads the play of the free safety and looks into the open "box" behind the linebackers' pass drops. A good play-action fake by the halfback and the quarterback will freeze the linebackers and the free safety long enough for the flanker (Z) to run his post route deep enough to occupy the free safety. If the post is run too shallow, the cornerback will follow, thereby enabling the free safety to defend the dig route. The tight end (Y) runs a drag route and looks for the opening between the inside linebacker's pass drops. The split end (X) runs a 14-yard dig route, looking to get into the open area behind the inside linebacker's drop and underneath the free safety. The fullback (F) runs a five-yard flat route after scanning for a linebacker blitz. The halfback (H) runs the normal 24 Inside Zone path and then executes a five-yard flat route. All factors considered, the halfback should be more concerned with executing a great fake, rather than getting out into his pass route.

On any play-action pass, we have the opportunity to keep our running backs in the backfield to block if they are needed. This opportunity is determined by the defensive front and the personnel we are facing.

Coaching Points for the Quarterback

The overall play of the quarterback is very critical to the success of the play-action attack. The following points are stressed to the quarterbacks:

- All action with the ball should be done at waist level. When the quarterback receives the ball from the center, he should bring it into his midsection and move toward the running back to execute the fake, while keeping the ball at waist level. At the mesh point, the quarterback sticks the ball out and fakes to the running back, before returning the ball to his own midsection.
- The ball should be extended to the running back to the point that it is held directly in front of him, clearly giving the defense the impression that an exchange will take place.
- Faking to the right side is usually easier for a right-handed quarterback. This type of player will require more practice to become effective at faking to his left side.
- Most fakes will take place on the quarterback's third step. Two to four extra steps are taken after the fake before the quarterback sets up in a position to release the ball. Normally, we run our play-action routes with a five-step drop.
- After faking the ball exchange with the running back, it is extremely important for the quarterback to move into the proper throwing position and snap his head around in order for him to make a proper read and see his receivers.
- The quarterback always has at least one primary target, one alternate option, and one possible outlet. The read is usually made long-to-short rather than short-to long, and the quarterback will throw to the short outlet if all other receivers are covered.

Making the Play-Action Package Work

Obviously, the play-action package is only effective when a team is able to run the ball effectively on a consistent basis. The better the running game, the more aggressive the linebackers become, and the faster the defensive backs will come up to support the run. It is also worth noting that the play-action pass works best when the opposition is playing a base defense, and the offense can anticipate how the defense will react based upon the scouting report. All factors considered, we prefer to throw play action against zone coverage in the secondary.

11

Incorporating the Option Game in the Zone Offense

It is obvious that a great deal of interest currently exists concerning zone running schemes at both the high school and college levels. We feel that interest in the zone offense is largely due to the fact that coaches are attracted by the concept of a single blocking scheme to account for all of the various types of modern defensive fronts defenses are currently playing. In addition, several defensive-minded coaches seem to prefer the fact that the zone gives offenses the ability to stay aggressive, regardless of the changing nature of a multiple-defensive structure from play to play. The zone also allows offensive linemen to be more aggressive and play with a defensive temperament. The zone not only makes them more physical, it prevents them from becoming passive.

The zone concept also gives offenses the opportunity to attack a variety of points within a given defensive structure without changing the play call. We have always felt that any type of cutback run is the most difficult play to defend, and the zone offense is primarily a cutback scheme. Every play has the chance to cutback, depending on the reaction of the defense. Most coaches like the fact that the zone offense is compatible with the play-action pass and naked concepts that are already being used to confuse and misdirect the defense.

More importantly, the zone offense provides teams with a simple, but sound and effective, plan to attack every possible defensive scheme that we might face. Our offense gets adequate practice repetitions and has great confidence in being able to execute our zone schemes. This confidence alone gives us a chance to win every game we play.

Installing an Option Scheme

In one recent season, we had two athletic quarterbacks who ran well. As a result, we started to examine blending some option plays into our zone running game. We wanted defenses to consider and practice option responsibilities, without changing our basic zone-blocking schemes. We ended up combining our 28/29 Stretch blocking scheme with an 18/19 Speed Option package. The entire offense had the exact same blocking assignments in 18/19 as they did in 28/29, with the exception of the fullback. In 28/29 Stretch, the fullback always blocks the force. In 18/19 Speed Option, we simply option the force and assign the fullback to help on the edge, while always working upfield and looking inside for a wrong colored jersey. Diagram 11-1 shows 18 Speed Option.

While still running an option scheme, we also run a play in which the Inside Zone play is simulated. This play is called 14/15 Option. The scheme is exactly the same as 24/25 Inside Zone for the offensive line and the wide receivers, but a load block scheme is used on the edge instead of attempting to turn it out. 14/15 Option is shown in Diagram 11-2.

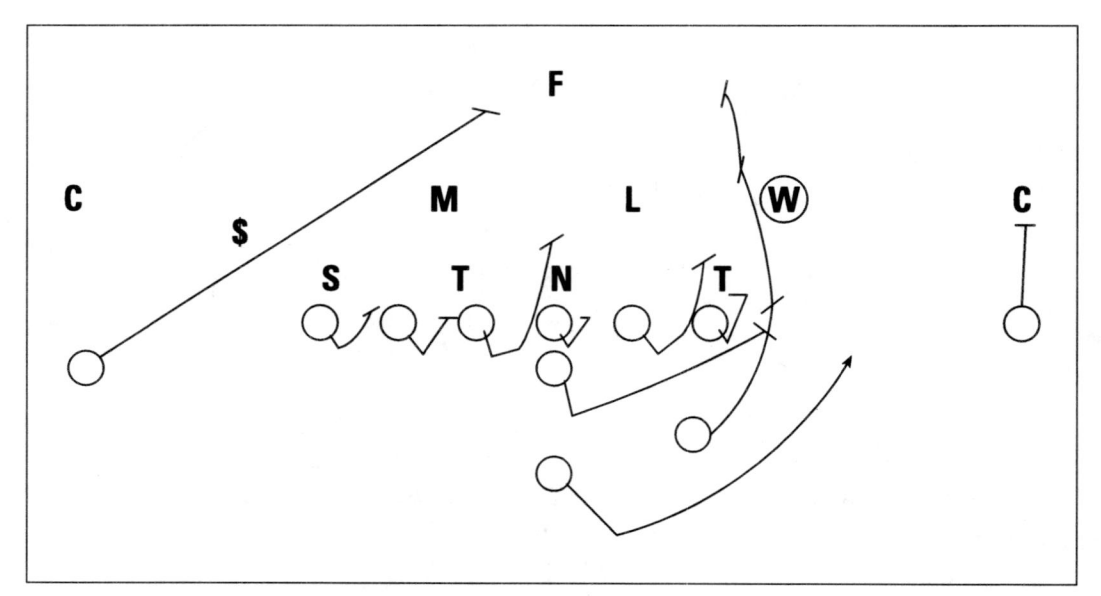

Diagram 11-1: Queen Left 18 Speed Option

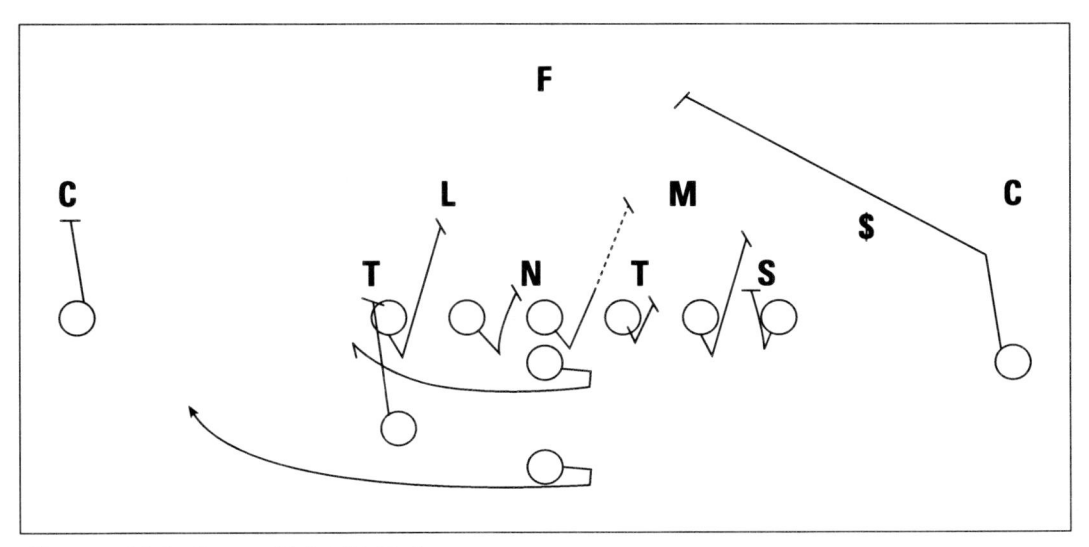

Diagram 11-2: Queen Right 15 Option

The backfield action is taught using what we call a Whirlybird option scheme. In this situation, the halfback lead steps like he does on the Inside Zone play, and then redirects the opposite way and gets in a pitch phase with the quarterback. The quarterback opens to the Inside Zone play and turns 180 degrees, trying to option the force element of the defense.

These two ideas represent extensions of the basic zone scheme that forces defenses to play (and practice) option assignments. We have also used Crack and Seal schemes with our option plays, as discussed earlier in this book.

The Flexibility of the Zone Attack

We believe that the zone can fit any team's personnel as it changes from year to year. For example, if a team has three great receivers, a one-back zone attack can be featured, as shown in Diagram 11-3. On the other hand, if teams have two great tight ends, they can feature a one-back attack with a two-tight end formation, as shown in Diagram 11-4. If teams have a great fullback, they can use any of the two-back formations discussed earlier in this book. The key point to remember is that the zone offense gives coaches the flexibility to adapt plays to fit their personnel.

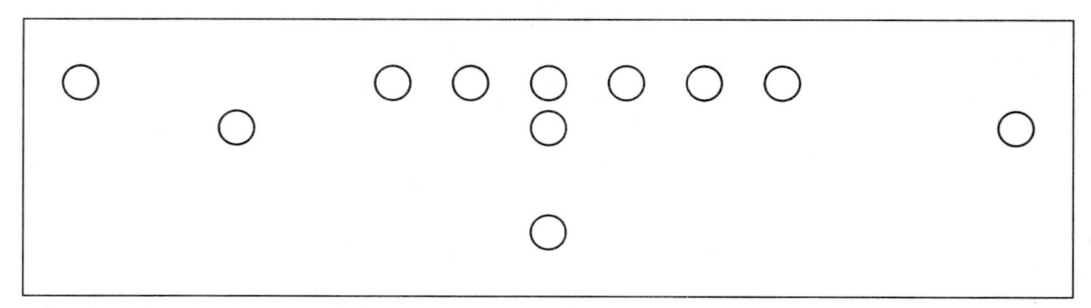

Diagram 11-3: Deuce Right

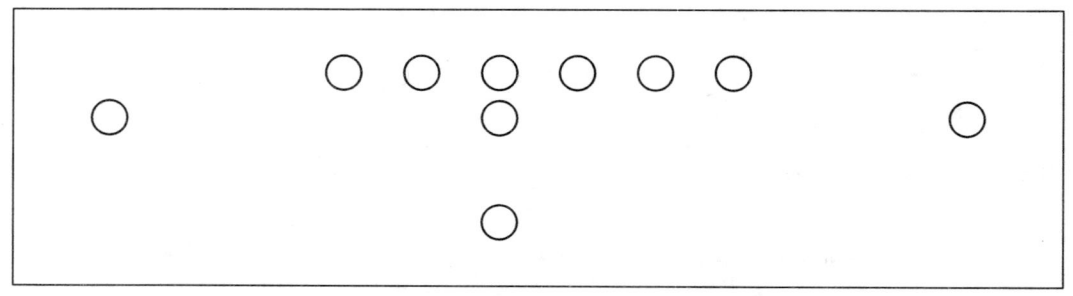

Diagram 11-4: Ace Right

12

Innovations in the Zone Running Attack

As evidence of our belief in, and commitment to, running the Inside Zone play and the Outside Zone play as the basis of our offense, consider the fact that in the six years since the first edition of *Coaching Football's Zone Offense* was written, we have not made any significant changes to the basic Inside Zone and Outside Zone blocking schemes that we utilize in our running attack at the University of Wisconsin-Whitewater. Our success has continued to increase our level of confidence in the philosophies that led us to choose this style of offensive attack. Our use of the basic schemes described in this book allowed us to have a player rush for 4,311 yards and 40 touchdowns in his career, setting school marks in both categories and becoming the first 4000 yard rusher in the history of UW-W Warhawk football.

As a point of fact, defensive philosophies and trends continually change and inevitably evolve. In this regard, one of the most difficult aspects about coaching on the offensive side of the football is making the necessary adjustments to deal with those changes while maintaining the integrity of the basic "bread-and-butter" schemes that you want to "hang your hat on" offensively. We think we have effectively done that with our Inside Zone and Outside Zone running schemes.

The majority of defenses that we are confronted with at our level tend to utilize schemes based on aggressive, attacking philosophies. We see a good deal of what we call "quarters coverage," where the defense wants to get the safeties involved in stopping the run in order to outnumber the offense at the point of attack. As a consequence, we have added some wrinkles to our basic Inside Zone and Outside Zone running schemes to slow down these aggressive, attacking fronts in order to take advantage of the changes we see from the defensive units that we face. As a result, our offensive attack has evolved, in the last five years, from essentially a two-back running attack to primarily a one-back running attack.

The major reason for this change is that the prevalent use of quarters coverage against two-back formations by defenses has made it very difficult for us to consistently run our Inside Zone play effectively out of a two-back set. Diagram 12-1 illustrates the problem caused by the alignments of safeties playing quarters coverage against a two-back formation.

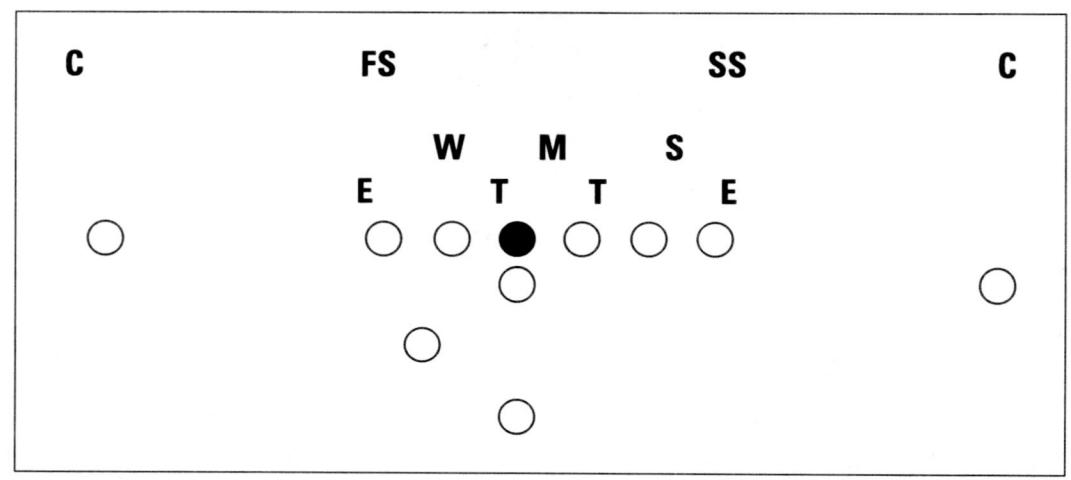

Diagram 12-1: Quarters coverage vs. a two-back set

Because of the depth that the safeties play at in quarters coverage and the way that defensive coaches teach them to read the release of the #2 receiver aligned on their side of the field, the safeties are able to provide very fast run support and "fit" into whatever blocking scheme the offense attempts to employ. While we have utilized the previously discussed "crack" scheme and made some of the aforementioned receiver adjustments with various levels of success, and while our play-action passing attack has been effective against quarters coverage, we have not found an effective way to run our base Inside Zone running play out of a two-back formation against this defensive scheme.

Our evolution to primarily a one-back running attack came about as a result of deciding to stop trying to line up in two-back formations and run our basic Inside Zone running play against quarters coverage. As a result, when we face quarters coverage, our first thought is to get into a one-back formation, similar to those illustrated in Diagrams 12-2 and 12-3.

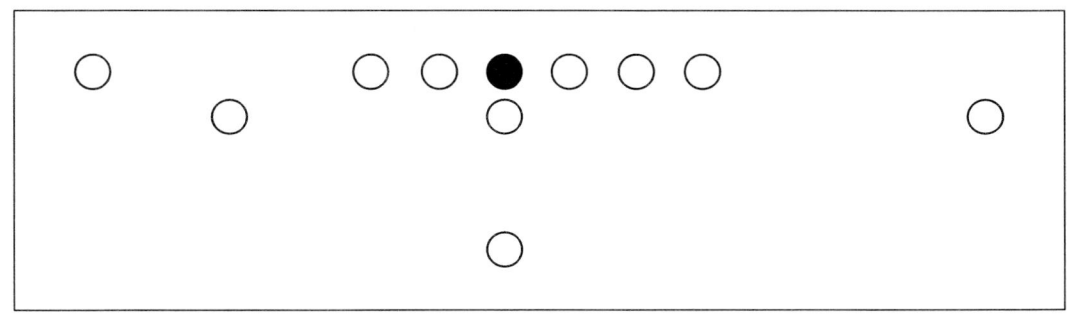

Diagram 12-2: Deuce right formation

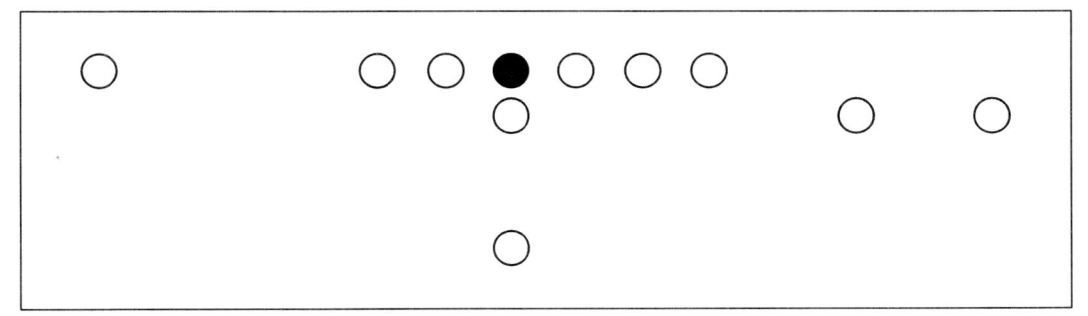

Diagram 12-3: Trey right formation

These formations tend to alter the alignment of the safeties, thereby forcing them to play wider and looser, and preventing them from being so focused on stopping the run. If the safeties remain overly conscious of our running attack, then our one-back formations allow us to exploit this aggressiveness and willingness to crowd the line of scrimmage with our passing attack. Our one-back formations enable us to alter the alignment of the defensive safeties and limit their ability to fit into our inside zone running scheme.

Diagram 12-4 illustrates the passing threat that a sound defense must account for when we line up in a one-back formation. The free safety lines up wider and plays looser than he does when there are two backs in the backfield, and he has no real threat to his deep quarter.

The difficulty that we have running our Inside Zone play out of our one-back formations is accounting for the defensive edge player on the split-end side of the

HAS TO DEFEND DEEP 1/4

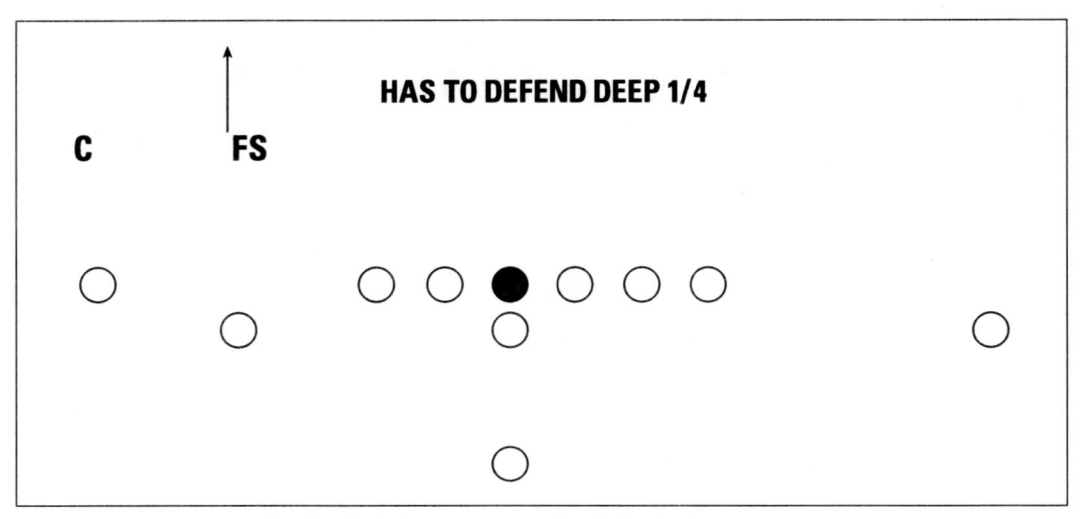

Diagram 12-4: Free safety's alignment vs. a one-back formation

formation. We can no longer utilize the "sift" technique, because there is no fullback in the backfield. The problem is related to the number of defenders that the defense places "in the box" (i.e., having to block eight defenders with only seven offensive players from a two-back formation). Our one-back formations dictate that we account for seven defenders with only six offensive players. The basic dilemma we face is being able to run our basic Inside Zone running scheme against a defense that chooses to keep seven in the box and outnumber us, as illustrated in Diagram 12-5.

In Diagram 12-5, the alignment of the receivers in our one-back formation leaves us no way to account for the weak outside linebacker with our Inside Zone running scheme. While the possibility of using "check-with-me" plays was addressed to declare

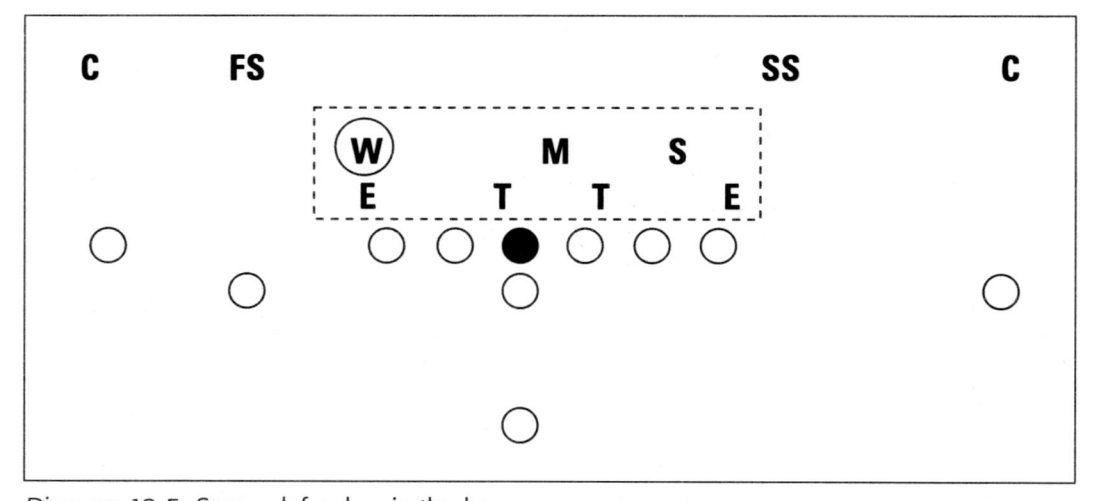

Diagram 12-5: Seven defenders in the box

at the line of scrimmage whether we were calling a running play or a passing play based on the quarterback's assessment of the weak outside linebacker's alignment was addressed earlier in the book, the ability of the defense to vary the alignment of the weak outside linebacker and disguise his responsibility on any given play still means that we will sometimes guess wrong and run a bad play into the strength of the defense. In order to make sure that we are always right and account for defenses that like to "stem" or move around prior to the snap of the football, we introduced what we call "orbit motion."

Orbit motion brings a receiver aligned to the outside back toward the quarterback, so that when the ball is snapped, the receiver is in position for a handoff from the quarterback as part of a reverse scheme. When the receiver does not get the ball, he is still in position to execute an effective handoff fake that simulates the reverse action and freezes the defense. Diagrams 12-6 and 12-7 illustrate orbit motion to the left ("Lee") and orbit motion to the right ("Ray").

The blocking scheme that we use in conjunction with orbit motion dictates that we account for the split-end side edge defender with the reverse or the reverse fake. The offensive tackle on the split-end side of the formation uses the "sift" technique, just as

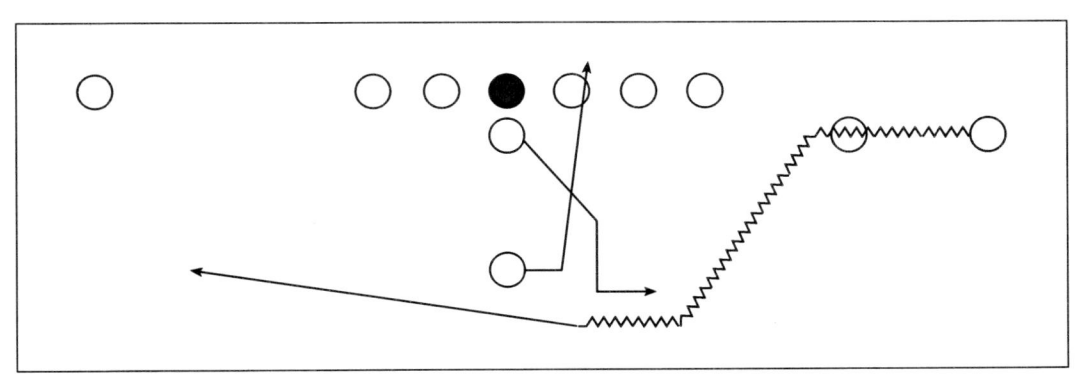

Diagram 12-6: Lee motion

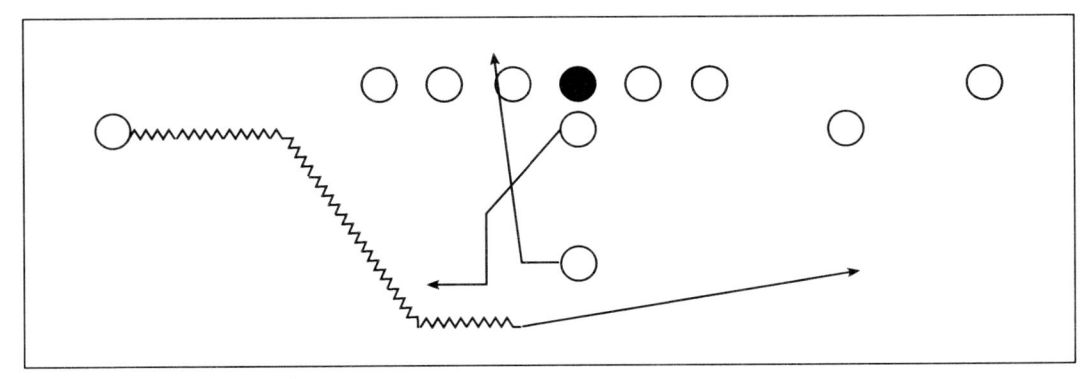

Diagram 12-7: Ray motion

he does when we run Inside Zone from a two-back set. We hold whoever is responsible for controlling the edge with the possibility that we are running the reverse. This concept is illustrated in Diagram 12-8.

In Diagram 12-8, the quarterback fakes to the receiver who is running orbit motion, and the offensive tackle sifts to the second level (linebacker level). We are able to run our basic Inside Zone running play from one-back formations without making any changes to our basic blocking rules, schemes, or techniques.

An example of an actual play that we can use to run the reverse is illustrated in Diagram 12-9. The reverse is an important complementary play to our Inside Zone running play. In our terminology, the particular reverse illustrated in Diagram 12-9 is called Trey Right Z Lee 24 Reverse.

The formation is Trey Right, and Z Lee tells the flanker that he will be in orbit motion to the left. 24 Reverse tells the tailback that he is faking 24 (our Inside Zone running

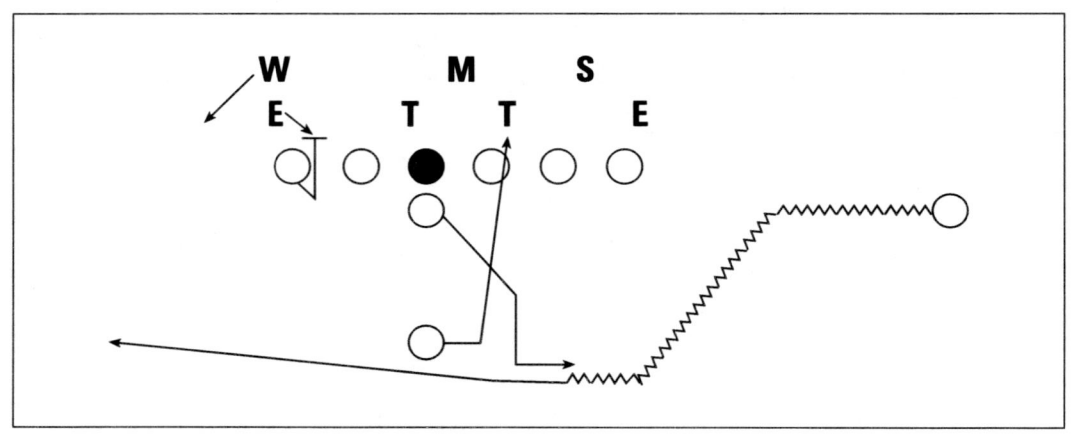

Diagram 12-8: Sift technique with reverse fake

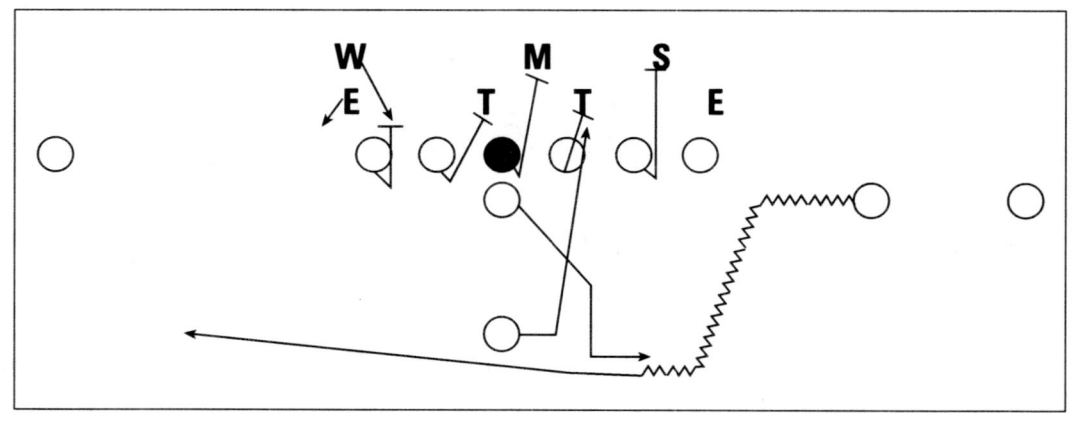

Diagram 12-9: Trey Right Z Lee 24 Reverse

play) and the receiver that he is getting the football, and that we are actually running the reverse. The beauty of this play for us is that we block it exactly like our Inside Zone running play. The Inside Zone running play and the reverse look exactly the same to the defense. The weak outside linebacker cannot cheat inside to stop the zone play without making the perimeter of the defensive structure vulnerable to the reverse.

The only minor adjustment that we make when we actually give the ball to the flanker and run the reverse involves the blocking assignment of the split end. It is the split end's job to block any defensive player who follows the flanker across the formation when he goes into orbit motion. We refer to this as a "crack" block, and how we use it to block the edge of the defense is illustrated in Diagram 12-10.

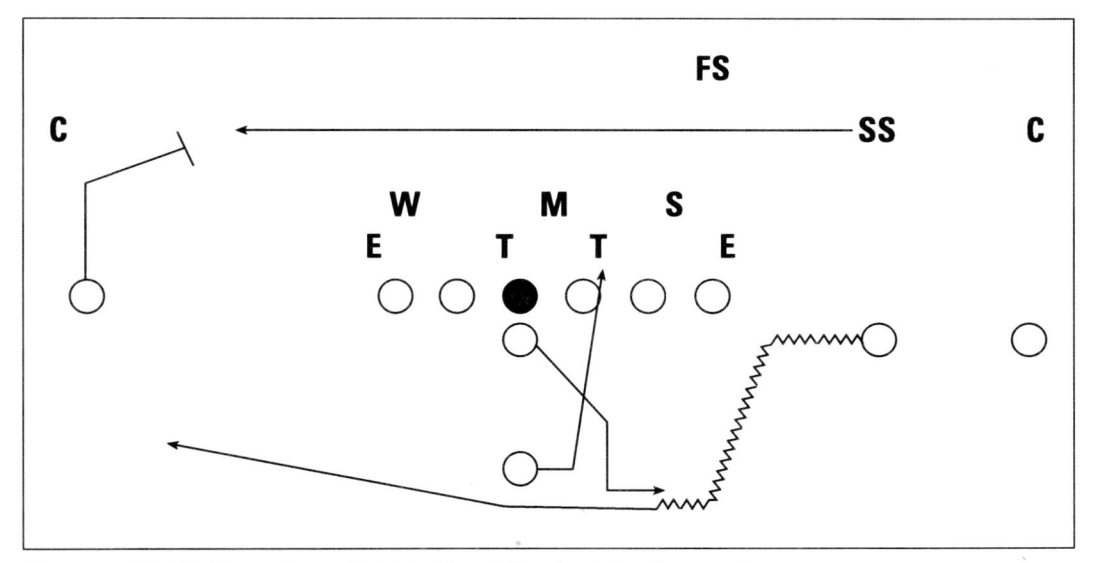

Diagram 12-10: The split end blocks the defender following motion

Because of the success we have had in utilizing orbit motion to help us effectively run our basic Inside Zone play out of one-back formations, some defenses choose to invert a safety or an outside linebacker against our one-back formations, or move one safety up and one safety back as soon as a receiver goes in orbit motion. If there is an inverted defender and we are running the reverse play, then the split end must block the inverted defender. This situation is illustrated in Diagram 12-11.

Basically, the split end is simply identifying how the defense is reacting to orbit motion and then making sure that his block accounts for their reaction, or adjustment. In this situation, only three choices really exist:

- If the safeties simply align wider and deeper to stay in quarters coverage and no defender reacts to the orbit motion, then the split end's blocking assignment stays the same.

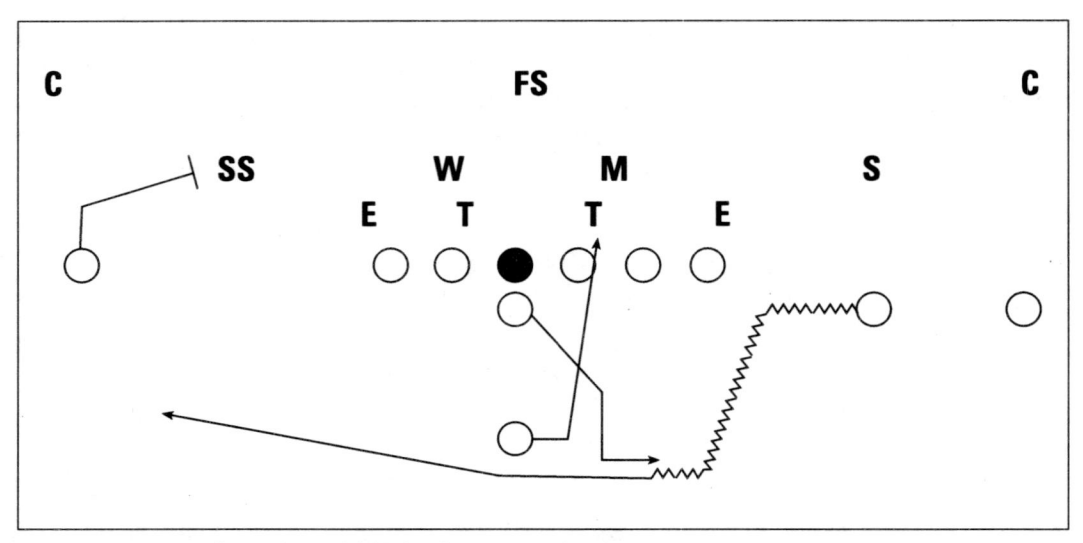

Diagram 12-11: The split end blocks the inverted safety

- If the safeties stay in their quarters coverage alignment and the defense deals with the motion by trying to have a defender follow the flanker across the formation, then the split end blocks the defender that follows the motion.
- If a defender inverts up to deal with the orbit motion that is coming toward him, then the split end blocks the inverted defender.

We have found this to be a simple and effective way to run our Inside Zone running play against teams that want to play quarters coverage against us. The threat of the reverse, and the susceptibility to the pass, that results from aligning in one-back formations has helped us to stay with our "bread-and-butter" Inside Zone running play against defenses that had previously given us a great deal of trouble when we were lining up in two-back formations.

As was discussed earlier in the book, we always incorporate some type of play-action passing attack into whatever Inside Zone or Outside Zone running play we are trying to run. The play-action passing series that we have incorporated into our one-back, orbit motion, Inside Zone (fake reverse) running scheme is what we call our "negative" series. An example of an actual play-action pass play that we use to complement our Inside Zone running play is illustrated in Diagram 12-12. In our terminology, the particular reverse illustrated in Diagram 12-12 is called Trey Right Z Lee 24 Negative.

The play actually consists of an Inside Zone running play fake to hold the middle of the second level (linebacker level), a reverse fake to the flanker in orbit motion to give some misdirection, and a flood route concept that allows the quarterback to read the coverage low (short)- to-high (deep). Both play fakes must be executed well so

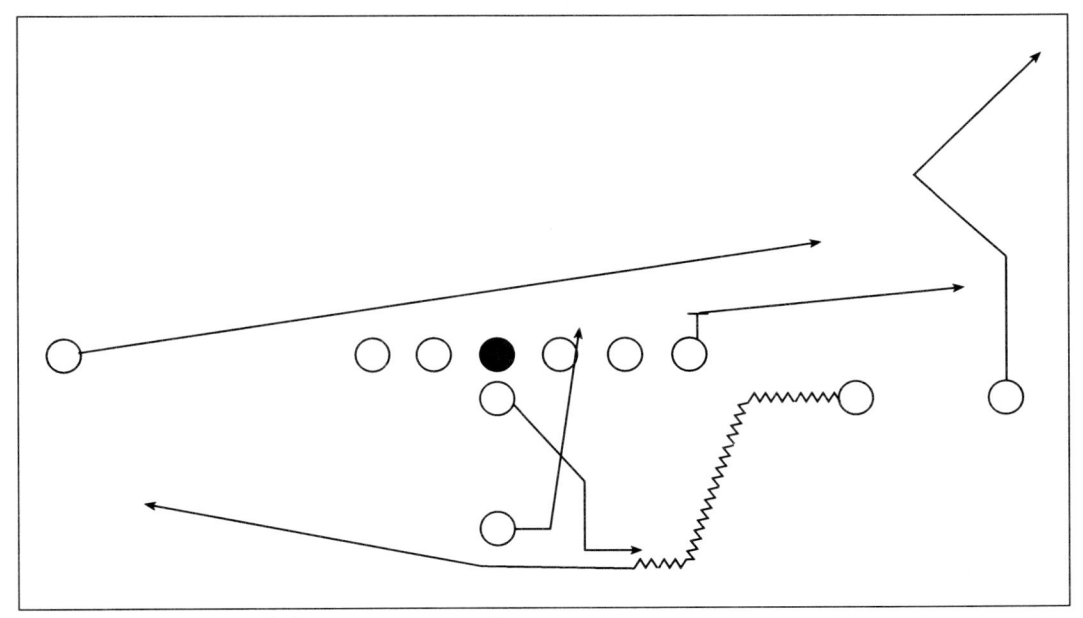

Diagram 12-12: Trey Right Z Lee 24 Negative

that the defense is forced to defend both the Inside Zone running play and the reverse. They are crucial to the overall effectiveness of the play. This play has been a fantastic red-zone option for us, as well as a great misdirection play out in the open field.

The tight end executes what we call a "slam" release from the line of scrimmage, blocking the defensive player aligned over him and obtaining an outside release that allows him to get to the flat quickly, while preserving a clear passing lane between him and the quarterback. The tight end must gain width and depth to a point five yards from the line of scrimmage and anticipate a quick throw from the quarterback in the event that he is pressured.

The playside receiver runs a post-corner route, doing his best to get outside leverage on the third-level (defensive back level) defender. The backside receiver runs a crossing route that gets him to a depth of 8-10 yards by the time he gets across the formation. The backside receiver adjusts his route to ensure that he fits into the flood concept, running behind the tight end and underneath the flanker, looking for the hole in the coverage. It is imperative that the backside receiver not stop his route too early or start to "settle" before he gets to the hole in the coverage caused by flooding the zone with three receivers.

To summarize the wrinkles that we have incorporated into our running schemes, we have simply tried to account for the defender responsible for the edge of the defense, without actually blocking him. We slow down his identification of, and reaction to, our Inside Zone running schemes by freezing him with a reverse fake, in order to remove him from the interior structure of the defense without having to block him. In order to run play A, we account for a particular defender by threatening him with play B, rather than blocking him. This same concept has been widely used by offensive teams that line up in one-back formations in an attempt to spread the defense with four receivers in order to open up running lanes for both their quarterback and tailback.

We call our version of this scheme 24 Read, and it incorporates the same basic blocking schemes as the other one-back running plays that are part of our attack. 24 Read is illustrated in Diagram 12-13.

The split-end side offensive tackle sifts the edge, and we account for the edge defender by threatening him with a potential run by the quarterback. Our quarterback, who is aligned in shot-gun formation, is taught to ride the tailback into the line of scrimmage, disconnect, and then run around the edge of the defense. We run the play as a true option read. If the defender outside of the split-end side offensive tackle closes (to the inside) fast, then the quarterback is taught to disconnect (i.e., keep the ball) and run around the edge of the defense. This situation is illustrated in Diagram 12-14.

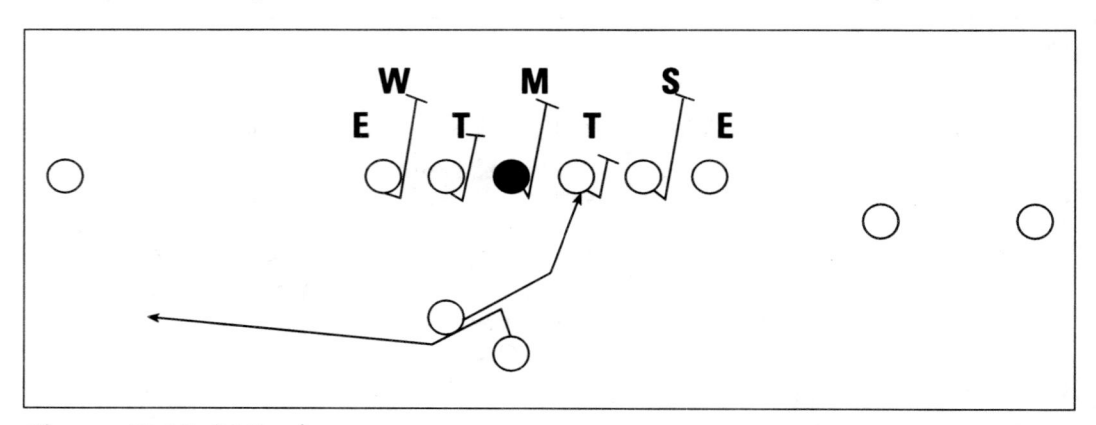

Diagram 12-13: 24 Read

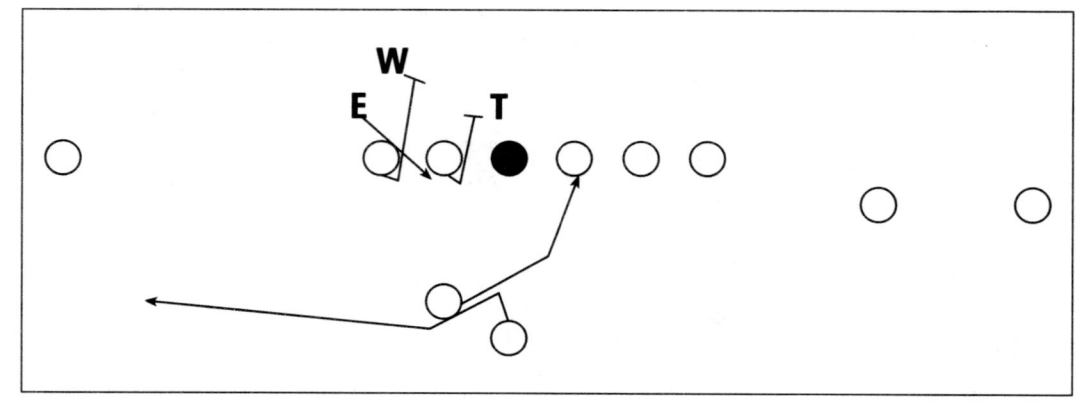

Diagram 12-14: 24 Read with quarterback disconnect (keep) and run

If the defender outside of the split-end side offensive tackle holds his ground or moves upfield (toward the line of scrimmage, but not to the inside), then the quarterback is taught to disconnect (i.e., give the ball to the tailback) and run around the edge of the defense. This situation is illustrated in Diagram 12-15.

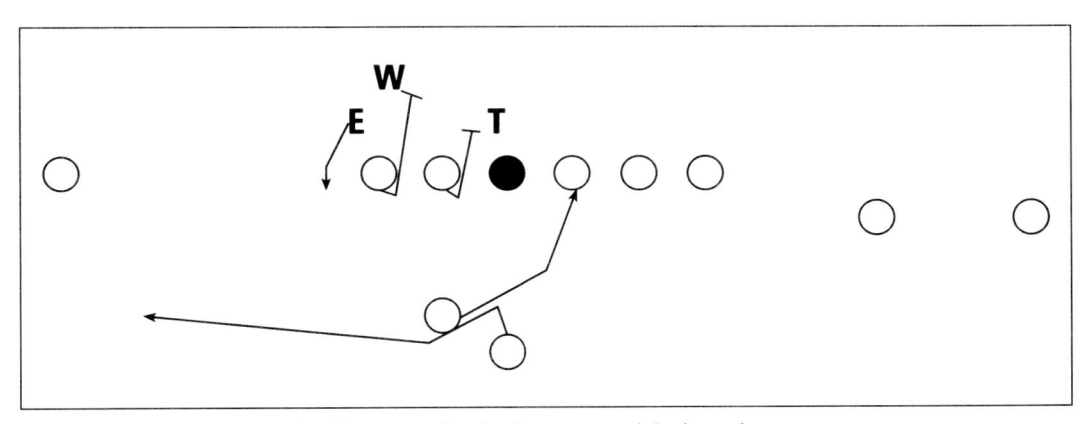

Diagram 12-15: 24 Read with quarterback disconnect (give) and run

Again, the beauty of this play for us is that we block it exactly like our Inside Zone running play. We have added an option concept and developed another way to slow down the edge defender who cannot cheat inside to stop the Inside Zone play, without giving up the perimeter of the defense to our quarterback who has a true run option.

The play-action passing schemes that we use in conjunction with 24 Read are similar to those discussed in Chapter 9. Diagram 12-16 illustrates a play-action pass based on "naked" series protection, while Diagram 12-17 illustrates a play-action pass based on "bootleg" series protection.

Hopefully, the innovations discussed in this chapter will be helpful to you in expanding the possibilities that you consider for your zone running attack. The key point that must be remembered is that the strength of the zone offensive attack lies in the simplicity of its running and passing schemes and the consistency and similarity of the techniques involved from play to play. This book was written so that you would be able to benefit from what we have learned from running this effective offensive attack. If it achieves its intended purpose, you will be able to achieve a similar level of success at whatever level you try to implement it. Good luck, and keep on zoning!

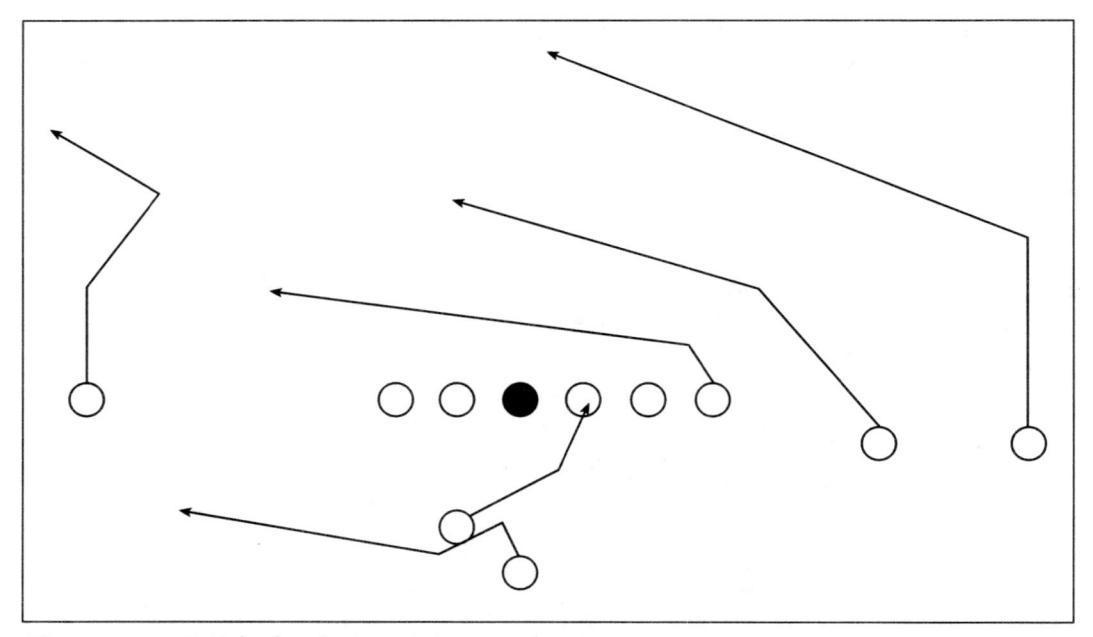

Diagram 12-16: Naked series pattern

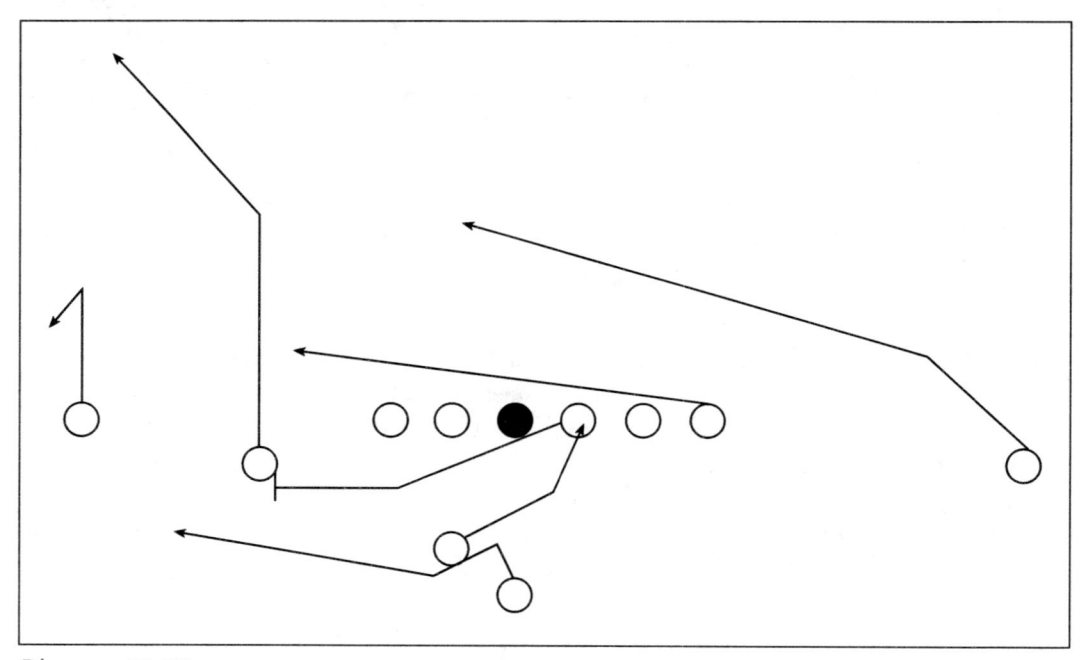

Diagram 12-17

About the Author

Stan Zweifel is the offensive coordinator and wide receivers/quarterbacks coach at the University of Wisconsin-Whitewater. Since joining the Warhawk's staff in 1990, Stan has helped develop the UW-W offense into one of the game's most potent attacks. He is widely respected for his knowledge of and his ability to teach the zone concept.

A graduate of the University of Wisconsin-River Falls where he was the Falcon's leading receiver for two seasons, and led the team in scoring in 1973, Stan began his coaching career at the interscholastic level, holding positions at Markesan, WI and New Ulm, MN high schools. He next moved to the collegiate level as the offensive coordinator at Northern Colorado University, before accepting the head coaching position at Yanton College (SD). He then served as the head coach at the University of Minnesota-Morris, before joining the UW-W staff.

A prolific writer, Stan has written or co-authored five instructional football books. He has also been featured on fifteen well-received instructional videos. In addition, he is a much sought-after speaker, who lectures widely at coaching clinics around the country on a variety of instructional and motivational topics. He also annually conducts one of the most successful offensive-defensive linemen instructional clinics in the country.

He and his wife, Diane, have four children, Saree, Shannon, Mark, and Mike.